"This volume provides a wealth of practice-based tools for mid-career faculty and for those who support them. It's like learning from the most generous and experienced colleagues you could hope to meet."

—Dr. **Christel Lutz**, *Director of Education, University College Utrecht; Principal Fellow, Centre for Academic Teaching and Learning, Utrecht University*

"This book is thoughtfully situated and relevant to the unique dilemmas, opportunities, and challenges of 'midcareer' faculty. Readers will benefit not only from the actionable recommendations offered but also the programmatic inspiration and institutional examples shared."

—Dr. **Jennifer Ng**, *Associate Vice Provost for Faculty Affairs, The University of Kansas*

"The coverage of topics in this book provides faculty, campus leaders, and faculty developers with ready to use information and materials to support mid-career faculty. Readers will find resources for immediate implementation, and importantly, mid-career faculty will find ways to ignite their passion in building their career pathway forward."

—Dr. **Pamela L. Eddy**, *Associate Provost for Faculty Affairs and Development and Professor, Higher Education, William & Mary*

A Toolkit for Mid-Career Academics

Mid-career faculty are the backbone of the college and university workforce and represent the largest population of faculty in the academy, yet they face myriad challenges that hinder career satisfaction and advancement.

This book offers action-oriented tools to engage (or re-engage) mid-career programming at the individual faculty, institutional, consortial, and grant-funded levels. Bringing together leading scholars and practitioners engaged in research and practice, this edited volume offers solutions to two driving questions faced by mid-career faculty: "what's next" and "how to navigate." This focus on both what and how highlights critical issues and challenges associated with mid-career coupled with specific tools and strategies to successfully navigate from diverse stakeholder perspectives. Jargon-free and rich with stories from the field, each chapter can serve as a stand-alone resource, be read in order as presented, or be read non-sequentially based on the reader's specific needs.

Mid-career faculty, including non–tenure-track and community college academics, will welcome the resources, tools, and strategies featured throughout this book, the "pocket professional development mentor," to help create more inclusive and equitable programming at multiple levels.

Dr. Vicki L. Baker, a Fulbright Scholar, is the E. Maynard Aris Endowed Professor in Economics and Management and department chair at Albion College. She is co-founder of Lead Mentor Develop, LLC. Vicki was recognized as a Top 100 Visionary 2021 in Education (GFEL) and a Top 10 Visionary in Education in 2023 by *CioLook* Magazine.

Dr. Aimee LaPointe Terosky is Associate Dean of the School of Education and Human Development and Professor of Educational Leadership at Saint Joseph's University. Dr. Terosky's expertise is school leader/faculty careers in K–12 and higher education. She has received her university's Teaching, Research, and Justice Merit Awards, including the Tengelmann Award for Distinguished Research and Teaching.

Dr. Laura Gail Lunsford is Professor of Psychology and Assistant Dean at Campbell University. She was an associate professor at the University of Arizona and has held academic leadership roles at NC State, Duke University, and UNC Wilmington. A Fulbright Scholar, she publishes on mentoring and leadership in the academy.

A Toolkit for Mid-Career Academics

Cultivating Career Advancement

Edited by Vicki L. Baker,
Aimee LaPointe Terosky,
and Laura Gail Lunsford

NEW YORK AND LONDON

Designed cover image: Getty Images

First published 2024
by Routledge
605 Third Avenue, New York, NY 10158

and by Routledge
4 Park Square, Milton Park, Abingdon, Oxon, OX14 4RN

Routledge is an imprint of the Taylor & Francis Group, an informa business

ISBN: 9781032550305 (hbk)
ISBN: 9781032550237 (pbk)
ISBN: 9781003428626 (ebk)

DOI: 10.4324/9781003428626

Typeset in Sabon
by Apex CoVantage, LLC

Access the Support Material: Routledge.com/9781032550305

We dedicate this book to all the mid-career faculty and academic leaders who devote their time, energy, and passion to supporting students, faculty, and staff. We see you, we hear you, and we support you!

Contents

Figures

Tables

Acknowledgments

Vicki would like to acknowledge the many partnerships she has forged over the past fifteen years across the academy that have allowed her to support faculty and academic leaders and that inspired this volume. She offers special thanks to the volume contributors for so willingly sharing their experiences, programming, and tools. Their knowledge will make the academy a better, more supportive place for mid-career professionals. Vicki is most appreciative of Aimee and Laura for their friendship and collaboration over the years and for making this volume a reality – they are the best! And finally, Vicki thanks her husband, Bryan, and two children, McKenna and Henley, for reminding her every day of how blessed life is.

From her master's and doctoral years to her current professional years, Aimee is thankful to be surrounded by exemplary faculty members who strive daily to provide meaningful contributions to knowledge and communities while also leading full lives. Many aspects of their advice and their models are embedded in her work today! She offers special thanks to Anna Neumann, Aaron Pallas, Catherine Hill, Jeffrey C. Sun, Katie Conway, Vicki L. Baker, Audrey Jaeger, KerryAnn O'Meara, Chris Healey, Terry Furin, and Kris Brown for their expertise in this scholarly area. And as always, she thanks Jeff, Ava, and Caitlin Terosky and Linda and Peter LaPointe for endlessly supporting Aimee's faculty growth!

Laura appreciates the academic leaders who advocate for faculty development and recognize the importance of supporting faculty members across their career spans. She is grateful to the volume contributors for sharing their resources to enhance mid-career faculty development. Special thanks to Vicki for being such a great long-time collaborator and to Aimee, her new collaborator. Laura also appreciates Campbell University's support to finish this volume through the Faculty Summer Research Awards.

As a team, we thank our editor, Meredith Norwich, and the entire editorial team at Routledge for supporting our vision and helping to make this volume a reality. We also thank Lynne Ferguson for her excellent copyediting and expertise.

Foreword

Over the past decade or so, mid-career faculty in higher education institutions have been garnering increasing attention in scholarship. This much-needed volume addresses what's next for mid- career faculty and then develops a road map of how to navigate the journey as a mid-career faculty member, develop skills, be purposeful, plan the study leave or sabbatical, and follow their passion by safeguarding time and space.

Most mid-career faculty are at the associate rank, who see themselves as stuck. The profile of full professors, particularly at R-1 institutions, is starkly male and white. According to the U.S. Department of Education's report, *The Condition of Education 2020 (NCES 2020–144)*, nationally, approximately 34 percent of full professors are women. But underrepresentation is particularly pronounced among women who are Hispanic or Latino and Black or African American or multiracial. White women hold 27 percent of full professor positions, Hispanic women hold 3 percent, Black women hold 2 percent, and Asian/Pacific Islander women and women who list two or more races each hold 1 percent. Why does this matter?

Full professorships are prestigious and obviously lead to higher salaries. According to the 2022 Eos Foundation's Women's Power Gap Initiative study, the American Association of University Women, and the WAGE project, in the U.S., women represent just 24 percent of the highest-paid faculty members and administrators at 130 leading research universities. Women of color are even more grossly underrepresented, at just 2 percent of top core academic earners. Not being promoted to full professorship exacerbates the pay gap. The trends show that institutions of higher learning have failed to harness the available expertise or build the talent of mid-career faculty. While talent and intelligence are evenly distributed in society, opportunities, and particularly opportunities for mid-career faculty, to move up the career ladder are lacking.

My own interest in examining satisfaction and recognition of mid-career faculty stemmed from my individual experience and what I saw in leading the institutional-level analysis of the COACHE survey data focused on associate professors. The intersections of the individual and institutional is critical to considering the provision of institutional resources and investment in mid-career faculty. As I reflect on those early days from my current vantage point in a university leadership position at Virginia Commonwealth University (VCU), I realize the importance of having individuals with knowledge and expertise to develop contextually meaningful initiatives and programs for mid-career faculty. Faculty skill development, explicated in this volume, is a major endeavor I am currently pursuing. Additionally, an intentional multi-pronged approach is essential to begin to move the needle for mid-career faculty.

Intentionality is a key concept of Section 1 of this volume. Aimee LaPointe Terosky notes that mid-career faculty often respond to others' agendas without a clear vision of their own priorities. Many mid-career faculty are often called upon to contribute to service work, take on administrative and leadership roles requiring considerable time and effort, and often with little professional development. Vicki Baker and KerryAnn O'Meara, among many other scholars, have called attention to institutional responsibility to ensure equitable teaching and service workloads. I may refine this to call for equitable workloads based on type of faculty appointment such as tenured versus non–tenure-track mid-career faculty. Emphasizing professional development and enabling mentoring relationships soon after faculty are tenured and/or promoted to the associate rank can set the stage for these faculty. A half-day orientation for newly promoted associate professors is the first step we have initiated at VCU. It will enable reflective planning for goal setting and prioritizing and serve as an opportunity for the attending faculty to self-select into a cohort that can meet at regular intervals. At the institutional level, the plan is to longitudinally track each cohort of faculty, which would also allow us to ensure that the faculty member is promoted in a timely manner. Hastings, in this volume, discusses a cohort model approach used by mid-career faculty to propose a career development project. Such an approach enables one-on-one and peer support to refine their ideas to seek funding.

Following up on this initial orientation based on needs is important to re-shape the experiences of mid-career faculty. Vicki Baker and colleagues provide a "toolkit" that comprises a wide range of prompts and forms for use by institutions. These tools range from setting goals to assessing grant opportunities, scaling up research, and assessing individual development plans using Vicki Baker's career advancement framework, Purpose, Scope, and Evidence of Impact (PSEI). Noting that experiences vary by type of institution, the volume includes efforts at a community college and liberal arts college.

Returning to the aforementioned point about the role of the institution, it is imperative to note the central role of leaders such as department chairs or heads, deans, and vice provosts for faculty affairs in developing a career trajectory for mid-career faculty. Their approaches to advising, mentoring, recognizing variations in needs by type of employment, and ensuring equity can go a long way in enabling change. Institutional leaders are also responsible for consistency in assessment of contributions, especially service and leadership. This aspect was the focus of my NCFDD webinar, Integrating Service and Leadership Contributions in Processes of Promotion from Associate to Full Professor, in their four-part series about preparing dossiers for promotion from associate to full professor, released in August 2022. Institutional accountability is no doubt coupled with the need for a faculty member to make judicious decisions about service and leadership roles.

Providing options for professional development and emphasizing the need for building skills to navigate career trajectories is one part of the equation. The other part of the equation is for mid-career faculty to take the time to utilize the initiatives. Mid-career faculty must find the time to invest in themselves – personally and professionally!

Collaborations and partnerships in utilizing the tools can further enhance the motivation of mid-career faculty. The volume is attentive to the role of consortiums and professional associations, which has not been extensively discussed in the past. Cross-campus efforts discussed by Boyd et al. can allow mid-career faculty to build broader networks while benefits are distributed beyond a single institution.

As mid-career faculty, administrators, and institutions initiate programs and workshops for mid-career faculty, we must balance between the ideal and the real. Programs and workshops must not only be carefully conceived and implemented but must be periodically assessed. Sustaining programs requires resources – funds and personnel – and commitments of institutions.

This book is a must-read for those involved in and committed to faculty development across the higher education landscape.

Mangala Subramaniam
Virginia Commonwealth University

Richmond
September 18, 2023

About the Editors

Vicki L. Baker, PhD, is at the forefront of innovation and strategy in faculty and leadership development. Recognized as a Top 100 Visionary in Education by the Global Forum for Education and Learning (2020–2021) and) and a Top 10 Visionary in Education in 2023 by *CioLook* Magazine, Dr. Baker was selected to join the 2023–2024 cohort of ACE Fellows. A faculty member and Fulbright Specialist Alumnus (Utrecht, Netherlands), she works to help faculty members, colleges, and universities thrive. She is the E. Maynard Aris Endowed Professor in Economics and Management at Albion College, where she serves as Chair of the Economics and Management Department. Prior to joining the academy as a faculty member, Dr. Baker worked at Harvard Business School (executive education) and AK Steel Corporation. She earned her PhD (higher education) and MS (management and organization) at Penn State University, her MBA at Clarion University of Pennsylvania, and her BS at Indiana University of Pennsylvania. She holds a certificate in human resource management (Villanova University) and is a Certified Professional in HR through the Society for Human Resource Management (SHRM).

Dr. Baker is the author of *Charting Your Path to Full: A Guide for Women Associate Professors*, lead editor of *Success After Tenure: Supporting Mid-Career Faculty*, and lead co-author of *Developing Faculty in Liberal Arts Colleges*. She recently published *Managing Your Academic Career: A Guide to Re-Envision Mid-Career* (Routledge/Taylor & Francis) and a New Directions in Higher Education volume, *Bridging the Research–Practice Nexus: Resources, Tools, and Strategies to Navigate Mid-Career in the Academy* (Wiley). She has written more than one hundred peer-reviewed journal articles, book chapters, invited opinion pieces for higher education news media outlets, case studies, and blogs on the topics of faculty and leadership development and higher education.

Dr. Baker's work has been featured in national/international media outlets including WalletHub, *Times Higher Education*, the Hechinger Report, the *Wall Street Journal*, the *Atlantic*, *USA Today*, the *New York Times*, the *Chronicle of Higher Education*, and the Huffington Post. She has conducted workshops and has given scholarly presentations and keynote addresses at professional associations including the Association for the Study of Higher Education, the Council for the Advancement of Higher Education Programs, the American Educational Research Association, and the Professional and Organizational Development Network in Higher Education (POD). Dr. Baker, along with Laura Gail Lunsford, is co-founder of Lead Mentor Develop, LLC, where she regularly consults with higher education and industry organizations on leadership, faculty development, change management, mentoring, and career advancement strategies.

Aimee LaPointe Terosky, EdD, is Associate Dean of the School of Education and Human Development and Professor of Educational Leadership at Saint Joseph's University in Philadelphia. Dr. Terosky's scholarly and practitioner expertise focuses on teaching and learning and school leader/faculty careers in K–12 and higher education as well as urban principal career vitality. Her recent research has been published in the *Review of Higher Education*, *Diversity in Higher Education*, the *Educational Administration Quarterly*, the *Journal of School Leadership*, the *Teachers College Record*, *Studies in Higher Education*, the *Journal of Excellence in College Teaching*, *School Leadership and Management*, *Innovative Higher Education*, and *Inside Higher Education*.

Prior to her arriving at Saint Joseph's in January 2011, Dr. Terosky served as the Assistant Principal of Public School #334 in New York City – which received the 2007 New York City Blackboard Award for Outstanding Public Middle School – and was an affiliate professor of higher and post-secondary education at Teachers College, Columbia University. Dr. Terosky received her BS in secondary education (social studies) from The Pennsylvania State University, her MA in school leadership from Villanova University, and her EdD in higher and postsecondary education from Teachers College, Columbia University. Her dissertation, *Taking Teaching Seriously: A Study of Professors and Their Undergraduate Teaching*, won the 2005 Bobby Wright Dissertation of the Year from the Association for the Study of Higher Education (ASHE), which is considered the highest dissertation honor in the field of higher education.

Over the past five years, Dr. Terosky received Saint Joseph's Teaching, Research, and Justice Merit Awards and was selected to serve as the liaison between Saint Joseph's University and Samuel Gompers K–8 school, a public community school in the School District of Philadelphia. The Saint Joseph's and Gompers Partnership has received more than $120,000 in grants and the Saint Joseph's Justice Award, Community Partner Award, and the PHENND Organization's Lindy Award for Excellence in K–12–Community–University Relations.

Laura Gail Lunsford, PhD, is a US Fulbright (Germany) alumna and Full Professor of Psychology and Assistant Dean of Psychology and Social Work in the School of Education and Human Sciences at Campbell University. She was previously a tenured associate professor at the University of Arizona; directed the Swain Center for executive education in the Cameron School of Business at UNC Wilmington; served as the Alumni Director at Duke University's Fuqua School of Business; and was the founding full-time Director of the Park Scholarships at NC State. She has published more than fifty peer-reviewed articles, chapters, and books on mentoring and leadership development, including the definitive *Mentors' Guide: Five Steps to Build a Successful Mentor Program*, now in its second edition, and the second edition of the textbook *Leadership: Leaders, Followers, Environments*.

Dr. Lunsford has presented on mentoring at conferences sponsored by the European Mentoring and Coaching Council, the American Psychological Association, the Association for Psychological Science, and the American Educational Research Association, among others. The Department of Education, the National Science Foundation, the Institute for Education Science, the LUCE Foundation, and the NC Collaborative have funded her work. The National Academies of Science, Engineering and Medicine (NASEM) appointed her to a consensus committee on effective mentoring in STEMM, which published one of their most frequently downloaded reports. She was recently appointed to a NASEM Roundtable on mentoring, well-being, and professional development.

In 2009, Dr. Lunsford was honored with the International Mentoring Association's Dissertation Award. Her BA and PhD are from NC State University and her MS is from UNC Greensboro. Along with Vicki Baker, she is a co-founder of Lead Mentor Develop, LLC, where she regularly consults with organizations on creating fantastic mentoring programs and providing mentorship education.

Volume Contributors

A. Mohammed Abubakar serves as an associate professor at the College of Business and Social Sciences, Antalya Bilim University, Antalya, Turkey. His research spans organizational behavior and the management information systems domain. His focus includes the socioeconomic implications of digital market platforms, online labor platforms, knowledge management, and workplace and employee relations.

Maria (Mia) E. Bertagnolli is Vice Provost for Faculty Affairs and a professor of biology at Gonzaga University. In her vice provost role, she supports the development of faculty by working on initiatives that foster a supportive, inclusive environment and excellence in scholarship and teaching.

Linda M. Boland is Professor of Biology and Associate Provost for Faculty at the University of Richmond, where she was also the founding director of a faculty development center for teaching and scholarship. Her research, with undergraduate student mentees, focuses on the molecular physiology of ion channels.

Diane E. Boyd is the Mary Seawell Metz '58 Executive Director of the Faculty Development Center and Associate Dean of Faculty Development at Furman University. She researches threshold concepts in the scholarship of teaching and learning, course design for educational equity, and increasing agency and vitality via values-infused mid-career programming.

Chrystal D. Bruce is a professor of chemistry at John Carroll University. In addition to supporting the advancement of mid-career faculty and systemic institutional change, her research interests include engaging undergraduate students in making meaningful contributions in computational chemistry and the teaching and learning of chemistry at the undergraduate level.

Kia Lilly Caldwell is the Vice Provost for Faculty Affairs and Diversity and Professor of African and African American Studies at Washington University in St. Louis. As vice provost, she supports the development of policies, practices, and programs that enhance faculty excellence, equity, and success.

Nancy L. Chick is Director of Faculty Development at Rollins College. After becoming a full professor of English in Wisconsin, she shifted her focus to the scholarship of teaching and learning (SoTL) and has authored and edited many publications on the results of SoTL projects and on the field of SoTL itself.

Monique N. Colclough is the Director of Programs and Initiatives at the Belk Center for Community College Leadership and Research at NC State University. Her community college and university work are centered on advocating for equity and student success through collective action with executive leaders.

Dawn Culpepper is a research assistant professor and an associate director of the University of Maryland ADVANCE Program for Inclusive Excellence, where she leads faculty development, education and training, and research and evaluation activities. Her research focuses on identifying strategies for enhancing diversity, equity, and inclusion in the academic workplace.

Seema Dahlheimer is a senior lecturer and an assistant director of the Engineering Communication Center and a faculty fellow in the office of the Provost at Washington University in St. Louis. Her research interests include equity and inclusion in higher education, community-engaged teaching, and reflective writing as a pedagogical tool.

Sarah A. Deal is a senior researcher at DVP-PRAXIS, which provides formative and summative evaluation and consulting services. Her action-focused evaluations and research focus on how community colleges can support students in achieving their goals.

Begüm Çubukçuoğlu Devran is a senior instructor in the Faculty of Education, Eastern Mediterranean University. Her research interests include teacher education, teachers' professional development, and educational technology. She holds a doctorate in education.

Megan Drinkwater is a professor of classics at Agnes Scott College, where she served as director of the Center for Teaching, Learning, and Professional Development. Her work there focused on faculty support across the career span and improving faculty governance processes.

Alev Elçi is an associate professor of educational sciences (educational/teaching technologies) and serves as the Managing Director for the Higher Education Professional Development Network YÖMEGA, Türkiye. She has fifteen years of industry experience and twenty years of academic experience. Her research areas include educational development, digital teaching and learning, technology-enhanced learning, social networks, learning communities, and narrative approaches.

Amy A. Eyler is a professor in the Brown School at Washington University in St. Louis, in the Graduate Program of Public Health. She is also a faculty fellow in the Provost's Office who supports faculty leadership and gender equity.

Patricia M. Flatt is a professor in and Chair of the chemistry department at Western Oregon University. Her research focuses on natural product biosynthesis in marine and freshwater cyanobacteria. At WOU, she has served as the coordinator for the STEM Scholars Center, supporting the advancement of women and underrepresented minority students.

Lauren Footman is the inaugural Diversity, Equity, and Inclusion Officer of Delaware County, Pennsylvania. Footman has been a diversity professional across the corporate, non-profit, and government sectors for the last decade as well as a coach and consultant.

Candace Hastings is the Director of Faculty Development at Texas State University. She spends her days learning what faculty need and developing programming to support those needs. A teacher at heart, she has spent her thirty-year career doing a little bit of everything, from teaching first-year English to doctoral-level research methods.

Chris Heasley is an associate professor of educational leadership and counseling and director of the IDEPEL (doctoral) program at Saint Joseph's University. His research focuses on the interconnectedness between educational environments and faculty/student outcomes in areas related to psychosocial development and socially constructed identities. *Untangling Leadership: Aligning Mind and Heart to Advance Higher Education* (Rowman & Littlefield, 2023) is his most recent book.

Tiffany N. Hughes is a doctoral student in the Department of Educational Leadership and Policy at the University of Texas at Austin. Her research primarily examines the experiences of minoritized students across graduate and professional postsecondary educational settings.

Sarah R. Kirk is Provost and Dean of Faculty and a professor of chemistry at Hobart and William Smith Colleges. In her various institutional leadership roles she has led institution-wide diversity initiatives in support of faculty and students focusing on such topics as faculty handbook revisions and recruitment and retention strategies.

Brooke Fisher Liu is a professor of communication at the University of Maryland. She is a former ADVANCE professor and an ADVANCE peer network co-facilitator. Her primary line of research examines how government messages, media, and interpersonal communications can motivate people to successfully respond to and recover from disasters.

Lori Markson is a professor of psychological and brain sciences and is the Faculty Director for Undergraduate Research at Washington University in St Louis. She is a faculty fellow in the Provost's Office to support mid-career faculty mentoring.

Lori Mumpower is Director of the Center for Teaching and Learning Excellence at Embry-Riddle Aeronautical University, Daytona Beach campus. Dr. Mumpower has been an educational development leader for the past ten years as well as a writing and speech teacher.

KerryAnn O'Meara is Vice President for Academic Affairs, Provost, and Dean of Teachers College, Columbia University. KerryAnn served as director of the University of Maryland's ADVANCE program for ten years, leading evidence-based interventions in inclusive hiring, third-space networks, workload reform, and faculty evaluation.

Taylor L. Pratt is a doctoral student, Center Manager for the SKILLS Collaborative, and the senior staff member for the UofL/Army Master

Educator Course (MEC) partnership at the University of Louisville. Her research focuses on supports for college students with disabilities, including inclusive and equitable teaching practices.

Richard J. Reddick is Senior Vice Provost for Curriculum and Enrollment and Dean of the Undergraduate College at the University of Texas at Austin. He is a professor of educational leadership and policy at UT and serves as a visiting associate professor and faculty co-chair for the Institute for Educational Management at Harvard.

Elizabeth S. Roberts-Kirchhoff is Assistant Dean for Academics and a professor of chemistry and biochemistry at University of Detroit Mercy. Her research interests include inclusive teaching strategies in the college classroom and institutional policies and practices that support diverse faculty and students in STEM.

Hala G. Schepmann is a professor of chemistry at Southern Oregon University. Her drug-discovery research focuses on the identification of bioactive natural products with pharmaceutical applications. Dr. Schepmann also co-founded and leads a university faculty alliance that supports the advancement of underrepresented faculty groups by advocating for supportive and equitable policies.

Staci Starck is the Budget and Human Resources Director of the Office of Admissions at Michigan State University, with more than a decade of experience in research grant management and administration. She is currently a doctoral student in the Central Michigan University Educational Leadership program.

Shantell Strickland-Davis is the Associate Vice President of Organizational Learning and Leadership Development at Central Piedmont Community College. She is the founding Executive Director of the Parr Center for Teaching and Learning Excellence at Central Piedmont. Her research agenda includes understanding the ways in which community college faculty are best supported through classroom instruction, assessment, and engagement.

Jeffrey C. Sun is Professor of Higher Education and Law, Distinguished University Scholar, and Associate Dean for Innovation and Strategic Partnerships at the University of Louisville. In addition, he directs the SKILLS Collaborative, a research and policy center examining workforce development and legal issues in career/professional postsecondary education. Dr. Sun's research and practice areas focus on higher education law and professional/career education policies and practice.

Katherine A. Troyer is the Director of The Collaborative for Learning and Teaching at Trinity University in San Antonio, Texas. Her bookshelves (which place SoTL books next to horror scholarship) reveal her interest in how spoken and unspoken fears – whether in a horror film or in the classroom – shape thoughts and ideas.

Victoria L. Turgeon is a professor of biology and neuroscience and a faculty ombudsperson at Furman University. Her research focuses on blood proteins that exacerbate spinal cord injury. She also led the development and implementation of the Community Engaged Medicine program, aimed at increasing healthcare provider diversity and addressing social determinants of health.

Deborah Vriend Van Duinen is the Arnold and Esther Sonneveldt Professor of Education at Hope College. She is the Director of the Big Read Lakeshore, an annual month-long reading program that impacts more than 20,000 readers of all ages. Her research areas include adolescent literacy, young adult literature, and community literacy.

Mary Katherine Watson is an associate professor of civil and environmental engineering at The Citadel. Her research focuses on understanding cognitive processes while undertaking sustainable design tasks and in online contexts. Dr. Watson directs the Excellence in Civil Engineering Leadership program, which supports the persistence and success of high-performing low-income students.

Jennifer Wojton is an associate professor of humanities and communication and the Coordinator for Faculty Mentoring Initiatives on the Daytona Beach Campus of Embry-Riddle Aeronautical University. Mentoring, as both a practice and an area for research, has been central to her career in academia. She also publishes scholarship in digital culture studies and fan studies.

Introduction

What's Next? and How to Navigate? Facilitating Mid-Career Advancement

Vicki L. Baker

"What's next?" is a question that my co-editors and I hear consistently from mid-career faculty and mid-level academic leaders across the academy. The mid-career stage is characterized by increased responsibility, diversified roles, and fewer milestones to traverse as one navigates it (Baker & Manning, 2021). Yet the mid-career stage is also a time of great opportunity (Baker & Terosky, 2021): a time to engage in intentional career planning to chart a path forward, regardless of whether one's professional aspirations keep one on the traditional faculty trajectory or inspire a pivot toward an administrative path or the pursuit of yet-to-be realized opportunities.

Traditionally, mid-career has been defined as the time following the achievement of tenure and promotion (where a tenure system is present), up to ten years prior to retirement (Baker, 2020). However, the editorial team of *A Toolkit for Mid-Career Academics* recognizes that individuals' lived experiences do not always result in a direct path within the academy as it has been characterized to date. Thus, we expand on the notion of mid-career, defined by Baker and colleagues previously (Baker, 2020; Baker et al., 2019), as we seek to be inclusive of the diversified appointment types and paths to mid-career. As such, mid-career also includes those who are seven-plus years past earning an advanced or terminal degree and who may occupy non–tenure-track (NTT) positions, whether full-time or part-time. Mid-career includes those faculty members who earned full professorship as well as those who may have joined the academy after shifting careers following significant time spent in another field or industry. Mid-career also encompasses personal and professional realities, which can include caregiving for school-aged children or eldercare for aging parents.

Given the diverse ways in which mid-career is experienced and navigated, our aim in this volume is to facilitate a reimagining of and reinvestment in the mid-career stage through the creation of a practical, hands-on resource that provides value at the individual faculty, institutional/programmatic, consortia, *and* grant-funded levels. Our goal is to equip scholars of faculty work, faculty developers, mid-career faculty members, and

DOI: 10.4324/9781003428626-1

institutional leaders (e.g., department chair, dean of faculty) with new ideas on how to build a sustainable, diversified portfolio of career advancement supports aimed at mid-career professionals.

Why a Toolkit for Mid-Career?

During the past two years, I (along with my co-editors) have worked with mid-career faculty and campus administrators as they sought to regain their footing post-pandemic. These individuals are capable, competent, and in need of support. Truth be told, I have yet to engage with a mid-career faculty member or administrator who does not see the value, and need, to strategically invest in the mid-career stage given the implications for individual-, departmental-, and institutional-level outcomes (Baker & Manning, 2021). Although our collective scholarship and practice to date has provided a deep dive into the "what's next?" question (Baker, 2022; Baker & Terosky, 2021; Baker et al., 2019), there is a need to move beyond the *what* and focus on the *how* of mid-career with corresponding tools and strategies.

A Toolkit for Mid-Career Academics features contributions from leading scholars, practitioners, faculty developers, and campus administrators, who provide answers to the "what's next" and "how to navigate" questions that are critical to advancement at mid-career. Our focus on what *and* how throughout this volume highlights critical issues and challenges associated with mid-career, coupled with specific tools and strategies to successfully navigate those challenges from diverse stakeholder perspectives. Anyone reading this volume will walk away with the ability to:

a. Identify individual developmental and/or programmatic needs at mid-career; utilize provided tools, resources, and strategies to address the needs.
b. Utilize and/or provide resources and examples to mid-career faculty and institutional/consortia leaders (e.g., department chairs, deans, provosts, executive directors) as they seek to adapt and develop successful programs for mid-career faculty in their own organizations.
c. Learn about and benefit from intentional efforts to incorporate diversity, equity, and inclusion (DEI) considerations into mid-career faculty programming.
d. Create a more strategic approach to mid-career faculty development that aligns with evaluation and advancement processes.

I want to highlight a few unique aspects of the work featured in the volume. First, DEI is foundational to the tools presented and is addressed explicitly in each chapter. We know the importance of acknowledging the barriers and burdens confronting mid-career faculty of color and other underrepresented populations. Thus, there is a need to be explicit about those barriers and to ensure the tools featured work in service of, not against, diverse populations of mid-career professionals. Second, several chapters focus on non–tenure-track mid-career faculty, which is a growing and underserved population in the academy. This segment of faculty has varied needs, and our goal is to help campus administrators and faculty developers learn how to better support and invest in career development for this population. Finally, the diversity of programs, institutions, and tools featured is intentional and a value added. Our hope is that faculty, administrators, and faculty developers adapt and adopt the featured tools for their purposes.

Volume Structure: How to Use the Volume

Given our aim of creating a user-friendly, accessible resource full of tools to support mid-career advancement, the volume is organized into four sections: Faculty Skill Development, Institutional Programming, Consortial and Professional Association Programming, and Grant-Funded Initiatives. Each section begins with a Section Introduction that provides a brief preview of the corresponding chapters and a summary of the main takeaways. Knowing the readership will be broad for this volume, the systematic guidance offered is intentionally accessible to academics and non-academics alike.

Each chapter in the volume can: (a) serve as a stand-alone resource, (b) be read in order, as presented, or (c) be read non-sequentially, based on the targeted needs of the reader. Chapter 19, the concluding chapter, summarizes the main themes across the volume sections and presents a practice agenda for mid-career advancement and career development.

Overview of the Volume

Section 1: Faculty Skill Development is focused on the individual faculty level. Section contributors provide critical advice that mid-career faculty and mid-career campus leaders need and want. Topics addressed include strategies to navigate and secure grant funding; sabbatical planning, execution, and re-entry; mentoring at mid-career; development of effective mentorship skills as a mid-career leader; and the crafting of a career that elevates passions and priorities. Through our scholarship and practice at mid-career, these topics get at the heart of what we hear consistently, regardless of institution type or appointment type.

Section 2: Institutional Programming features a number of exemplary programs that have been developed with mid-career faculty members' needs in mind while also centering the importance of advancing institutional priorities. Section 2 highlights programming that is guided by an inclusive definition of mid-career, thus facilitating the inclusion and engagement of NTT faculty. Some of the featured programs are rooted in a cohort model; each of the programs focuses on supporting mid-career skill development, with methods ranging from supporting faculty learning to enhancing teaching excellence. Institutions represented include a Hispanic-serving institution, a selective liberal arts college, a master's college/university, a doctoral university (with very high research activity), and a community college.

Section 3: Consortial and Professional Association Programming highlights the power of collective engagement at the consortial and professional association levels. As we all know, few institutions have the resources needed to sustain a robust portfolio of mid-career-focused supports. Thus, the advantages are immense of leveraging cross-institutional collaborations to pool resources (e.g., financial, intellectual) and co-create and co-disseminate knowledge. Section 3 showcases efforts to support mid-career faculty and mid-career leaders from the Associated Colleges of the South (ACS); YÖMEGA, the Higher Education Professional Development Network in Türkiye; Community College Teaching and Learning Hubs in North Carolina; and the Council for the Advancement of Higher Education Programs (CAHEP), housed within the Association for the Study of Higher Education (ASHE) professional association.

Section 4: Grant-Funded Initiatives provides a road map for those who aspire to secure funding and to inspire possibilities for what can be accomplished. Included in this section are discussions of efforts that are active in terms of grant status and others that need to be sustained once initial grant funding ends. Of particular importance are the lessons that can be learned through collaboration and capacity building when mid-career faculty and administrators work together. Featured programs include regional inter-institutional alliances in STEM fields of primarily undergraduate institutions (PUIs), faculty peer networks in the University of Maryland ADVANCE program, a partnership between higher education and the military, and humanities-based grant-funded work aimed at serving mid-career faculty.

The Power of a Mid-Career Community

I wrote this introduction after spending two days in Chicago at the American Educational Research Association (AERA), where I, along with Aimee LaPointe Terosky, Chris Heasley, and Meghan Pifer, facilitated a Division-J mid-career faculty workshop. We are fortunate to have such opportunities to engage in community with diverse scholars, practitioners, and administrators who seek guidance on how to navigate the *what* and *how* questions to inform their own career advancement and who also want to provide a better foundation for guiding the faculty peers they are tasked with supporting. This book was inspired by interactions with these individuals and by their follow-up emails and communications. Funding and travel are still constrained, and not all institutions can enlist the support of my consulting company Lead Mentor Develop, LLC, to develop custom faculty development/career advancement programming. Yet mid-career individuals are yearning for support and to learn from others, a lesson reinforced at AERA. This volume is for them: the mid-career faculty, the administrators, and the faculty developers who enlist our support and who trust us to show care and compassion for their mid-career experiences.

My hope is that they will feel seen and heard as they work through the chapters in this volume; that they learn from the triumphs and missteps outlined here; and that they are inspired to both advance their own careers and support mid-career faculty on their own campuses or in their consortia or professional associations. If they read something in this volume that resonates, I hope they will reach out to the talented contributors featured here to let them know. I also hope they will reach out to me to let me know how and in what ways this volume emboldened them. Happy reading!

References

Baker, V. L. (2020). *Charting your path to full: A guide for women associate professors*. Rutgers University Press.

Baker, V. L. (2022). *Managing your academic career: A guide to re-envision mid-career*. Routledge.

Baker, V. L., Lunsford, L. G., Neisler, G., Meghan, J., Pifer, M. J., & Terosky, A. L. (2019). *Success after tenure: Supporting mid-career faculty*. Stylus.

Baker, V. L., Lunsford, L. G., & Pifer, M. J. (2019). Patching up the "leaking leadership pipeline": Fostering mid-career faculty succession management. *Research in Higher Education*, *60*, 823–843.

Baker, V. L., & Manning, C. (2021). A mid-career faculty agenda: A review of four decades of research and practice. *Higher Education: Handbook of Theory and Research*, *36*, 419–484.

Baker, V. L., & Terosky, A. L. (2021). Spotlight on mid-career: Research and practice considerations for faculty and institutional leaders. *New Directions for Higher Education*, *193/194*, 5–10.

Section 1

Faculty Skill Development

Aimee LaPointe Terosky

Although the unsustainable nature of the contemporary faculty career requires attention at the institutional level, the following chapters share individual strategies ("tools") for navigating mid-career in the academy. The range of strategies addresses: (a) grant proposals and logistics, (b) sabbatical planning and implementation, (c) academic leaders' mentoring skills, (d) supportive networks to advance mid-career professional and personal goals, and (e) career design that elevates priorities. As a collective, the chapters in this section all speak to two key concepts: the power of *intentionality* and the value of *relationships*.

In terms of *intentionality*, this section's authors warn against a common threat during mid-career: being governed by others' agendas without a clear vision of one's own priorities. Once faculty members receive tenure and are promoted, it is common practice in higher education to call on them to assume service, administrative, and leadership roles at disproportionate levels and often with little to no professional development or support (Baker et al., 2018). As such, mid-career faculty often feel stuck, overworked, and disengaged from the very passions that drew them to their careers in the first place (Neumann & Terosky, 2007). To counter this threat, this section provides tangible tools that guide mid-career faculty, including reflection exercises that enable them to (re)engage with professional and personal vitality and action planning steps around goals and milestones that safeguard space for priorities.

In terms of *relationships*, the chapters in Section 1 illustrate the value of relationships at mid-career, specifically relationships that support (re)designing the career in ways that elevate priorities despite the very real context of increasing administrative, service, and leadership roles. Throughout this section's chapters, the authors identify tools for accessing, expanding, and developing professional networks that foster productivity, effectiveness, and joyfulness. For example, they promote the development of collaborative teams for grants, supportive networks across the full sabbatical experience, enhanced mentoring approaches that motivate

DOI: 10.4324/9781003428626-2

colleagues, collegial relationships that promote mid-career faculty members' professional goals alongside the maintenance of holistic and complete personal lives, and considerations of positive relationships in one's workload. Although relationship building might seem like a commonsense strategy, it is surprisingly challenging today given limits on discretionary time and constrained opportunities for interpersonal interactions due to rising workloads and new patterns of working remotely since the COVID-19 pandemic.

Each chapter in this section draws on the concepts of intentionality and relationships in developing tools that mid-career faculty can immediately put into practice. In Chapter 1, Starck highlights a collaborative model for grant writing and management that is grounded in community-of-practice and social networking theories. She exemplifies intentionality through all phases of grant writing by applying a tool that guides mid-career faculty in determining team members, workload distribution, timelines, and budgets. Starck demonstrates, vis-à-vis her Grants Tool, that positive grant experiences rely on intentional team composition and logistics, relationship-oriented team management, and mutually beneficial contributions.

Aligned with Starck's approach to grants, in Chapter 2, Boland and Baker share a Sabbatical Planning Worksheet that facilitates mid-career faculty members' reflections on their sabbatical goals, the action items needed to bring those goals to fruition, and the ongoing redesigning of the sabbatical experience. Beyond intentionality, they also highlight the value of relationships during the sabbatical, specifically by emphasizing the sharing of goals and outcomes with department chairs and accountability partners. Boland and Baker also highlight the relationship with the self, often overlooked in mid-career faculty careers, by stressing the importance of safeguarding the sabbatical as a source of rejuvenation.

Reddick and Hughes offer a tool that consists of reflective prompts, garnered from their experiences leading professional development sessions, especially their work with the mid-career faculty workshops offered annually by the Association for the Study of Higher Education and the American Educational Research Association. In Chapter 3, they first share their own sound advice (and that of others in the literature) for fostering mid-career goals, such as being strategic with research and service and intentionally seeking out supportive mentors; then they offer actionable prompts to engage readers in their own career and life reflections.

In Chapter 4, Lunsford and Baker explain two tools that holistically guide mid-career academic leaders through mentoring activities, one of which increases awareness of contextual factors that impact working conditions and the other which identifies pathways for expanding professional networks. Through their Environmental Scan and Developmental Network Analysis worksheets, Lunsford and Baker fill a void in the professional development of academic leaders (e.g., department chairs, deans, directors) by providing tools to enhance academic leaders' skills in mentoring others. Both of the earlier-noted concepts of intentionality and relationship building are presented in this chapter, as the authors' tools guide mid-career academic leaders (and the colleagues they are mentoring) to better understand the contexts in which their work is embedded and to more effectively leverage the potential networks that can build social capital and deliver potential resources.

This final chapter, by Terosky and Footman, also highlights intentionality and relationship building through their Job Crafting Action Plan tool. Job crafting, the career design model highlighted in Chapter 5, calls on mid-career faculty to proactively reflect on teaching, research, and service priorities and then apply the job crafting model, which includes steps to maximize tasks, relationships, and mindsets that promote their goals. A key aspect of job crafting is building positive and supportive relationships, in which mid-career faculty are prompted to consider which colleagues or work contexts best serve their priorities.

In closing, the individual-level tools highlighted in Section 1 serve as powerful strategies to help faculty assume agency at mid-career. When discussing agency, or an individual's "power, will, and desire to create work contexts conducive to their thought over time" (Elder, 1997, pp. 964–965), it is important to note that intentionality and access to relationships/ networks is a privilege and does not present equitably for all mid-career faculty. Past scholars and practitioners have inflated the power of the individual in pursuing intentional action plans and accessing networks with little regard for the dominant white cisgender male culture that characterizes higher education. As such, the tools presented in this section strive to balance the perspectives and actions that individual faculty can apply to (re)claim their careers within institutional and societal realities that hinder the enactment of such tools for mid-career faculty who are members of minoritized communities.

References

Baker, V. L., Lunsford, L. G., Neisler, G., Pifer, M. J., & Terosky, A. L. (2018). *Success after tenure: Supporting mid-career faculty*. Sterling, VA: Stylus.

Elder, G. H. (1997). The life course and human development. In W. Damon & R. M. Lerner (Eds.), *Handbook of child psychology* (5th ed., pp. 939–991). Wiley.

Neumann, A., & Terosky, A. L. (2007, May/June). To give and to receive: Recently tenured professors' experiences of service in major research universities. *Journal of Higher Education, 78*(3), 282–310.

Chapter 1

Demystifying Grants

Strategies to Take Your Research to the Next Level and Get Funded Through Collaborative Networking

Staci Starck

Overview

This chapter is geared to mid-career faculty members who are navigating grant processes, striving to scale up their research, and applying for high-dollar awards. The success of faculty in the promotion and tenure process, especially in reaching the rank of full professor, can be dependent on research output and productivity. To produce large, robust research studies, it is essential for faculty to secure sponsored research funds, for which they need to submit proposals to government agencies or foundations. Grant proposals generally comprise an abstract, detailed narrative, budget details, and a statement of work. The grant world is increasingly competitive, and having multiple grant proposal rejections is discouraging.

Early-career grant obtainment, high-quality proposal content, topic choice, and social networking have all been identified as indicators for success in getting a research proposal funded. Through the power of social networks, mid-career budding principal investigators can strengthen grant proposals by drawing on the collective knowledge, experience, and resources of those in their networks. Faculty members who intend to scale up their research by broadening its scope, increasing the funding amount, or seeking longer-term funding should consider utilizing social networks to grow collaborative research teams that will facilitate this growth.

Program Focus

Prior research has identified various indicators of success in obtaining grant funding. Career stage is one indicator. Securing grant funding in early to mid-career has an incredible impact on the likelihood of receiving future funding. One significant finding is that researchers who fail to secure funding early in their careers are less likely to submit subsequent grant applications, suggesting that early success can have a positive impact on the confidence needed to keep applying for grants (Bol et al., 2018).

DOI: 10.4324/9781003428626-3

Early-career investigators who were successful in securing subsequent funding had strong grant-writing abilities at the time of their first application and were scored better, submitted applications more frequently, and renewed more applications. Diversity in sponsor applications and being at an institution that already has a high number of funded awards (Haggerty & Fenton, 2018) were also indicators of success.

The content in the proposal is another indicator of success for a funded proposal. Topic choice for the grant proposal appears to have an impact on the likelihood of receiving funding (Hoppe et al., 2019). Proposals with abstracts that are written in a confident manner with more complex wording are more likely to be funded, indicating that language choice and author voice have an impact on the likelihood of funding (Markowitz, 2019).

Intra-institutional support (i.e., research enterprise, attendance at grant-writing seminars, statistical consulting, etc.) and networking through mentorships help grow the collaborative building blocks that early-career faculty need to develop their skills as grant writers and to ultimately be successful in obtaining funding (Leberman et al., 2016).

Collaborative networks are also an indicator of success. Experience on collaborative teams has been identified as a factor in the facilitation of professional growth and the development of academic identity (Leibowitz et al., 2014). The strength and size of social networks positively impact the number of proposals submitted, and additionally, the likelihood of receiving an award (Haller & Welch, 2014). Institutional affiliation does appear to create a familiarity bias, which impacts the scoring of grant applications (Tamblyn et al., 2018). A larger and more diverse research team across multiple institutions also may have a positive impact on the likelihood of being funded.

Needed Skill

Grant-writing workshops are often offered to faculty to develop the specific skills required for grant narrative composition but often fail to address some of the other skills required for grant management. To scale up research studies and obtain larger research grants, it is also essential to build research teams.

This chapter will address the importance of building research networks, strategies to build a community of scholars, and practical considerations for managing a cross-institution grant-funded research project.

Rationale

Securing grants to sponsor research activity is increasingly important across many institutions, colleges, and universities, which often depend on a certain amount of sponsored funding to supplement their annual operating budget. Scholarship is an expectation for faculty, even those with tenure, and there is very little opportunity for internal funding to sponsor research. Therefore, faculty members are expected to apply for grants to sponsor their research and gradually scale up over time. However, it is incredibly difficult to obtain large-scale grants as an individual principal investigator. It is imperative that faculty grow their social networks, or professional connections, to build teams that will increase their likelihood of success in being awarded funds.

The expectations and workload for faculty gradually increase over time (Baldwin et al., 2008). The work required for full-scale research studies is best shared with a community of scholars to increase scholarship output. Increasing scholarly generativity will add to a mid-career faculty member's CV and will only help their chance of getting funded.

Equity and Inclusion Considerations

Prior research shows that there are demographic considerations that may impact the likelihood of receiving funding. There is a strong correlation between race and likelihood of receiving research funding, even though application review is not supposed to include demographic data (Ginther et al., 2011; Ginther & Schaffer, 2016; Hoppe et al., 2019; Zimmerman, 2022). White investigators are more likely to receive funding than Black, Asian, and Hispanic investigators irrespective of education or training (Ginther et al., 2011). White principal investigators (PIs) are more likely to receive funding than all PIs of color, and Black/African American PIs are less likely than all other racial groups to receive grant funding (Ginther et al., 2011).

Additionally, institutional affiliation and collaborative networks have been identified as key contributing factors for grant award success. Bias does seem to impact the scoring of grant applications due to familiarity with institutional affiliation (Tamblyn et al., 2018). Faculty at smaller institutions or at universities with less prestige will be negatively impacted, as they do not have the power of a big name to boost their credibility. Faculty that are part of a large collaborative professional network are more likely to submit more grant proposals and more likely to receive funding (Haller & Welch, 2014). Intentionally seeking to create more racially diverse research teams and submit collaborative proposals can be one method to address racial inequity in research funding.

Theoretical Grounding

The theoretical framework for this chapter utilizes the concept of a community of practice and social networking theory. A community of practice is a group that forms naturally around a common topic of study and that is stimulated by active discussion about good ideas (Wenger et al., 2002). Communities of practice are created through the act of making professional social connections. They facilitate conversations that deviate from the norm and creative thinking about topics that may be unconventional or novel (Wenger et al., 2002).

Tool

In the section that follows, I provide a tool that fosters strategies around grants, especially strategies around collaboration. The tool consists of a series of critical questions in four sections that support mid-career faculty during the stages of grant writing and building a collaborative research team. Section 1 focuses on the rationale and logistics of networking, Section 2 emphasizes the logistical implications of collaborative research roles, Section 3 homes in on budgetary considerations, and Section 4 highlights the logistical implications of a timeline for collaborative research. Helpful hints garnered from the wisdom of practice follow each section of reflective questions. The sections on the tool and the reflective questions are written in a voice directed at mid-career faculty members.

Section 1: Rationale for and Logistics of Networking

- Who am I working with now? Who have I worked with in the past? Who do I know now that I haven't yet collaborated with?
- Who is studying the same topics as me?

In creating a team with other faculty members with similar research interests, you can both strengthen your proposal and eliminate one potential grant competitor. Another advantage is that combining research interests in a collaborative manner strengthens the proposal. By creating teams with related but different research interests, you add topic diversity to your proposal.

Seek out diversity in all areas; gender, ethnic background, geography, institutional affiliation, area of study, etc. Network with people who have similar or related research interests at conferences. One way to facilitate these connections is through volunteerism via reviewing proposals, moderating panel discussions, and sitting on committees for conference organizations.

- Who is presenting on similar topics at conferences?
- Who is doing cutting-edge research in emerging areas of interest?

Remaining updated on current research will not only help you stay ahead on future research needs but also keep you in the loop regarding who is conducting research that is similar to yours (Yousoubova & McAlpine, 2022). It is best to stay relevant and to keep apprised of your competition.

- Are there pre-existing mentoring networks within my institution or professional organization?

There are a few models for large-scale network development. The National Research Mentoring Network (NRMN) serves as a model for strategic research collaboration through mentoring (Jones et al., 2017). The Grant Writing Coaching Program seeks to team up less-experienced grant writers in minority groups with senior researchers to develop grant-writing and management skills across institutional lines (Weber-Main et al., 2020).

Building relationships with senior researchers extends beyond developing skills in grant narrative writing. The opportunity to do collaborative research can facilitate knowledge transfer from senior researchers to budding principal investigators about grant management skills, including managing budgets, maintaining publication schedules, and reporting to sponsors.

Section 2: Logistical Implications of Collaborative Research Roles

When forming a team, it is important to have explicit discussions about the role each member will play (i.e., principal investigator, co-principal investigator, senior researcher, etc.), along with the tasks each team member will accomplish (e.g., primary grant writing, editing, or budget coordinating).

Below is a list of critical questions that can help you craft a well-rounded research team and define each person's respective role. This section will outline some of the roles and tasks that should be considered when planning a larger-scale research grant and can be used to facilitate a discussion between team members about who might take on the various roles.

- Who will be responsible for the overall proposal? Will there be shared ownership over the entire study, or will each team member be responsible for a distinct area of the study? Who has the most grant management experience?
  - The principal investigator (PI) is ultimately responsible for all aspects of the grant: management of the team, oversight of budget and financial transactions, data management, scholarly output, and reports to the sponsor. The main grant will be housed at the home institution of the PI, which will have oversight over any subcontracts issued to other institutions.
  - There may be one or more co-principal (Co-PI) investigators (depending on sponsor rules) for shared ownership and management of the

grant. Each co-PI is responsible for the oversight and management of their respective budget at their home institution. Some sponsors will issue separate awards directly to institutions of co-PIs to allow for multiple PIs to have equal authority over their own grant, allowing for separate but related collaborative workflows.

- What are the strengths of each team member? Are there any content gaps that should be filled?
- A senior researcher may be a faculty member or a post-doctoral researcher at one of the PI/co-PI's institutions. They may also be a faculty member at a separate institution and can be issued a subcontract at their home institution. The senior researcher will ultimately be responsible for the oversight of their subcontract but will have less management responsibility with regard to the overall grant. This role is generally held by earlier-career scholars or scholars who bring a different specialized skill set (e.g., a statistician).
- Will this research grant incorporate students?

  - Employing graduate research assistants on research grants can be mutually beneficial. Students can gain research experience and build their curriculum vitae. Graduate research assistants often focus on doing literature reviews, collecting data, and analyzing the data – tasks that are often time-consuming and monotonous.
  - Undergraduate research assistants can often serve as the assistants to the graduate research assistants. This provides undergraduate students with important research opportunities and gives graduate students an opportunity to provide mentorship and supervision.

- Does the research team have the capacity to manage the logistical aspects of the grant?

  - A professional project manager coordinates the study as a whole and builds bridges to maintain communication across the entire research team. The primary objective of this role is to know everything there is to know about the project, linking important considerations regarding data collection/analysis, budget, sponsor guidelines, scholarly output, and schedule.

Section 3: Budgetary Considerations

When developing your budget, know who will be paying for what. Following are some important questions to consider.

- How much of my time will I need to accomplish the work that I am promising to the sponsor? How much time is needed for a course buyout?
- Will we be meeting in person? Where will we meet? Who will pay for any shared expenses?

- Which budget will pay for which initiative/supply order? Does this align with the institution of the partner who will oversee this work?
- Is the budget realistic for the scope of work proposed?

For cross-institution collaboration, there will need to be a primary institution that is submitting the proposal, and all other institutions will be included in the grant as subcontracts. This doesn't detract from your scholarly contribution or reduce your collaboration in this project; it is just a way to determine how funds will be organized and disseminated. Be sure to have explicit discussions at the proposal stage about costs and consider which budget will absorb them.

Section 4: Logistical Implications and Timeline of Collaborative Research

It is essential to set a timeline for grant submissions. Each faculty member should work with their institution's research administrator or other staff members to align the team's proposal schedule with the program office's deadlines. Once a grant is awarded, it is equally important to set a schedule for the duration of the grant to meet the required milestones.

Table 1.1 is a suggested timeline to consider when planning a grant submission and some questions that should be considered during each stage.

Table 1.1 Grant Submission Timeline

Stage	Task
Pre-proposal development	• Who could be added to the research team so that it is more diverse? • What are areas of emerging research and future study? • Is this topic relevant to the field of research? • What initiatives are sponsors looking to fund? (Search grants.gov to seek opportunities available from many major federal sponsors in one place: https://www.grants.gov/web/grants/search-grants.html.) • How can this topic be aligned to meet the criteria of the request for proposal (RFP)? • Could this proposal be formatted for submission to multiple sponsors?
Proposal submission	• What role will everyone on the team fill? What are the responsibilities and expectations for each role? • What is the ultimate goal of the project? Is the scope of work mapped out across a realistic timeline? • Does the budget support the proposed work? • Who will write each section of the proposal? What is the timeline to submit this proposal on time, according to each institution's deadlines?

(Continued)

Table 1.1 (Continued)

Stage	Task
Award/project start	• What is the timeline and task list for this project? (A Gantt chart, process map, and work breakdown structure can all be very helpful. OSU provides a helpful toolkit for project management: https://ccts.osu.edu/content/project-management-research.) • What non-salary expenses are in the budget? When will these expenditures occur? • What is the data management plan? (DMP Tool can help create a data management plan in accordance with sponsor requirements: https://dmptool.org/.) • Have all regulatory reviews (e.g., IRB, IACUC) been submitted in compliance with institutional requirements?
Ongoing	• How often will the team meet? • Will there be subteams to manage specific tasks?
One year in	• Is an annual report required by the sponsor? Will budget expenditure progress be included in this report? • What are the milestones for the next year? (Use this time to reflect on what went well, what processes need refinement, and what might need to be adjusted for the expected timeline to be achieved.)
Grant end/closeout	• What is required to prepare to close out the grant? (Two to three months before a grant closes out, the team must prepare to meet that date.) • Have all publication submissions occurred? • Is the work of the study complete? • Have most expenditures been spent or encumbered? (In the instance that grant objectives have not been met and there are some funds remaining, check with your sponsor to see if a no-cost extension may be granted to extend the grant period.)

Lessons Learned

As a research management professional, I developed the tool (i.e., reflective questions on grants followed by wisdom of practice) showcased in this chapter over the course of many years of working with collaborative research teams. Through my experiences with collaborative research teams, grant writing, and using this chapter's tool, I share three key lessons learned. First, there are many ways to structure research projects, and the success of receiving grant funding can be highly dependent on how well constructed the research plan is in the proposal. When planning a research proposal for a large-scale project, it is helpful to have as many details as possible planned out to indicate to sponsors that the team is prepared to quickly launch it. Second, the proposal is the story of the research plan. As such, writers should ensure that the narrative flows well, that all details are accounted for, and that there are no surprise plot twists. This can be challenging with a larger team, but a well-planned project can be successful. Third, grant writers should build up their grant activity over time. Mid-career faculty should plan to gradually scale up and build a grant portfolio that supports research interests around a given topic. Grant funding leads to more grant funding, so in consideration of future projects, design your studies as a series of stages, always keeping in mind the next project.

Conclusion

In summary, one way to increase the likelihood of having a successful grant experience is to design a diverse research team that matches the scope of work. A diverse research team means that each member will have varying degrees of expertise in the subject matter and varying levels of experience working on grants. When seeking out members for collaborative research teams, it is a good idea to work with faculty who have significant experience in managing research teams; these collaborators can serve as role models when the time comes to strategize for future projects. Once these skills have been learned, practiced, and refined, mid-career faculty should be intentional about networking with junior faculty in order to assist in developing the next generation's grant management skills.

References

Baldwin, R., DeZure, D., Shaw, A., & Moretto, K. (2008). Mapping the terrain of mid-career faculty at a research university: Implications for faculty and academic leaders. *Change: The Magazine of Higher Learning, 40*(5), 46–55.

Bol, T., De Vaan, M., & van de Rijt, A. (2018). The Matthew effect in science funding. *Proceedings of the National Academy of Sciences of the United States of America, 115*(19), 4887–4890. https://doi.org/10.1073/pnas.1719557115

Ginther, D. K., Kahn, S., & Schaffer, W. T. (2016). Gender, race/ethnicity, and National Institutes of Health R01 research awards: Is there evidence of a double bind for women of color? *Academic Medicine: Journal of the Association of American Medical Colleges, 91*(8), 1098–1107. https://doi.org/10.1097/ACM.0000000000001278

Ginther, D. K., Schaffer, W. T., Schnell, J., Masimore, B., Liu, F., Haak, L. L., & Kington, R. (2011). Race, ethnicity, and NIH research awards. *Science (New York, N.Y.), 333*(6045), 1015–1019. https://doi.org/10.1126/science.1196783

Haggerty, P. A., & Fenton, M. J. (2018). Outcomes of early NIH-funded investigators: Experience of the National Institute of Allergy and Infectious Diseases. *PLoS One, 13*(9), e0199648. https://doi.org/10.1371/journal.pone.0199648

Haller, M. K., & Welch, E. W. (2014). Entrepreneurial behavior of academic scientists: Network and cognitive determinants of commitment to grant submissions and award outcomes. *Entrepreneurship Theory and Practice, 38*(4), 807–831. https://doi.org/10.1111/etap.12022

Hoppe, T. A., Litovitz, A., Willis, K. A., Meseroll, R. A., Perkins, M. J., Hutchins, B. I., Davis, A. F., Lauer, M. S., Valantine, H. A., Anderson, J. M., & Santangelo, G. M. (2019). Topic choice contributes to the lower rate of NIH awards to African-American/black scientists. *Science Advances, 5*(10), eaaw7238. https://doi.org/10.1126/sciadv.aaw7238

Jones, H. P., McGee, R., Weber-Main, A. M., Buchwald, D. S., Manson, S. M., Vishwanatha, J. K., & Okuyemi, K. S. (2017). Enhancing research careers: An example of a US national diversity-focused, grant-writing training and coaching experiment. *BMC Proceedings, 11*(Suppl. 12), 16. https://doi.org/10.1186/s12919-017-0084-7

Leberman, S. I., Eames, B., & Barnett, S. (2016). Unless you are collaborating with a big name successful professor, you are unlikely to receive funding. *Gender and Education, 28*(5), 644–661. https://doi.org/10.1080/09540253.2015.1093102

Leibowitz, B., Ndebele, C., & Winberg, C. (2014). 'It's an amazing learning curve to be part of the project': Exploring academic identity in collaborative research. *Studies in Higher Education, 39*(7), 1256–1269. https://doi.org/10.1080/03075079.2013.801424

Markowitz, D. M. (2019). What words are worth: National Science Foundation grant abstracts indicate award funding. *Journal of Language and Social Psychology, 38*(3), 264–282. https://doi.org/10.1177/0261927X18824859

Tamblyn, R., Girard, N., Qian, C. J., & Hanley, J. (2018). Assessment of potential bias in research grant peer review in Canada. *CMAJ: Canadian Medical Association Journal, 190*(16), E489–E499. https://doi.org/10.1503/cmaj.170901

Weber-Main, A. M., McGee, R., Eide Boman, K., Hemming, J., Hall, M., Unold, T., Harwood, E. M., Risner, L. E., Smith, A., Lawson, K., Engler, J., Steer, C. J., Buchwald, D., Jones, H. P., Manson, S. M., Ofili, E., Schwartz, N. B., Vishwanatha, J. K., & Okuyemi, K. S. (2020). Grant application outcomes for biomedical researchers who participated in the National Research Mentoring Network's Grant Writing Coaching Programs. *PLoS One, 15*(11), e0241851. https://doi.org/10.1371/journal.pone.0241851

Wenger, E., McDermott, R., & Snyder, W. M. (2002). Seven principles for cultivating communities of practice. *Cultivating Communities of Practice: A Guide to Managing Knowledge, 4.*

Yousoubova, L., & McAlpine, L. (2022). Why is the proposal alone not sufficient for grant success? Building research fundability through collaborative research networking. *Innovations in Education and Teaching International, 59*(1), 93–103. https://doi.org/10.1080/14703297.2021.1997784

Zimmermann, A., Klavans, R., Offhaus, H. M., Grieb, T. A., & Smith, C. (2022). Award rate inequities in biomedical research. *PLoS One, 17*(7), e0270612. https://doi.org/10.1371/journal.pone.0270612

Chapter 2

Faculty Re-Engagement

A Sabbatical Planning Guide to Support Productivity and Well-Being

Linda M. Boland and Vicki L. Baker

Overview

For tenured mid-career faculty, a sabbatical reprieve from the challenges of balancing teaching, research, and service provides both time and an environmental context that may reinvigorate their scholarly or creative endeavors (Baker & Boland, 2023). Members of the academy found they needed to reset their scholarly and creative goals following the global pandemic, just as they do at intervals of seven years (most commonly) when they take sabbaticals. New investments in career development supports are critical to ensuring that diverse and talented faculty members thrive. The sabbatical is an opportunity for them to contribute to their own growth, development, and well-being while helping to advance institutional aims and priorities.

The focus of this chapter is on providing a robust sabbatical tool that aids mid-career faculty members in being intentional with sabbatical planning and engagement as well as re-entry following the sabbatical. The sabbatical, as a considerable institutional investment in labor reallocation, provides time away from standard responsibilities on the assumption that mid-career faculty will return with new energy, creative ideas, and a readiness to re-engage with individual and institutional goals. The sabbatical is perhaps the single most important chance to facilitate faculty advancement and well-being; careful consideration of how to take advantage of this opportunity at mid-career is important for both the faculty member and the institution (Schabram et al., 2023). Our goal is to provide mid-career faculty with the needed support to realize the power of the sabbatical.

Program Focus

Given the duration of the typical career, faculty may experience multiple opportunities to take a sabbatical, each with unique alignments with career progression. The first sabbatical is certainly a critical one, with newly tenured associate professors often eligible in the year or two following promotion and a positive tenure decision. Additional sabbaticals may align with

DOI: 10.4324/9781003428626-4

promotion to full professor and other career advancement milestones before retirement. These multiple opportunities for sabbaticals amplify the importance of having a useful and adaptable tool to support sabbatical success.

For mid-career faculty who are not eligible for a sabbatical or who are unable to earn a sabbatical due to limited institutional resources, the tool featured can be repurposed for other time periods in which a break from the cognitive overload of the academy is realized. These could include an intersession, a summer break, or an academic term with reduced responsibilities. The approaches outlined in this chapter are designed for use by mid-career faculty primarily, but they can also be used to guide the work of department chairs, deans, and faculty developers who provide much needed mentoring support to mid-career faculty members.

What is described in this chapter is the foundation of a webinar prepared and delivered for the National Center for Faculty Development and Diversity (NFCDD) and piloted in a program for mid-career faculty at the University of Richmond.

Needed Skill

Among the sabbatical resources available, most focus on the planning stages (Bass et al., 2020; Sparks, 2022). Effective planning is certainly a necessary component to achieving success, and it provides a critical foundation on which to build. However, we argue that support around sabbatical execution and academic re-entry once the sabbatical is over are also important to ensuring success and achievement of outlined aims and objectives.

To that end, one needed skill for effective sabbaticals is employing the concept of reverse engineering, in which intended goals are deconstructed by modeling the steps and resources needed for a successful plan. Such a skill requires reflection on desired objectives. Asking *What will success look like at the end of my sabbatical?* helps foster this skill and allows intentionality in planning across all three phases of the sabbatical, as outlined in our previous work (Baker & Boland, 2023). We urge faculty to take time to consider this question, as initial answers are often overly ambitious or narrowly focused on scholarly or creative output when there should be a holistic approach that emphasizes the value of well-being and the rejuvenation of creative and intellectual energy, which are also sabbatical goals.

Rationale

By mid-career, faculty have often established a reputation for expertise in teaching and/or scholarly/creative works (Baker & Manning, 2021). However, reports of being stuck, overloaded, or without direction are also common, and thus faculty require sabbatical plans that are both realistic and aspirational (see Chapter 11 on a consortial approach to mid-career faculty development). A recent report published by the American Association of University Professors provided a snapshot of IPEDS data corroborating the challenges for full-time women faculty and faculty of color (Colby & Fowler, 2020). The findings revealed underrepresentation of women in higher academic ranks (e.g., associate, full), overrepresentation of women in non–tenure-track appointments (e.g., adjunct, contingent), and underrepresentation of faculty of color in higher academic ranks (e.g., associate, full). These trends justify the need for high-impact faculty development opportunities, such as sabbaticals, to support career advancement.

For tenured mid-career faculty, the second sabbatical is sometimes positioned at a time of increased responsibilities for institutional service that might coincide with consideration for promotion to full professorship (Poissant, 2022). The timing varies for everyone, but certainly if promotion has not yet been achieved by the time of the second sabbatical, it is essential to finalize specific projects that can ensure the success of the promotion. We advocate for careful planning of this pre-advancement sabbatical as well as taking advantage of mentorship to ensure one's scholarly or creative portfolio meets institutional expectations. If advancement is the near-term goal, decisions about projects and associated timelines should fit the goal. For example, ensuring that work that is already in the publishing pipeline is accepted would be a much higher priority than initiating a highly ambitious project that may take longer to complete despite the potential for higher impact.

Our practical strategies acknowledge the challenges experienced by mid-career faculty whose sabbatical was disrupted and/or delayed due to the global pandemic. For many, this resulted in two years of lost productivity and momentum (Byrd, 2020). Based on our interactions with faculty across the academy and at our own institutions, we feel that many faculty need guidance and resources to recalibrate and re-envision next steps. The sabbatical planning worksheet featured in this chapter is one such resource.

Equity and Inclusion Considerations

Although the intended audience for this chapter is the mid-career faculty member seeking support as they prepare for and engage in a sabbatical, we agree with Freeman and Baker (2022) that "a sole focus on faculty agency neglects the inherent biases that permeate the academy, creating barriers to inclusivity in promotion policies and practices" (para 5). Advancement of mid-career faculty from underrepresented groups in the academy may require more transparent processes for support and faculty development regarding sabbaticals. Likewise, the unwritten expectations relating to sabbatical productivity need to be made more explicit.

An institutional action proposed by Freeman and Baker (2022) focuses on an analysis of career advancement and faculty recognition trends. Given that the sabbatical may be *the* high-impact professional development resource that enables faculty to meet critical professional goals to facilitate career advancement, administrators need to be more intentional about tracking time to advancement for women, women faculty of color, and faculty of color compared to other demographic groups (Freeman & Baker, 2022). This knowledge would enable campus leaders to provide needed mentoring, sponsorship, and other interventions such as one-to-one coaching and reviews of sabbatical proposals and plans as a means of countering the trend of women faculty and underrepresented minority faculty taking longer to reach full professorship (Baker, 2020; Freeman & Baker, 2022).

We also advocate for holistic support for faculty who have been managing the hidden labor of supporting an increasingly diverse student population. Women and faculty of color disproportionately serve as advisors to students of color (Matthew, 2016; Shalaby et al., 2020), and they have a greater-than-average workload with regard to committee service as institutions work to ensure diverse representation on faculty committees (Matthew, 2016). Increasingly, we understand the added emotional labor for faculty of color and recognize the importance of a focus on regaining energy, well-being, and joy during sabbaticals (Baker, 2020). The tools provided here elucidate approaches and questions that help expose a type of "hidden agenda": the expectation for excellent sabbatical outcomes without the provision of sufficient support to achieve them.

Conceptual Grounding

We framed the sabbatical in three phases: pre-sabbatical and proposal, mid-sabbatical, and post-sabbatical (Baker & Boland, 2023). Our focus was on equipping faculty developers and others tasked with supporting faculty (e.g., department chairs, deans) with the needed resources to better mentor faculty members preparing for sabbaticals.

The aim of our original model was to highlight the importance of articulating goals and envisioning a scholarly/creative project plan. Managing aspirations and being thoughtful about the various resources available (e.g., financial, human, physical, intellectual) for help in executing plans is critical at this stage. To support faculty while they are engaged in their sabbatical (mid-sabbatical), we offered actions to help faculty developers guide faculty to an effective sabbatical experience, including finding one's workflow, using a pipeline framework to manage multiple projects at various stages, and building in points to check in with trusted mentors (and other accountability checks). Finally, the post-sabbatical phase focused on helping faculty members maintain momentum once they return to the academy. With the support of faculty developers, we suggested engaging in reflective practices, articulating dissemination plans, and mapping out next steps to best position faculty members to continue the great work initiated while on sabbatical.

In this chapter, we expand upon our original three-phase sabbatical model to focus on the faculty perspective, especially the intentionality required to plan and execute each stage successfully. As such, our enhanced model considers the purpose and planning during pre-sabbatical, the completion of goals while finding balance during the sabbatical, and reflection and re-entry during the post-sabbatical. Each phase is rooted in a question directed to the faculty member – *What does success look like?* – followed by another question – *What actions are needed to achieve success?* – as driven by a reverse engineering framework.

Tool

We offer a sabbatical planning worksheet titled Phases of the Sabbatical: A Tool for Faculty at Mid-Career that guides faculty members through the enhanced stages of our sabbatical model. For each stage, we offer critical considerations salient to the specific stage along with guiding questions to facilitate planning and reflection.

Phase 1. Pre-Sabbatical: Purpose and Planning

Pre-sabbatical planning requires purposeful action as faculty seek to identify at least two measurable outcomes for the sabbatical period; such planning can occur three to twelve months prior to the start of the sabbatical. To facilitate purposeful action, the worksheet tool (Table 2.1) includes space for critical considerations including markers of success, corresponding activities (or actions), existing and needed resources, and timeline. We strongly advise that the first outcome be a specific goal related to well-being (e.g., self-restoration, physical wellness); questions about what success looks like and how it will be measured may be applied to a well-being goal. Success may be a new habit or practice to support well-being in ways that can and will be sustained upon re-entry. For a scholarly/creative goal, the nature of the end product will vary by discipline but should represent something tangible (e.g., presentation, publication, exhibit) that can be communicated in a future sabbatical report, annual report, or advancement portfolio.

Although it is not uncommon for a faculty member to conceive a sabbatical plan close to the institutional deadline for a proposal (especially for the first sabbatical), a delayed start to phase 1 is limiting. Lead time is needed to meet with mentors and/or collaborators; to conceptualize, write, and wait for reviews of grant or fellowship applications; and to negotiate or plan for needed resources. Effective planning is particularly important to avoid overlooking the need for a well-being goal. Even mid-career faculty pursuing a second sabbatical can be challenged by a planning stage that fails to allow for time to be purposeful and to seek support from mentors, their chair, or faculty development personnel.

Table 2.1 Phase 1 Planning Worksheet

Phase 1. Pre-Sabbatical: Purpose & Planning

Goal- *Critical to near-term and future career goals*	**Markers of Success-** *Evidence of achieving a goal*	**Activities** *Planned steps to reach a goal*	**Needed Resources-** *Financial (e.g., grant funds)* • *Human (e.g., mentor)* • *Intellectual (e.g., professional development programming)* • *Physical (e.g., workspace)*	**Existing Resources**	**Timeline to address the markers of success**
1. Self-care or well-being goal					
2. Scholarly/ creative goal					

Key Questions:

- How do my sabbatical goals position me for my next career goal?
- How do my sabbatical goals align with the institutional mission?
- What funding can I apply for to support my plan?
- Who have I asked for feedback on my plan?
- What is a weakness of my plan? How will I minimize or overcome this?

Phase 2. Mid-Sabbatical: Completing and Finding Balance

Sabbaticals present a chance to re-invent one's scholarly/creative efforts through learning, collaboration, or self-training (Gernon, 2020). We recommend that this concept be incorporated into the purpose and planning worksheet (Phase 1). Unforeseen and interesting opportunities may arise while completing a sabbatical, and some may have a high potential to contribute to an effective and rewarding sabbatical experience. It is unfortunate if Phase 1 is over-planned to such a degree that new opportunities to explore and learn are seen as stressors. To minimize this, we propose building in time for new adventures that may also foster creativity and inspiration. Phase 2 is the time to heighten awareness of key opportunities that you want to take advantage of, such as establishing an unanticipated collaboration or learning new skills. Unplanned and unexpected opportunities may further advance short- and long-term goals; the ability to take advantage of them only works if you have not over-planned in Phase 1.

We also emphasize balancing near-term and longer-term goals when completing the sabbatical and regularly revisiting goals with the worksheet tool. For faculty taking a first sabbatical, the recency of a tenure and promotion decision may tip the balance to longer-term goals that can be carried forward post-sabbatical. For faculty taking a sabbatical within a year or two of seeking a second promotion, the balance may tip to near-term goals that can directly and quickly impact the promotion portfolio. And, for mid-career faculty who are taking a sabbatical after promotion to full professor, the balance might have more similarity to that of the first sabbatical: in other words, the goal might be to continue successful projects and generate new ideas for achieving long-term goals.

Wherever a faculty member is in their career path, the common features of the second phase of the sabbatical are the needs to complete one's goals and to maintain balance. The worksheet for the second phase (Table 2.2) accounts for the need for revisions at mid-sabbatical.

No sabbatical goes exactly as envisioned, and it's important to normalize this by anticipating that changes will be made, even with the best of planning. Regarding the well-being goal, even with relief from typical academic responsibilities, it is difficult to form new habits, and achieving a well-being goal can be a challenge when scholarly goals seem more important. For the scholarly/creative goal(s), the activities or the resources identified in Phase 1 of the sabbatical may be revealed as insufficient or misaligned with the scholarly goal(s). For these types of challenges, accountability partners are likely to be critical. Whenever accountability partners are not available, careful use of the sabbatical tool and its guiding questions can serve as a form of accountability.

Table 2.2 Phase 2 Planning Worksheet

Phase 2. Mid–Sabbatical: Completing & Finding Balance

Goal *Status update or revision (for all columns)*	Markers of Success	Activities	Management of Current Resources	New Resources Needed	Timeline
1. Self-care or well-being goal					
2. Scholarly/creative goal					

Key Questions

- What am I finding useful about my well-being goal?
- How am I balancing well-being goals with scholarly goals?
- How am I balancing sabbatical goals with near-term and long-term career goals?
- Do I need to discard or reframe any goals?
- What am I learning that is new or unexpected (about me, my goals, the world)?
- Are my timelines still appropriate or do they need revision?
- What new ideas do I want to record for the future without distracting from my sabbatical goals?

We advocate for strong scholarly/creative outcomes during a sabbatical, and yet the success of the sabbatical requires a special attention to balance in Phase 2. Balance includes maintaining progress on the well-being goal identified in purpose and planning, as well as maintaining progress on a specific scholarly/creative goal(s), while allowing for unscripted experiences that promote continuous learning.

Phase 3. Post-Sabbatical: Reflection and Re-Entry

The post-sabbatical period is temporally unique, and we advise that it be initiated at least two weeks prior to the sabbatical end date and continue for several weeks thereafter. These bookends provide an intentional period to reflect on sabbatical goals and to re-energize immediately prior to re-entry to maintain momentum. For ambitious faculty, it can be tempting to work on scholarly goals right up until the sabbatical end date, but this approach conflicts with the balance that was realized in Phase 2. And just as in Phases 1 and 2, we advocate for first considering the primary well-being goal and how to carry it forward once time becomes more constrained post-sabbatical. Careful consideration of approaches and/or attitudes that supported well-being in Phase 2 and discussion with accountability partners may help sustain momentum for effective practices in the post-sabbatical phase.

When using the featured sabbatical tool (Table 2.3), we also advocate for reflection on scholarly/creative goal(s). If a goal was not completed as planned, post-sabbatical is the critical time to reframe the goal and plan for the next phase of success in consideration of near- and long-term career goals. If promotion to full professor is desired soon after the sabbatical, decisions about publishing, exhibiting, or performing work should be priorities during the post-sabbatical stage.

Reflection during the post-sabbatical phase should include consideration of the persons you will consult to expand the success of the sabbatical. Reflection and re-entry are active processes, not simply a halt in the practices that were effective during the sabbatical. The worksheet tool for Phase 3 provides a guide for reflection and planning that mimics the reverse engineering process used in Phase 1. Although well-designed studies on the impact of a sabbatical on scholarly productivity or quality do not exist (Hallock, 2014), we know that critical reflection is a common component of professional development in any field. A final component of this phase is writing about what you learned and produced relative to your sabbatical goals and meeting your institution's requirements for a post-sabbatical report.

Table 2.3 Phase 3 Planning Worksheet

Phase 3: Post-Sabbatical: Reflection and Re-Entry

Goal *Revised from mid-sabbatical and any additional revisions*	Markers of Success *Evidence of achieving a goal*	Plans for Disseminating My Work *Where and when*	What I Learned That I Will Carry Forward *About me, my goals, the world*	Post-Sabbatical Conversations *Chair, mentor, collaborators, dean, grants office*	Conversation Topics *Sabbatical outcomes, next steps, future resources, career advancement*
1. Self-care or well-being goal 2. Scholarly/creative goal					

Key Questions

- What practices that supported my well-being will I continue post-sabbatical?
- What goals were completed and what markers of success will I communicate in a report?
- What additional goals will I discard, reframe, or carry forward?
- When and where will I disseminate my scholarly/creative work?
- How will I continue to engage with collaborators or new networks?
- Who will I talk to about my sabbatical and its impact on my career goals?
- What am I most looking forward to, upon re-entry?

Lessons Learned

Mid-career is a prolonged period of time for associate professors and post-tenure faculty and typically has the largest representation of an institution's faculty. Our faculty development work has revealed that many faculty at this stage would benefit from effective goal-setting and action plans. There are many nuances to mid-career that are impacted by time in rank, assumption of major leadership roles, timing relative to caregiver responsibilities (especially for women faculty), and the impact of hidden service for faculty of color. We have also observed considerable differences in the purpose and planning, completion and balance, and re-entry phases of a sabbatical for those faculty who are taking a first sabbatical and those who are taking a second sabbatical. The sabbatical tool featured in this chapter supports mid-career faculty and also may serve as a guide for their mentors.

Conclusion

The sabbatical is a high-impact professional development opportunity, one we have both benefited from immensely. Through our work as faculty developers, we observed a need for a tool that guides faculty members through the three stages we've outlined to ensure more holistic professional development and the advancement of goals aligned with purpose. We believe faculty members and institutions alike would benefit from more attention and intention related to sabbatical planning, execution, and re-entry.

Completion of this chapter's Sabbatical Planning Worksheet requires setting priorities and identifying related actions. At each phase, once the worksheet is full, we recommend sharing it with mentors and/or a department chair for feedback to inform revisions. It's important to consider priorities when listing goals; taking a holistic approach, we have recommended that the first goal address restoration, cognitively, emotionally, and physically. A second goal should be the highest priority scholarship/creativity goal. If nothing else is achieved during the sabbatical, be clear on these two goals. This focus gives meaning to planning and execution across all phases and is a much-needed approach to fully realizing the power of the sabbatical.

References

Baker, V. L. (2020). *Charting your path to full: A guide for women associate professors*. Rutgers University Press.

Baker, V. L., & Boland, L. M. (2023). Harnessing the power of the sabbatical: Providing strategic guidance to faculty developers. *Journal of Faculty Development*, 37(3), 48–53.

Baker, V. L., & Manning, C. E. (2021). A mid-career faculty agenda: A review of four decades of research and practice. *Higher Education: Handbook of Theory and Research*, *36*, 419–484.

Bass, E. J., Caldwell, B. S., Cao, C. G., Lee, J. D., & Miller, C. (2020, December). Planning the sabbatical: Potential benefits, options, and strategies. In *Proceedings of the Human Factors and Ergonomics Society Annual Meeting* (Vol. 64, No. 1, pp. 582–586). SAGE.

Byrd, W. C. (2020). Pandemic sabbaticals and faculty inequality. *Inside Higher Ed.* www.insidehighered.com/advice/2020/07/28/sabbaticals-are-career-opportunity-everyone-should-have-despite-pandemic-opinion#:~:text=Sabbaticals%20are%20invaluable%20opportunities%20for%20faculty%20members.%20They,a%20specified%20time%20to%20support%20research%20and%20writing

Colby, G., & Fowler, C. (2020). Data snapshot: IPEDS data on full-time women faculty and faculty of color. *AAUP.* www.aaup.org/sites/default/files/Dec-2020_Data_Snapshot_Women_and_Faculty_of_Color.pdf

Freeman, S., & Baker, V. L. (2022, July 22). Revolutionizing promotion to full professor. *Inside Higher Ed.* www.insidehighered.com/advice/2022/07/22/academe-should-revise-promotion-process-full-professor-opinion

Gernon, T. (2020). A sabbatical reboot. *Science*, *370*(6517), 738–738. www.science.org/doi/10.1126/science.370.6517.738

Hallock, K. F. (2014). Sabbaticals. *Workspan*, *57*(12), 12–13. https://archive.ilr.cornell.edu/sites/default/files/fielduploads/node_workspan/file/Dec2014-Sabbaticals.pdf

Matthew, P. A. (2016, November 23). What is faculty diversity worth to a university? *The Atlantic.* www.theatlantic.com/education/archive/2016/11/what-is-faculty-diversity-worth-to-a-university/508334/

Poissant, S. (2022). *Planning for a productive and restorative sabbatical.* University of Massachusetts Amherst, Office of Faculty Development. Mid-Career Faculty Workshop Series. www.umass.edu/faculty-development/events/planning-productive-and-restorative-sabbatical#

Schabram, K., Bloom, M., & DiDonna, D. J. (2023, February). Research: The transformative power of the sabbatical. *Harvard Business Review.* https://hbr.org/2023/02/research-the-transformative-power-of-sabbaticals

Shalaby, M., Allam, N., & Buttorff, G. (2020, December 18). Gender, COVID, and faculty service. *Inside Higher Ed.* www.insidehighered.com/advice/2020/12/18/increasingly-disproportionate-service-burden-female-faculty-bear-will-have

Sparks, T. D. (2022). Tales from Sabbatical I: Planning your leave. *Matter*, *5*(6), 1623–1626. https://doi.org/10.1016/j.matt.2022.04.020

Chapter 3

Critical Considerations at Mid-Career
How Mentoring Can Help You at This Stage

Richard J. Reddick and Tiffany N. Hughes

Overview

Mentoring has been promoted as a necessary skill for career advancement, particularly in early career stages. However, the need for revisiting and augmenting the developmental networks of the scholar at the mid-career stage is critical: associate professors report the lowest levels of satisfaction among professorial ranks (Jaschik, 2012). As former director Kiernan Mathews of the Collaborative on Academic Careers in Higher Education (COACHE) stated, this finding revealed "how all of the mentorship, the protections of time, the clear policies and formal milestones that faculty had as assistant professors are lifted when they become associates" (Jaschik, 2012, n.p.).

In this chapter, we share our experiences of working with post-tenure, mid-career faculty via workshops presented at annual meetings of the Association for the Study of Higher Education (ASHE) and the American Educational Research Association (AERA). Additionally, the senior author has reviewed many promotion dossiers and witnessed the impact of critical developmental interventions on careers and also, regrettably, how the lack of attention to their development can lead to less optimal outcomes for faculty. With critical considerations of their research trajectory, life circumstances, professional aspirations, and campus/community service, we maintain that mid-career scholars can realize more satisfying and rewarding outcomes for the next stage of their academic and personal development.

Program Focus

The shift in priorities that academics encounter at mid-career deserves time and intention. Often, mid-career faculty begin to tackle new professional and intellectual goals. This chapter will focus on the factors that they should consider at this stage while also reflecting on how mentoring and network relationships can facilitate faculty members' success.

DOI: 10.4324/9781003428626-5

Needed Skill

Mid-career is a transitional period for academics as they shift their focus from achieving tenure to utilizing their skills and knowledge in ways that have an enduring impact on their field(s). To successfully navigate this transition, scholars must engage in significant personal reflection, thinking about their feelings, behavior, and underlying motivations. For example, it is ideal to assess one's mentoring network – which arrangements are meaningful and which are no longer serving either or both individuals' needs. This also provides insight into what mentoring relationships need to be developed. Through reflection, mid-career academics are better able to assess their current goals and may also gain insights into how to bring them to fruition.

Additionally, mid-career academics must practice communicating their needs to key persons in their networks. To this point, mentoring relationships may previously have been focused on acclimating to one's field, department, college, and institution and positioning oneself for promotion. At mid-career, the scholar's needs have likely changed: it is time to adjust while alerting their network to these new goals.

Rationale

Too often, mentoring networks and dyads are thought of as permanent; however, these relationships must be assessed and refreshed as one's career advances. Mentoring relationships evolve: sometimes, they become friendships and peer arrangements, and sometimes, they cease to exist when the parties involved find that the relationship no longer serves their needs. Such a critical self-reflection provides clarity for mentees and mentors and reaffirms supportive relationships while allowing those that are no longer valuable to end (or to evolve into less intimate associations).

Equity and Inclusion Considerations

Equity and inclusion should underpin all that we do, not only for the benefit of students and colleagues but also for the benefit of our professional output. At the mid-career stage, scholars should consider how equity and inclusion are manifested in relationships (as both mentor and mentee), research, and professional engagement (both on campus and at large). If, during this reflection, scholars identify areas where equity and inclusion are inadequate, they can adjust the approach, worldview, and/or boundaries to better reflect more equitable outputs and expectations.

Conceptual Grounding

In this section, we discuss the conceptual framework of the mid-career faculty workshops we offer at the annual meetings of the Association for the Study of Higher Education (ASHE) and American Educational Research Association (AERA). Within the broader workshop, we lead a section on the role of mentors or networks in advancing mid-career professional and personal goals. The following key concepts, drawn from both the literature and our wisdom of practice in higher education, frame the tool of reflective questions utilized in the workshop. The concepts consist of independence and status in research, fostering complete lives, pursuing professional aspirations, and engaging in campus and community service.

Research: Independence, Leadership, and Status in the Field

There are a range of academic careers and institutional types; our vantage point is from an R1, heavy-research-activity institutional context, but we acknowledge the landscape for promotion varies greatly among R1s, R2s, and teaching-intensive institutions. If one considers the three-legged stool that characterizes academic careers, research is often considered the most critical, overshadowing the other two legs, the pillars of teaching and service (Ezell et al., 2019).

Mid-career is a time to assert scholarly independence. This is gauged differently across subfields and disciplines, but the question to ask is, "How am I regarded by colleagues as a contributor to knowledge in the field?" This can be measured in many ways, including by scholarly output, where you are the sole, senior, or lead author; by projects for which you are the principal investigator on a grant, or co-investigator; by demonstrable mentoring of students, post-doctoral fellows, or junior scholars in your research field; and by creation of a foundational research product (e.g., book, article, monograph, creative project) for which you are the lead or sole author. These outputs signal to colleagues that you are staking out new ground in the field and exerting leadership in that quest.

If you have previously considered yourself more of a mentee, now, you should be engaging in a critical reframing to become both mentee and mentor. It's likely that this is already happening – by advising students in a lab or by collaborating with them on research projects, for example. If you have just reached the status of promotion and/or tenure, you might find it difficult to see yourself as senior. We encourage you to consider the perspective of the scholars who look to you for guidance. Mid-career faculty occupy a critical role: often engaged in vibrant projects interesting to new scholars, you might be more approachable and collaborative with emergent researchers. You may also represent identities that students may not see in the field (race/ethnicity, sexual orientation, gender identity, ability status, neurodiversity, and first generation, among others), introducing for them the possibility of an academic career.

Because of this reality, it is important to share your experiences navigating an academic career. For emerging scholars, personal anecdotes and stories of success and struggle are important messages presenting a realistic picture of their potential careers. For those climbing the ladder behind you, your mid-career status represents success – regardless of your own reflections on the journey thus far. Securing an academic job, completing a terminal degree, publishing, and collegiate teaching may seem routine to you, but these are experiences that junior scholars may not have navigated. Furthermore, more senior scholars may gloss over these experiences. We all have our personal levels of comfort about sharing – but those reflections can be powerful.

On the question of scholarly independence, your relationship with your doctoral advisor, post-doctoral supervisor, or other foundational mentor can be complicated: sometimes, the advice is, "Never publish with your advisor." This is somewhat glib, but establishing scholarly independence means working on projects and advancing knowledge without those early mentors. However, access to data, labs, and other resources may make such relationships difficult to detach from. Remember the rationale for the continued collaboration, but also establish other opportunities to publish, obtain grants, and present papers independently. Discuss this with senior scholars at your institution and at other institutions you might aspire to work at in the future.

Life Circumstances: You Deserve to Be Complete

Many of us pursued promotion to mid-career with zeal, forgoing time with loved ones and other activities that complete us. In many ways, this is a criticism of the pace of academic careers (Catterall et al., 2019). However, at mid-career, there is an opportunity to reassess how you spend time. In your early career, you expend effort setting up a lab, creating syllabi, and networking. Now, you can reflect on what makes you the most creative, most innovative, and happiest. You probably won't get much external direction on this: your teaching, research, and service is akin to a perpetual motion machine, and you likely can't just hit the stop button. But take time – officially, through sabbaticals (if available), or just by carving out opportunities to think about how you can sustain your career.

This advice can be a relief: academics who have worked relentlessly, from graduate school to post-docs to the job market to promotion, are potentially hearing "Take a break!" for the first time. But it's a break with a purpose: spend time journaling, reflecting, and planning. When navigating this experience in the past decade, the senior author reflected on being "present" – not just being physically there but eschewing the distractions of research and administrative responsibilities to engage authentically with friends and family. By committing to putting personal fulfillment first, Rich gradually learned to strategically say no to more commitments. This reflective process answers the following questions:

- Why am I doing this?
- What's the best outcome from doing this, and how likely is it to happen?
- What will be lost if I don't do this?
- Are there other ways of achieving this goal than this process?
- Will this activity lead to happiness – and how soon will it manifest?

(Reddick, 2023)

Many obligations will be eliminated by asking these questions. Very few opportunities are truly once in a lifetime. Being at mid-career also means you have more options. If the pace of your career is off, you can consider if you are in the right institutional space. As historian Butch Ware has said, "Promotion and tenure is a national, or international, assessment of your standing in the field." More people now know of your stature, and the possibilities for change are more abundant.

This reflection should be a shared one: consult with your colleagues and loved ones regarding where and when you are most enthusiastic and happy and where and when you are least so. Though you should filter these conversations through your own perspective, it can be enlightening to hear others reflect on your work–life balance. This advice from the safety briefing on airplanes is profound: "Put your own mask on before helping others." You cannot be of help to anyone if you do not exercise self-care. After promotion and tenure, Rich reflected on graduate school: while he was working and dissertating, he also found time for hobbies like cooking and playing music. Once Rich was on the tenure track, these activities disappeared completely. Post-tenure, he decided to rekindle these joys, and Rich found himself more effective and focused after disengaging from work.

In our ASHE and AERA workshops, we have been intrigued by the varied interests that scholars rediscover or engage with once they have a chance to reflect on what's important to them. Exercise, travel, pets, the arts, and simple "down time" – all emerge as choices that energize mid-career scholars and provide the motivation to take on the additional responsibilities of leading and creating with brio.

Professional Aspirations

One post-promotion revelation is the range of ways in which you can fashion an academic career. Focusing intently on research and teaching is certainly the most evident. But there are other pathways in academia. Administrative leadership is an option, both in the institutional context (shared governance, program directorships, department chairships, and so on) and in scholarly associations (editorial boards, elected roles, meeting chairs). We believe that all mid-career folks should explore and sample some of the different aspects of leadership. Diverse voices and experiences are sorely needed, and you might find yourself intrigued by the possibilities.

It is critical to enlist your circle of mentors in your initial forays into leadership. Some of us will be nominated or recognized as having leadership potential. Many of us will be overlooked during these hidden processes, so we strongly recommend meeting with department chairs, deans, and scholarly association leaders to inform them that you are interested in leadership. You can be specific about what types of opportunities you are interested in – ones that allow you to continue teaching and researching, ones that are time limited and/or project based, ones that speak to your interests and commitments (social justice, DEI, serving certain communities), or ones that are aligned with your scholarly interests, to name a few parameters. It should never be a secret that you, as a mid-career scholar, are seeking chances to grow as a leader.

Simultaneously, we recommend that you seek out leadership development opportunities. These can be in your institutional setting and can include seminars, courses, and academies that provide opportunities to develop networks and that provide insight into leadership roles. These workshops and courses are sometimes part of the checklist that leaders consult when appointing or evaluating new leaders. Although these sessions are valuable because of the exposure they afford to pathways and considerations for leadership in the institutional context, you should cultivate your own leadership philosophy, derived from your own experiences and reading.

There are professional development institutes nationwide that are focused on preparing emerging leaders in higher education. Programs such as the American Council on Education Fellows and the Harvard Institutes for Higher Education, among others, introduce scholars to networks and leadership roles. Our advice is to investigate these opportunities, and if you find a good match, propose that your institutional leadership support your application.

Academic societies and organizations are additional venues for trying on leadership roles. A specific concern may spur your leadership involvement:

this book project is very much an example of such an organic leadership opportunity, in which many of us came together, with varying levels of familiarity with one another, because we had a shared interest in scholarly career development. This community has led to regular collaboration on the ASHE and AERA workshops for multiple annual meetings. In doing this work that we find fulfilling and essential, we have also established leadership that is recognized in our field.

The experiences you have in leadership are worthwhile opportunities for reflecting on what you might do next. Leadership is a challenge, but it should also be rewarding. If a particular experience is stressful, it's important to note what made it that way and pursue opportunities that differ from it in key ways. Even though you might be mid-career, you are still encountering experiences for the first time, and it's okay to reflect, "Well, I don't want to do *that* again." Part of the reward for reaching the status of mid-career is being able to determine the ways in which you are best suited to serve.

Campus and Community Service: Meaningful Work Beyond Your Lab

As scholars who research historically marginalized communities in higher education, we know that most scholars from underrepresented populations are engaged in service, notably enhancing the representation of their communities on campus (Reddick et al., 2021). We acknowledge that many mid-career scholars reading this are already engaged in this work at a high level, but mid-career is an opportunity to change your vantage point and think broadly about serving in a way that has a sustained impact.

Many of these opportunities are wonderful and career enhancing (Eldeirawi et al., 2023). Others, not so much: we advise mid-career faculty to never commit to projects, chairships, or other service commitments on the spot. Leverage mentors and unit leaders as intercessors and consult with them about the pros and cons of any opportunity. Not all service is created equal: opportunities have differing levels of prestige and time investment. It's important to note that many opportunities will appear out of the blue, so no matter what you have planned, it's good to keep some time and space in the calendar free for these novel chances.

Service can also be a web of entanglements obstructing needed time for publishing, researching, and teaching. "Stalling out" mid-career is a risk, considering that there are more responsibilities than there are people. When one additionally counts social loafing and the "privilege payoff" – how majority scholars acquire time and benefits as they are not shouldering institutional efforts to advance equity and inclusion – mid-career scholars, particularly those from underrepresented communities, are at risk of falling into a cycle of constant service obligations that do not advance their careers. Attend to service opportunities that are fulfilling and uplift communities, as long as they are feeding your soul and your values. When this is no longer the case, it may be time to reassess.

A last consideration is that service can be a spotlight on the causes you value. As a mid-career scholar, your service contributions can have an outsized effect and may result in others becoming aware of and/or championing similar causes. Social media and virtual communities have aided in amplifying, magnifying, and clarifying a multitude of discourses that may not otherwise have opportunities to gain traction, unpacking the hidden curricula of academia and highlighting inequity and injustice – as well as positing strategies to address these shortcomings (Reddick, 2016). Think of the impact of digital movements such as #BlackLivesMatter, #MeToo, and other activist spaces. We envision a future in which the world of academia will better recognize the organizational and collective impact of social media, but in the meantime, we recommend learning to leverage these platforms to support communities and causes.

Tool

With this wisdom of practice in mind, we next share a tool created for the ASHE and AERA mid-career professional development sessions offered at the annual conferences. The tool is a series of reflective journal prompts for mid-career scholars to assess current goals and priorities, which will assist academics with the critical considerations that should be weighed at this stage of their professional development. We also include the ASHE/AERA Mid-Career Mentoring Guide used during the conference workshop, which has guided the crafting of this chapter and which can be used to inform how scholars evaluate peer networks and manage relationships.

Mid-Career Reflection Prompts

Instructions:

These reflective prompts invite you to consider areas of your professional and personal lives and evaluate your current desires, goals, and priorities at mid-career.

STEP 1: Please record your answers to the prompts that follow.

Research:

- What is your current level of contribution to your field? What project or research product would you like to lead?
- How are your mentoring relationships with other scholars (seniors, peers, and juniors)? Which should be further developed or improved?

Prioritizing Life Circumstances with Work Responsibilities:

- Have you developed a habit of overwork? Or do you carve out appropriate amounts of time for both work and leisure?
- Are there hobbies, interests, or relationships that you have neglected on your academic journey? How might you re-engage in leisure activities or reconnect with friends and family?

Professional Aspirations:

- What is your leadership philosophy? What core values would you bring to leadership?
- What leadership role would you like to fill? How can you prepare yourself to meet that challenge?

Campus/Community Service:

- What issues/causes do you want to advocate for?
- Which organizations would you like to partner with to make an impact?

STEP 2: Next, consider who among your mentor network might help you best complete a self-assessment and who might help you achieve any goals from the list that follows in the Mid-Career Mentoring Guide (Figure 3.1). Make a note of their name by the associated reflection and make an intention to seek their counsel as you work toward these priorities in the future.

MID-CAREER MENTORING GUIDE

"IN SUM, THE FINDINGS OF THE CURRENT WORK SUGGEST THAT MENTORING NETWORKS, RATHER THAN MENTORING DYADS, ARE CRITICALLY IMPORTANT IN CAREER DEVELOPMENT." (DECASTRO ET AL. 2014)

Prepared by Richard J. Reddick, Ed.D.
@DrRichReddick

MID-CAREER MENTORING SHOULD TAKE INTO ACCOUNT:

Research
Life Circumstances (family, lifestyle, interests beyond work)

Professional Aspirations (leadership, public scholarship)
Campus/Community Service (working on issues you care about, that are visible and rewarding)

SUPPORT FROM LEADERSHIP

- Make sure your department chair/dean knows what your goals are, so when opportunities arise they can assist you.
- As a tenured faculty member, you have greater visibility on campus. Leverage this visibility through *thoughtful* engagement with the larger university.
- If useful, seek out leadership opportunities on campus (e.g., emerging leader workshops), through professional orgs (e.g., ASHE, AERA Division J), and through professional development (e.g., ACE Fellows, Harvard Institutes for Higher Education).

PEER MENTORING

- At this level, peer mentorship becomes more essential. Some of the best advice might come from colleagues in the same stage of career and life as you!
- Think of how peers and near-peers can assist you with:
  o Research goals (grants, authorship, editorship opportunities)
  o Professional goals (consulting, planning convenings)
  o Lifestyle goals (accountability groups, support networks)

SEEKING MENTORSHIP

- Seek mentors locally AND nationally/internationally.
- The path to full professor has many routes, and it's useful to have advice about how to navigate.
- Your career might continue at your current institution... and it might not.
- Think of promotion as a national discussion on your career—it's important to have perspectives and feedback on your body of work.

MENTORING HAZARDS

- Mid-career mentoring hazards include your own bandwidth as a mentor...
  o You will likely take on a more senior role developing other scholars.
- Evolving relationships
  o Someone you considered to be a mentor might now be more of a peer—so the relationship changes
- Toxic relationships
  o Rivalries, abusive, and otherwise subtractive engagements.
  o We should talk more about these complications!

MANAGING MENTORS

- Resist the ancient advice of having only one mentor.
  o Seek out those who are doing things in their lives and careers that you'd like to emulate.
- Don't underestimate the value of mentoring-at-a-distance.
  o Coffee at conferences, with the occasional email/text/Zoom chat can be incredibly effective.
- Your mentoring journey is *your* mentoring journey.
  o There's no need to gauge your mentoring experience against others, if it's working for you and your mentor.

LOOKING AHEAD...

- Be mindful of relationships that aren't working.
  o Tenure is a good time to assess if your mentoring relationships are working as you would like them to.
- Some mentors might move to the "occasional advisor" or "friend" role.
  o Others might be removed altogether!
- Remember—it's your career.
  o Be receptive to advice and know the pros and cons of your choices...
  o ...but your identity, life circumstances, and quality of life might filter how you utilize this advice.

AERA Mid-Career Faculty Pre-Conference Workshop - April 2022
richard.reddick@austin.utexas.edu

Figure 3.1 Mid-Career Mentoring Guide

Lessons Learned

As rewarding as reaching the mid-career milestone can be, there are hazards and concerns to attend to. First, mid-career scholars experience the liminality of inside status but not necessarily the ultimate decision-making ability. In many ways, mid-career status can be frustrating because it is precisely the stage at which one knows the systems that uphold institutional inertia but may lack the standing to make change occur. Equally important is the realization that as vital as developmental relationships are – coaching, sponsorship, and mentoring – mid-career is where many of these relationships undergo redefinition.

Your standing and stature in the field may mean these relationships shift: on the positive end of the spectrum, coaches, sponsors, and mentors may become peers and friends (Grant-Vallone & Ensher, 2017). However, we should be cognizant of the potential for these relationships to shift in less positive ways: they can become complex and even competitive as you seek out similar opportunities. On the negative end, relationships can take a toxic turn – perhaps fueled by the insecurity of the senior member or by a realization on the part of the junior member that the relationship is not healthy or is even abusive (Knippelmeyer & Torraco, 2007). Mid-career is a good time to reassess these connections and to evaluate if they are working optimally for both parties (Eldeirawi et al., 2023). At the same time, mid-career scholars may find themselves at a point at which they can expand their mentoring practice to impact more junior colleagues or deepen their investment in existing relationships. This reflection is needed and encouraged.

Conclusion

Mid-career scholars are at a crossroads regarding their involvement in developmental relationships, including mentoring. Gaining status and credibility among peers while serving as a role model and guide for the next generation of scholars can be challenging. Significantly, examining your journey at this stage can provide the motivation and momentum to advance to whatever you envision at the senior level: refining your research agenda; accounting for your unique and important lifestyle aspirations; reflecting on your preferred career pathways, which can include leadership within your institution, field or subfield, or community; and deciding how you intend to serve in multiple contexts.

All these inflection points demonstrate the need to have a constellation of mentors and advisors as you plot the next steps in your journey. At the same time, having the confidence to consider the perspectives of those you trust while determining for yourself what is best for your circumstances is a critical aspect of navigating your course. Whatever direction you choose, whatever path you take, we hope this chapter has provided some assistance – and validation that the direction you pursue is within your grasp. As you are mentored and mentor others, remember your hard work and commitment to reach this place in your career. There are many directions in which you can go, but you fully have the ability to decide which step to take. We hope the strategies outlined in this chapter serve as a road map on your way.

References

Catterall, K., Mickenberg, J., & Reddick, R. (2019). Design thinking, collaborative innovation, and neoliberal disappointment. *Radical Teacher*, *114*, 34–47.

Eldeirawi, K. M., Hershberger, P. E., Pickler, R. H., Wyatt, G. K., & Zerwic, J. (2023). Embracing midcareer in the tenure system. *Journal of Professional Nursing*, *44*, 12–16. https://doi.org/10.1016/j.profnurs.2022.10.010

Ezell, D., Gala, P., & Tillmani, F. (2019). The journey of a PhD: The transition from grad student to tenure track faculty and the three-legged stool. *Journal of Faculty Development*, *33*(3), 49–56.

Grant-Vallone, E. J., & Ensher, E. A. (2017). Re-crafting careers for mid-career faculty: A qualitative study. *Journal of Higher Education Theory and Practice*, *17*(5), Article 5. https://articlegateway.com/index.php/JHETP/article/view/1533

Jaschik, S. (2012, June 4). Unhappy associate professors: Preliminary results of national survey find their job satisfaction in many areas lags those at assistant and full ranks. *Inside Higher Ed*. www.insidehighered.com/news/2012/06/04/associate-professors-less-satisfied-those-other-ranks-survey-finds

Knippelmeyer, S. A., & Torraco, R. J. (2007). Mentoring as a developmental tool for higher education. *Online Submission*. https://eric.ed.gov/?id=ED504765

Reddick, R. J. (2016). Amplify, magnify, clarify: Using social media to promote scholarship. In M. Gasman (Ed.), *Academics going public: How to write and speak beyond academe* (pp. 55–70). Routledge.

Reddick, R. J. (2023). *Restorative resistance in higher education: Leading in an era of racial awakening and reckoning*. Harvard Education Press.

Reddick, R. J., Taylor, B. J., Nagbe, M., & Taylor, Z. W. (2021). Professor beware: Liberating faculty voices of color working in predominantly white institutions and geographic settings. *Education and Urban Society*, *53*(5), 536–560.

Chapter 4

Effective Mentoring Conversations with Faculty

A Guide for Department Chairs, Directors, and Deans

Laura Gail Lunsford and Vicki L. Baker

Overview

> I think we have, as an institution, learned to network really well around teaching and pedagogy both amongst ourselves and in our wider professional affiliations. I think you are suggesting we do the same around the question of mentoring – that it be an explicit goal going forward, and not just for chairs. This is important.
>
> – Associate Provost, Liberal Arts College

This quote is from an associate provost who contacted us through our consulting firm, Lead Mentor Develop, LLC, to request support in guiding and professionally developing department chairs around enhanced mentoring approaches. Academics are trained in their disciplinary areas and spend decades developing competence and subject matter expertise. However, unless one's disciplinary area is leadership and/or management, there is little to no explicit training to develop the skills needed to effectively mentor junior faculty. Furthermore, even organizational scholars may not be good organizational practitioners (Fulop, 2002).

Mentoring and coaching others are key leadership skills emphasized in this chapter. Across the academy, mentorship of faculty members is touted as a critical and necessary source of support (Pololi & Knight, 2005; Sorcinelli & Yun, 2007). Development of formal mentorship skills is even more important as the academy becomes more diverse and leaders are expected to foster an inclusive working environment (Dahlberg & Byars-Winston, 2019; Lunsford, 2021; Maas et al., 2020). The ideas presented in this chapter are grounded in the National Academies' definition of mentorship (Dahlberg & Byars-Winston, 2019): "A professional, working alliance in which individuals work together over time to support the personal and professional growth, development, and success of relational partners through the provision of career and psychosocial support" (p. 2)

DOI: 10.4324/9781003428626-6

The chapter's aims are twofold: First, we seek to help mid-level leaders navigate critical mentoring conversations via appreciative inquiry (AI) and motivational interviewing (MI), which we define later in this chapter. Second, we provide mid-career faculty with the knowledge and ability to use the featured tools, the Environmental Scan and the Developmental Network Assessment, to aid career advancement. The tools and techniques featured here support competency development in the areas of motivation, engagement, and communication to facilitate positive behavioral change. Based on our partnerships with institutional leaders (e.g., provosts, deans, unit heads, and department chairs) across the academy, we argue for the importance of intentional investment in the areas of AI and MI to foster a supportive and collegial environment that inspires and promotes thriving.

Program Focus

As we have stated previously, "the development of academic leaders is at a critical juncture, as evidenced by increased attention on the challenges and opportunities experienced by those currently in and aspiring for careers in academic administration" (Baker et al., 2019, p. 823). Faculty members in leadership roles on their campuses have a robust and ever-evolving portfolio of responsibilities, which might include chairing their departments and supporting early-career colleagues' career advancement (Baker & Manning, 2021), and these require intentionality and the cultivation of requisite skills. Simultaneously, there are contextual challenges in the academy that inhibit one's ability to lead and mentor effectively. For example, the global pandemic had immediate negative effects on faculty members. *Pandemic burnout* (Gewin, 2021) has been documented as resulting from increased workload, derailed research agendas, job stress, and mental distress.

Another contextual challenge that could hinder academic leaders' mentoring capacities relates to the conception of faculty members as knowledge workers (Lunsford & Padilla, 2022), defined as individuals who generate value through their minds, requiring a range of technical, social, emotional, and higher cognitive skills that require constant attention (Drucker, 1959). Faculty members often have greater loyalty to their discipline than to the organization in which they are employed. Thus, academic leaders have to transition from their own role as a faculty member, in which they may have provided only discipline-specific mentoring, to providing more general mentoring to help their colleagues succeed in the institution (and not just their discipline).

The academy, to develop these mentoring skills, needs to equip mid-level academic leaders with the tools (and competencies) to develop others. For example, chairs have little control over faculty activities; they do not hire or fire full-time faculty members. A bad leader (e.g., a weak department chair) could essentially be ignored by faculty members until another one arrives, resulting in a focus on individual pursuits rather than departmental priorities. A good leader (e.g., a strong divisional dean), on the other hand, may invigorate a department or division. We advocate for a focus on the development of effective mentoring skills to promote collegial and empathetic interactions within departments.

Needed Skills

In our research on mid-career faculty succession management (Baker et al., 2019), we learned that the mid-career faculty members in leadership roles (e.g., department chair, program director) were interested in working with a coach or mentor if made available. These faculty members sought to support the career advancement of their colleagues while developing their own skills and competencies. The identified needs (e.g., supporting career advancement and growth of colleagues) require effective mentoring conversations that lead to behavior change. These conversations require persuasive and motivational language, both of which are a focus of this chapter's tools. Persuasion involves changing someone's attitude. For example, a department chair may need to persuade a faculty member to clarify elements in their syllabus to reduce student complaints or to engage in more scholarly activity. Work motivation involves goal-oriented, voluntary behavior (Kanfer et al., 2017). Knowing what to ask and how to ask requires intentionality. Such skills may result in both more effective informal "hallway" chats and the formal conversations that occur in, for example, annual performance discussions. Thus, this chapter helps academic leaders ask better questions that motivate and inspire their departmental colleagues.

Rationale

Our research on mid-career faculty leadership development is clear and alarming; "faculty members are both unprepared for leadership roles and need encouragement to develop their leadership aspirations" (Baker et al., 2019, p. 834). Faculty leadership does not just happen. It must be cultivated in intentional, strategic ways (Baker et al., 2017). The tools featured in this chapter support campus leaders in asking questions that persuade and motivate (what do you enjoy?) rather than threaten or coerce (you might not get tenure).

We agree with Gmelch (2002), who stated, "If it takes seven to 14 years to develop and refine disciplinary expertise as a faculty member, why does the academy continue to believe it can 'build a chair' during a weekend workshop?" (p. 2). The tools and strategies outlined in this chapter move beyond the weekend workshop model to instead focus on providing ongoing developmental support that benefits those in leadership roles and the individuals in their departments.

Equity and Inclusion Considerations

Undergirding AI and MI is identity work. That is, academic leaders need to gain insight into their preferences and biases as they seek to understand the identities of the faculty members whom they support. Cultural humility is an important aspect of this work, which involves self-reflection, respect, and empathy (Foronda, 2020). Learning to ask rather than assuming supports open dialogue.

In our work, we find that academic leaders share stories about challenging faculty members whom they perceive as disinterested, uninvolved, not a good fit, or even actively at odds with departmental aims. Yet when we express curiosity about the supposed poor performance or unwillingness of a faculty member, we usually discover missed opportunities to build trusting relationships in which faculty members' interests are recognized and supported in ways that align those interests with institutional goals.

Mentorship is an essential leadership skill. People reach out to us through Lead Mentor Develop, LLC, because they want to do better and are not quite sure how to get there. Well-intentioned academic leaders often lack the knowledge to navigate challenging conversations and are eager to learn how to identify and address the biases and toxic perspectives that permeate the academy. Using the tools described in this chapter, we help academic leaders learn more about faculty members as people and what is important to them to feel a sense of belonging in the academy. And we provide the needed tools to mid-career faculty as they navigate their career journey.

Conceptual Grounding

Academic leaders play a crucial role in inspiring and motivating followers to achieve organizational goals. Such leaders have titles like department chair, director, dean, or unit head. Yet these front-line and middle-management roles are challenging, and faculty members often feel unprepared to assume these roles. Developing and supporting others is one of the main tasks of academic leaders; their work in this space can be supported via techniques from appreciative inquiry and motivational interviewing.

Developing Others

Faculty members are experts in their disciplines but often have underdeveloped skills in the areas of leadership and management of others. Based on the literature, reflective listening promotes belonging and recognizes the whole person (Dahlberg & Byars-Winston, 2019). The competency of developing others involves effective social and networking skills, including communication, empathy, persuasion, and conflict management (Jokinen, 2005). Yet as faculty members move into front-line and middle-management positions, there is often a tough transition from self-management to other-management (Floyd, 2016; Gonaim, 2016).

Indeed, the first leadership role for many faculty members often becomes their last leadership position because of negative experiences (Baker et al., 2019). In part, these negative experiences arise because of a failure to recognize that leadership is a process between leaders and followers, not a person (Lunsford & Padilla, 2022). Our work with hundreds of faculty members supports the scholarly findings, which indicates a need for more professional development to help faculty members mentor others effectively. In particular, we find that leaders want more training in how to use motivational language to effect behavior changes in their mentoring conversations with faculty members.

The ability to ask meaningful questions is a skill that can and should be developed. Effective questioning helps leaders understand the needs and perspectives of their followers, and it also builds trust, which fosters collaboration and engagement. When leaders ask questions in a way that encourages reflection and dialogue, they can promote deeper learning and encourage their followers to take ownership of their work, leading to a more productive and fulfilling academic experience for all.

Appreciative Inquiry and Motivational Interviewing

The tools we highlight in this chapter are grounded in *appreciative inquiry* (AI) and *motivational interviewing* (MI). AI and MI have been found to promote behavior change across a range of contexts and settings (Alston-Mills, 2011; Cooperrider & Whitney, 2000; Miller & Rose, 2009; Rollnick et al., 2010). AI developed out of work on organizational change (Cooperrider & Srivastva, 1987) and focuses on creating change by identifying and building upon what could be and on individual and organizational assets. A key element of AI is that inquiry and problem solving start with a grounding in a positive past (Cooperrider & Whitney, 2000). AI is characterized by a 4-D cycle (see Figure 4.1) that includes (a) Discovery (inquiries about positive change or what has worked well in the past, (b) Dream (identifying the results-oriented vision related to what was discovered), (c) Design (creating possibilities), and (d) Destiny (achieving purpose and learning agility).

By using an AI approach, leaders foster a positive and optimistic organizational culture that emphasizes the potential for growth and success.

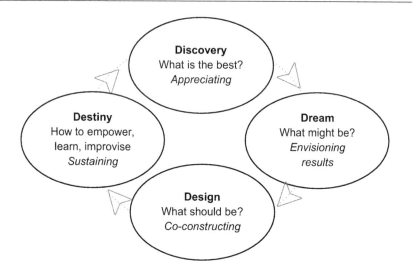

Figure 4.1 4-D Cycle of Appreciative Inquiry

This approach encourages leaders to ask questions that promote a focus on what is working well rather than getting stuck on complaining about problems. AI fosters a sense of collaboration and a shared vision for the future. Additionally, AI helps to build resilience and innovation as leaders and followers are encouraged to seek out new and creative solutions to challenges. An illustrative example is the use of AI to re-envision peer evaluation in an academic department: faculty members used the AI cycle to transform an impersonal evaluation of tenure-track faculty to a process that celebrated success and felt collegial (Oxendine et al., 2022).

MI focuses on supporting *change talk*. This approach originated in behavioral interventions to reduce alcohol use. It recognizes the importance of individual motivation in changing behaviors. In particular, the goal is to create a safe, non-threatening space in which to engage a person in arguing for change rather than telling them what needs to change. This approach has expanded to non-therapeutic settings. Although it takes considerable training and observation to be a competent MI practitioner, we have found that elements of this approach are useful tools for academic leaders. There are ways to ask questions that engage faculty to identify areas for change.

Tools

This section presents two tools, rooted in the tenets of AI and MI, that faculty leaders can use to engage in collegial, supportive mentoring conversations with faculty members: the Environmental Scan and the Developmental Network Assessment.

Environmental Scan

The Environmental Scan draws on an AI approach to recognize assets and successes before envisioning future successes (see Table 4.1). This tool might be used as part of an annual review process or mid-tenure review conversation (Lunsford, 2019). After using this tool for several years, we identify 10 questions that work well.

We recommend that the faculty member be given the questions in advance of a formal meeting focused on career advancement needs: this way, the faculty member has a chance to prepare or even write down their answers. The academic leader then walks through the questions and answers presented in the Environmental Scan in a formal meeting with the faculty member.

Table 4.1 Environmental Scan

Environmental Scan: Instructions
The questions below ask you to consider your accomplishments and resources as you envision the next year or stage of your career. Record your responses to the 10 questions below.

1. Make a list of all the people you would thank; all the possible funders of your work; and all the professional societies or connections that provided you support.
2. Who at your institution holds a position to which you aspire (formally or informally)?
3. Who at another institution has a position to which you aspire (formally or informally)?
4. What do you really enjoy doing?
5. With which professional associations do you affiliate?
6. What other professional associations align with your interests?
7. What do you need to learn to take you to the next level professionally?
8. What strengths do you underuse at present?
9. With whom do (or might) you enjoy collaborating?
10. What self-care do you need to enact to stay refreshed and excited in your career?

Next, organize your responses into your goals and then two sets of resources. First, list your goals (aspirations). Second, list your personal resources (skills, joyful activity, personal network of support). Third, list is who is accessible to you (at work and through your professional affiliations).

Developmental Network Assessment

This assignment works well at times of transition – for example, when there is a newly hired or promoted professor – or as part of an annual review process. This tool helps faculty members recognize that a different developmental network might be needed in their new role. As part of an annual review, it can help faculty members identify new people who can support their new goals, such as redesigning a course or writing a book proposal.

As a first step, academic leaders should provide the worksheet to a faculty member to complete in advance of a planned meeting (see Table 4.2). Using MI strategies around change talk, academic leaders can reflect on the results with a faculty member by making observations and asking questions such as the ones that follow.

- (Observation): It looks like you have a well-developed network to support you in the area of [name goal]. There appear to be opportunities to identify others to support you in the areas of [name goal(s)].
- (Motivating language): What are your thoughts on how you plan to work with [initials] in the coming year on your goal?
  - (Scaling question): On a scale of 1 (well-intentioned but not likely) to 10 (doing it the moment we finish our conversation), what number reflects your motivation for moving forward on your plan?
  - Why is your number a [number mentioned] rather than [a lower number]? [Note that this question supports the faculty member in expressing motivation to engage in the behavior rather than you telling the person what to do.]
- Who do you know now with experience in [goal]?
- How might you identify others who have accomplished [goal]?
- Use the scaling question to ask about moving forward with identifying others.

Developmental Network Assessment Worksheet

Instructions

- Step 1: Write the initials of up to seven people who have provided you professional support in the *last year* in the shaded boxes.
- Step 2: In the first column, write three to seven areas you would like to develop in the next one to three years.

- Step 3: Mark an X where a person has provided or could provide support to you on the development goals.
- Step 4: Circle any blank cells. These are opportunity areas to develop your mentoring network.

Table 4.2 Developmental Network Assessment Worksheet

	Person 1	Person 2	Person 3	Person 4	Person 5	Person 6	Person 7
Development Goals ↓							
1.							
2.							
3.							
4.							
5.							
6.							
7.							

Lessons Learned

We have been fortunate that our work in Lead Mentor Develop, LLC, has facilitated partnerships across the academy. We have engaged with academic administrators from a range of institutional settings seeking to provide resources and tools to both their aspiring and their firmly situated campus leaders. They recognize and appreciate the need to invest in one of their most critical resources, mid-career faculty who take on leadership roles. As part of our conversations, we regularly hear that work overload is a reality for mid-career leaders and the faculty they support and that current professional development is lacking. Failure to provide such professional development has far-reaching consequences that influence student, faculty, and staff experiences. Our aim is to equip academic leaders with tools that are readily available, can be incorporated into existing processes, and will support thriving at all levels.

We have learned three critical lessons that will benefit others seeking to use the tools and conceptual grounding presented in this chapter. First, academic leaders appreciate tools they can use immediately and as part of their regular career development processes (e.g., yearly evaluations). As part of our workshops, we have academic leaders first use the tool with one another in pairs. We believe it's important for academic leaders to get the needed training and skill development and to experience the tools in the context of their own professional and personal development prior to facilitating others' engagement with the tools. We find they learn how to use the tools and that they can also share personal experiences with working through the tools and frameworks, which helps to foster trust.

Second, although we advocate for use of these tools as part of one's professional development portfolio, we find that the Environmental Scan is particularly effective for new faculty members or faculty members who are recently promoted (e.g., mid-career). These are important transition times, when an assessment and "stock-taking" of resources and re-envisioned goals is needed. Faculty members usually appreciate these conversations, which support them in identifying new ideas or resources they had not considered previously.

Third, having a visual accounting of needs and available mentors is crucial to career advancement. The Developmental Network Analysis encourages faculty to think about their needs and to create a visual inventory of those individuals who provide related support. Faculty cannot be strategic and intentional about building a board of advisors, as we refer to it, without engaging in an activity that seeks to facilitate an accounting of each. Only until someone is clear on the human resources (e.g., mentors, supporters) they have at hand can they be deliberate about fostering relationships to advance areas of need.

Conclusion

Developing academic leaders' capacity for effective mentorship yields individual and institutional benefits. As with most skills, some people are naturally better at mentorship than others. However, mentorship is a skill that can and should be developed in all academic leaders. We advocate for an intentional focus on professional development to help academic leaders develop a framework for effective mentorship that involves learning how to regularly engage in supportive and motivating conversations. This chapter provides two tools that can guide such conversations at key points in a faculty member's career.

References

Alston-Mills, B. (2011). Using appreciative inquiry to promote diversity in higher education. *Journal of Diversity Management (JDM)*, 6(3), 1–6.

Baker, V. L., Lunsford, L. G., & Pifer, M. J. (2017). *Developing faculty in liberal arts colleges: Aligning individual needs and organizational goals*. Rutgers University Press.

Baker, V. L., Lunsford, L. G., & Pifer, M. J. (2019). Patching up the "leaking leadership pipeline": Fostering mid-career faculty succession management. *Research in Higher Education, 60*, 823–843.

Baker, V. L., & Manning, C. E. (2021). A mid-career faculty agenda: A review of four decades of research and practice. *Higher Education: Handbook of Theory and Research, 36*, 419–484.

Cooperrider, D., & Srivastva, S. (1987). Appreciative inquiry in organizational life. In R. Woodman & W. Pasmore (Eds.), *Research in organizational change and development* (Vol. 1, pp. 129–169). JAI Press Inc.

Cooperrider, D. L., & Whitney, D. (2000). A positive revolution in change: Appreciative inquiry. In *Handbook of organizational behavior, revised and expanded* (pp. 633–652). Routledge.

Dahlberg, M. L., & Byars-Winston, A. (2019). *The science of effective mentorship in STEMM*. National Academies of Science, Engineering, and Medicine.

Drucker, P. (1959). *Landmarks of tomorrow*. Heineman.

Floyd, A. (2016). Supporting academic middle managers in higher education: Do we care? *Higher Education Policy, 29*, 167–183.

Foronda, C. (2020). A theory of cultural humility. *Journal of Transcultural Nursing, 31*(1), 7–12.

Fulop, L. (2002). Practicing what you preach: Critical management studies and its teaching. *Organization, 9*(3), 428–436.

Gewin, V. (2021). Pandemic burnout is rampant in academia. *Nature, 591*(7850), 489–492.

Gmelch, W. H. (2002). The call for department leaders. Paper presented at the Annual Meeting of the American Association of Colleges for Teacher Education. https://files.eric.ed.gov/fulltext/ED460098.pdf

Gonaim, F. (2016). A department chair: A life guard without a life jacket. *Higher Education Policy, 29*(2), 272–286.

Jokinen, T. (2005). Global leadership competencies: A review and discussion. *Journal of European Industrial Training, 29*(3), 199–216.

Kanfer, R., Frese, M., & Johnson, R. E. (2017). Motivation related to work: A century of progress. *Journal of Applied Psychology, 102*(3), 338.

Lunsford, L. G. (2019). Mapping your mentoring network. In V. Baker (Ed.), *Charting your path to full: A guide for women associate professors*. Routledge.

Lunsford, L. G. (2021). *The mentor's guide: Five steps to build a successful mentor program*. Routledge.

Lunsford, L. G., & Padilla, A. (2022). *Leadership: Leaders, followers, environments*. World Scientific Publishing.

Maas, B., Grogan, K. E., Chirango, Y., Harris, N., Liévano-Latorre, L. F., McGuire, K. L., Moore, A. C., Ocampo-Ariza, C., Palta, M. M., Perfecto, I., Primack, R. B., Rowell, K., Sales, L., Santos-Silva, R., Silva, R. A., Sterling, E. J., Raísa R. S., Vieira, R. R. S., Wyborn, C., & Toomey, A. (2020). Academic leaders must support inclusive scientific communities during COVID-19. *Nature Ecology & Evolution, 4*(8), 997–998.

Miller, W. R., & Rose, G. S. (2009). Toward a theory of motivational interviewing. *American Psychologist, 64*(6), 527. https://doi.org/10.1037/a0016830

Oxendine, S. D., Robinson, K. K., & Parker, M. A. (2022). Transforming departmental culture: Empowering a department through appreciative inquiry. *To Improve the Academy: A Journal of Educational Development, 41*(2).

Pololi, L., & Knight, S. (2005). Mentoring faculty in academic medicine: A new paradigm? *Journal of General Internal Medicine, 20,* 866–870.

Rollnick, S., Butler, C. C., Kinnersley, P., Gregory, J., & Mash, B. (2010). Motivational interviewing. *British Medical Journal, 340,* 1242–1245. https://doi.org/10.1136/bmj.c1900

Sorcinelli, M. D., & Yun, J. (2007). From mentor to mentoring networks: Mentoring in the new academy. *Change: The Magazine of Higher Learning, 39*(6), 58–61.

Chapter 5

Safeguarding Space

A Job-Crafting Action Plan That Elevates Mid-Career Priorities

Aimee LaPointe Terosky and Lauren Footman

Overview

Following tenure and promotion, academic faculty members confront new responsibilities that they were previously shielded from during their pre-tenure years, such as taking on department or university leadership roles or mentoring junior faculty. With rising responsibilities, mid-career faculty report higher levels of dissatisfaction than faculty at any other academic rank (Mathews, 2014), oftentimes citing a lack of training and support for their new roles (Misra et al., 2011) and diminished time to pursue the scholarly and teaching passions that originally drew them to the profession (Neumann et al., 2006). In this chapter, we highlight a strategy that assists mid-career faculty members in identifying and intentionally (re)integrating priorities through a practice called the Job-Crafting Action Plan.

Program Focus

During professional development sessions that we have run throughout our careers, we have consistently been asked the same question: "How do I learn how to say no?" With further discussion, we often uncover a deeper concern facing professionals at mid-career: "How do I safeguard space for my professional priorities in my post-tenure career?" The response we provide is far more nuanced than just saying "no." We work with mid-career faculty on job crafting, a strategy put forth by organizational psychologists Berg et al. (2013). Job crafting is defined as "the process of employees redefining and reimagining their job designs in personally meaningful ways" (Berg et al., 2013, p. 81) and consists of three components: task, relational, and cognitive crafting, all of which we describe in greater detail later in the chapter. Job crafting addresses two needed skills related to mid-career: a sense of agency and career design skills.

DOI: 10.4324/9781003428626-7

Needed Skills

In the field of sociology, agency is defined as an individual's "power, will, and desire to create work contexts conducive to their thought over time" (Elder, 1997, pp. 964–965). Applied to higher education, O'Meara and colleagues (2008) defined agency as strategic and intentional views or actions toward goals that matter to the faculty member. Often, mid-career faculty find their sense of agency constrained following the realized goal of tenure and promotion that consumed much of their professional direction since joining the faculty ranks. Studies show that mid-career academics can face a period of stagnation (Baker & Manning, 2021) as they recalibrate to new roles and responsibilities expected of tenured faculty and to potentially new scholarly or teaching agendas (Terosky et al., 2014).

Relatedly, the needed skill of career design, defined as individuals' perspectives and actions taken to construct and pursue their professional priorities and responsibilities and maintain their vitality, is heightened at mid-career as most of the protections afforded to junior faculty (e.g., time for research, reduced service work, course releases) go by the wayside following the award of tenure. Mid-career faculty at all institutional types find themselves vulnerable to a barrage of requests to fill leadership and/ or academic administration roles, oftentimes without any form of preparation, mentoring, or professional development . . . and let's be honest, perhaps even with a sense of obligation rather than any real interest.

Rationale

Typically characterized by the metaphor of an overloaded plate, mid-career is a time when a sense of agency and well-honed career design skills are needed more than ever. Other than set teaching and shared governance meeting times, academics largely control how, when, and where they work. Although this working schedule can be viewed as a blessing, it can also be a curse, because without intentional reflection, planning, and follow-through around the use of time, academics can find their sense of agency lacking and their ability to design meaningful and sustainable careers limited. That's where the practice of job crafting comes into play.

Equity and Inclusion Considerations

Job crafting that promotes a sense of agency and intentional career design can present differently for women and faculty of color who are underrepresented in the academy. The extant literature has fully documented two phenomena present in academic career culture – ideal workers and invisible labor – that disproportionately impact academics who are not white, cisgender men (Acker, 1990; Perez, 2021). The ideal worker is characterized as someone who devotes their full attention and energy to their work without considering outside commitments or distractions, such as caregiving, personal interests, and community engagement, to name a few (Acker, 1990; Shahjahan, 2020; Williams, 1989). Invisible labor is unrecognized and unrewarded work, and in the higher education context, it is oftentimes related to a commitment to uplifting students and communities that are often overlooked (Shavers & Moore, 2014). Likewise, much of the professional development programming striving to foster work–life balance or sustainable careers overlooks how race and gender identity, as well as departmental cultures, influence career advancement (Kulp et al., 2019), especially in light of the pervasive narratives, such as "prove them wrong" or "be twice as good," that characterize many Black and Brown faculty members' experiences (Shavers & Moore, 2014). These phenomena oftentimes place the onus of responsibility for agency and career design on the shoulders of the individuals themselves rather than highlighting issues of patriarchy, racism, and classism in the academy (Barnett, 2020; Griffin, 2019; Griffith & Ford, 2022). This chapter focuses on individual navigational strategies to address equity challenges and builds on past research on faculty work activity dashboards that provide visualizations for workload transparency (O'Meara et al., 2020), institutional agents that place senior colleagues in positions of advocacy (Bensimon et al., 2019), and discussions of quantitative and qualitative metrics of tenure and promotion. Although equity and inclusion are not the specific focus of this chapter, we recognize that significant reform is needed at the institutional level in order to foster sustainable faculty careers that embrace equity.

Conceptual Grounding

This chapter introduces a mid-career tool, the Job-Crafting Action Plan, which is conceptually grounded in the work of Berg et al. (2013). Job crafting is a strategy to redefine and reimagine a career in personally and professionally meaningful ways. It comprises three components: task crafting, relational crafting, and cognitive crafting, described in detail in what follows. To successfully job craft, individuals must first engage in self-reflection, a mental exercise focused on understanding their priorities or what brings them meaning and what they hope to contribute. With self-reflection on priorities, individuals can better identify if/when their priorities align (or do not align) with their enacted life choices.

In the following sections, we define each of the three components of job crafting, followed by a real-world case to ground this conceptual model in practice. For context, our case is about Linda, an associate professor of biology at a comprehensive university with expertise in tick-borne diseases. Prior to receiving tenure, Linda emphasized traditional scientific research, but then post-tenure, she found herself overextended in service, leadership, and advisory roles at levels disproportionate to those of her departmental colleagues.

Task Crafting

Task crafting is defined as a strategy that advocates for removing and adding career responsibilities to better align professional priorities or contributions with time use. Before faculty members can add or subtract responsibilities, they must first actively reflect on the best uses of their time and talents as well as their sources of joy in their careers. In this way, faculty members are not just learning how to say "no," although that is a part of it, but also figuring out what they want to say "yes" to. By increasing the ratio of yeses to nos, faculty members will likely contribute fairly to the university's workload but in ways that bring them more joy.

What does task crafting look like in practice? Take the case of Linda, the associate professor of biology, who serves as our model. Through self-reflection, Linda recognized that she would like to shift from traditional science research to community-engaged research in her post-tenure career. More specifically, she would like to take her scientific research on testing for tick-borne diseases to a broader, non-academic audience, namely medical doctors and their patients. In order to bring her community-engaged work to fruition, Linda knew she needed to task craft, or adjust how she spent her time and talents. As such, she intentionally arrived two days early to an academic conference to use a faculty work activity dashboard that would chart her current service and leadership roles (see O'Meara et al., 2020). Through this reflection, Linda compiled a list of her yeses and nos (projects that add or detract from her priorities) and set a timeline for redesigning how she spends her time. As a woman faculty member in a male-dominated department, her decisions and subsequent action items would be strengthened by her use of faculty work activity dashboards, because they serve as visual datasets demonstrating her contributions to the department.

Relational Crafting

Relational crafting is identifying effective professional relationships and maximizing time spent engaging in those relationships. Here, faculty members ask themselves, "What people do I enjoy working with? What work styles do I prefer?" The goal is to spend more time in professional responsibilities that foster positive professional relationships and preferred working styles (e.g., online work vs. face-to-face meetings, time efficiency vs. community building, participation in standing committees vs. task-based committees, etc.). As a strategy, relational crafting is helpful in completing less desirable work that is required of faculty members to run a university or be good academic citizens as well as in finding additional networks for supporting current and future priorities. The latter benefit is especially important for women and faculty of color, who can identify institutional agents or senior colleagues who hold forms of power and who can advocate for their goals (Bensimon et al., 2019).

While Linda was charting her workload, she also took into consideration relational crafting by ranking committees in terms of the efficiency of the chair and the interdisciplinary composition of each. Although one of her committees does not directly align with her established priority of community-engaged work, she decided to remain on the committee for three reasons: (a) the committee chair is organized, efficient, and complimentary, (b) the fellow committee members come from a range of disciplines and often provide new perspectives for Linda, and (c) the committee is in a needed shared governance area and serves as an important contribution on Linda's part to the university (as noted in her faculty work activity dashboard).

Cognitive Crafting

The final component of job crafting is *cognitive crafting*, which is changing perceptions about the tasks and relationships that make up work. In other words, faculty members ask themselves, "How can I adjust my mindset in relation to X, or how do I recommit so that this task is more joyful and less burdensome?" At times, a new perspective on a task might spur pathways or networks for opportunities that advance priorities in unexpected ways.

With her heightened prioritization of community-engaged work on tick-borne diseases, Linda engaged in cognitive crafting by rethinking her role as the chair of her university's assessment committee, a notably time-consuming and challenging task. With a decision to move away from seeing assessment work as merely compliance and instead viewing it as a source of learning, she immersed herself in the teaching and learning literature. In time, with this mindset, she not only found the assessment committee work more interesting but also found new and creative ways to merge her teaching, research, and community-engaged health policy work.

Tool

We share here a mid-career faculty tool called the Job-Crafting Action Plan, which is designed to safeguard space to elevate priorities at mid-career. This tool reflects the collective wisdom of the literature in education and organizational psychology (especially Berg and colleagues), more than 100 research participants in our studies over the past 20 years, and more than 250 of our various attendees at professional development sessions.

The Job-Crafting Action Plan includes two key activities: self-reflection on professional priorities across one's teaching, research, service, and leadership roles (see Table 5.1) and then action plans related to task, relational, and cognitive crafting (see Table 5.2). In the first section (Priorities at Mid-Career), mid-career faculty can ask themselves the following self-reflective prompts:

- What do I enjoy doing at work? What brings me the most joy?
- What do I want my contributions to be?
- What responsibilities align my talent, my interests, and the needs of my community or institution?

In the second section, Job Crafting at Mid-Career, mid-career faculty align their priorities with the three components of job crafting (task, relational, and cognitive). To assist, mid-career faculty can reflect and act on the following prompts:

- *Task crafting:* Are there ways to remove tasks or reduce the time spent on tasks that do not align with my priorities?
- *Relational crafting:* Are there ways to surround myself with colleagues who follow a working style that fits with me? Are there ways to work alongside colleagues who inspire me rather than drain me?
- *Cognitive crafting:* Are there ways to reframe a task that better match my interests or open up new possibilities?

Table 5.1 Priorities at Mid-Career

Teaching Priorities
Research Priorities
Service Priorities
Leadership Priorities

Table 5.2 Job Crafting at Mid-Career

Task (Aligned with Priorities)	Action Item	Timeline	Status
Relational (Aligned with Priorities)	Action Item	Timeline	Status
Cognitive (Aligned with Priorities)	Action Item	Timeline	Status

Job Crafting Action Plan: The Case of Linda

To exemplify the Job Crafting Action Plan, we return to the case of Linda, our associate professor of biology who set out to bridge her research and teaching on tick-borne diseases with her service and leadership in community-engaged health policies and practices. In Table 5.3 (Priorities at Mid-Career), Linda identifies priorities around community-engaged work in the main areas of her faculty work: in teaching around service-learning and public intellectualism; in research around new forms of testing for tick-borne diseases that can be used in doctors' offices; in service around advocacy for community-engaged scholarship on her campus; and in leadership around faculty development and assessment of community-engaged work. Note: Linda has additional professional priorities beyond community-engaged work, but we home in on one priority for the sake of clarity in this exercise.

In Table 5.4 (Job Crafting at Mid-Career), Linda aligns her priorities in teaching, research, service, and leadership with the three forms of job crafting, with specific action items and timelines for completion. For task crafting, she outlines responsibilities to add or subtract from her workload based on their proximity to her priorities around community-engaged work. Through relational crafting, Linda identifies positive collegial contexts that uphold her preferred working style and potentially create new networks for collaboration. Finally, with cognitive crafting, she realigns key leadership roles with her community-engaged work priorities.

Table 5.3 Priorities at Mid-Career: Linda

Teaching Priorities

Expand teaching to include service-learning courses (that engage students in public health and laboratory research around testing for tick-borne illnesses)

Integrate projects into classes on strategies for translating research language to public language (for later use with doctors' offices and patients)

Research Priorities

Translate scientific literature and research findings on testing of tick-borne illnesses for general public consumption; work toward creating informational tools and sessions for medical professionals and/or families/patients

Revamp laboratory experiments to have a new focus on inexpensive forms of testing for tick-borne illnesses per recent scientific discoveries

Service Priorities

Create networks and pathways to foster interest in service-learning and community-engaged work

Advocate for community-engaged work to be recognized as a valuable form of faculty work

Leadership Priorities

Move into leadership in faculty development on campus to promote public consumption of research, especially scientific research for public policy

Revise university assessment committee, per role as chair, to include teaching and learning literature and practices around service-learning and community-engaged work, going beyond current focus on traditional general education learning objectives

Table 5.4 Job Crafting at Mid-Career: Linda

Task Crafting	Action Item	Timeline	Status
Reduce departmental committees and advising responsibilities (after conducting a workload dashboard)	Meet with department chair to review faculty work activity dashboard; highlight discrepancies in equitable workload across department; resign from one departmental committee and reset student advising numbers to fair distribution	By May 2023	

Task Crafting	Action Item	Timeline	Status
Add in tasks related to community-engaged work (including professional development and tenure/promotion guidelines and service-learning)	Identify and meet with stakeholders in university's Center for Community Engagement; join workshops or sessions offered by the center; request to join the advisory board; enroll in teaching a future service-learning course; participate in service-learning course preparation programs	2023–2025	

Relational Crafting	Action Item	Timeline	Status
Increase networks with local communities for public health policy outreach around tick-borne illnesses	Email and meet with local pediatricians to listen and share ideas about translating scientific research to medical practitioners and families/patients; based on meetings, select two best aligned (in terms of working style and disposition) pediatrician partners to pilot a tick-borne informational session	2024–2025	
Reduce committees that do not generate positive relational or working-style experiences; determine future plan on avoiding negative committees	Resign from faculty sub-committee that meets monthly regardless of need; create a "cheat sheet" for questions about committee's culture and working style, time demands for future requests	By May 2023	

Cognitive Crafting	Action Item	Timeline	Status
Find pathways for assessment to support service-learning and community-engaged work	Conduct literature review (with GA support) on literature and assessments around service-learning and community-engaged work	Fall 2024	

(Continued)

Table 5.4 (Continued)

Cognitive Crafting	Action Item	Timeline	Status
Determine ways to align time and priorities in departmental meetings when relevant	Identify ways to make departmental meetings more efficient, which increases time for potential professional development around community-engaged work and public intellectualism	Spring 2025	
Create new ways of approaching compliance tasks on assessment (and other) committees	Develop collaborative opportunities for writing compliance reports with positive colleagues (internal and external to university); share resources on best practices for reporting	2023-ongoing	

Lessons Learned

Through our work on job crafting with faculty members like Linda, we have gained insight into what helps and hinders participants who undertake the Job-Crafting Action Plan. In general, we have found that most people are keenly aware of what is not working at mid-career but often feel stuck in their current professional situation. This requires repeating: almost always, the core issue is not knowing how to reflect on priorities or develop action steps; the core issue is more about finding the space – both physically and emotionally – to undertake these important career design strategies with a sense of agency. It is also important to note that finding space is not and should not be the sole responsibility of the individual faculty member, as academic leaders, especially department chairs, significantly influence the workloads and time allocations of faculty members. As such, much of the work needed in this realm is raising awareness, educating, preparing, and supporting academic leaders as catalysts for equity-oriented change in their departments and beyond (Kulp et al., 2019; O'Meara et al., 2020).

This point leads to our final lesson learned about the efficacy and utility of the Job-Crafting Action Plan – the need to address the dominant narrative at mid-career that the onus of responsibility rests solely on the individual faculty member's shoulders. Currently, it is mid-career faculty who are expected to carry the lion's share of service and leadership roles; it is mid-career faculty who are expected to figure out new ways of time management or technological efficiencies or simply to just work harder. Even mid-career faculty foster this narrative, as we often hear our participants ask, "Who else will do it?," or state, "I have to do it because I'm good at [fill in the blank]." Through our lessons learned, we have found that we need to address the psychological burden of the onus of responsibility carried by most of our mid-career faculty participants just as much as we need to model the benefits of job crafting.

Conclusion

In this chapter, we highlight the Job-Crafting Action Plan strategy as a means of intentionally elevating priorities at a complex career stage. By fostering a sense of agency and career design skills, job crafting calls on faculty members to push back on the notion that mid-career is devoid of opportunities to bridge priorities with professional responsibilities. Through self-reflection on priorities in four areas of faculty work (i.e., teaching, research, service, and leadership) and subsequent action plans around job crafting (i.e., task, relational, and cognitive crafting), mid-career faculty members can better safeguard space for their mid-career priorities. Although this chapter focuses on individual-level actions, we highlight the need for institutional responsibility for addressing inequitable workloads and cultures.

References

Acker, J. (1990). Hierarchies, jobs, bodies: A theory of gendered organizations. *Gender & Society*, 4(2), 139–158.

Baker, V. L., & Manning, C. (2021). Preparing the next generation of institutional leaders: Strategic supports for mid-career faculty. *To Improve the Academy: A Journal of Educational Development*, 40(1). https://doi.org/10.3998/tia.963

Barnett, R. (2020). Why diversity, equity, and inclusion matters in US higher education. *Perspectives in Education*, 38(2), 20–35. http://dx.doi.org/10.18820/2519593X/pie.v38.i2.02

Bensimon, E. M., Dowd, A. C., Stanton-Salazar, R., & Dávila, B. A. (2019). The role of institutional agents in providing institutional support to Latinx students in STEM. *The Review of Higher Education*, 42(4), 1689–1721.

Berg, J. M., Dutton, J. E., & Wrzesniewski, A. (2013). Job crafting and meaningful work. In B. J. Dik, Z. S. Byrne, & M. F. Steger (Eds.), *Purpose and meaning in the workplace* (pp. 81–104). American Psychological Association. https://doi.org/10.1037/14183-005

Elder, G. H. (1997). The life course and human development. In W. Damon & R. M. Lerner (Eds.), *Handbook of child psychology* (5th ed., pp. 939–991). Wiley.

Griffin, K. A. (2019). Institutional barriers, strategies, and benefits to increasing the representation of women and men of color in the professoriate. *Higher Education: Handbook of Theory and Research*, 35(1), 277–349.

Griffith, T. O., & Ford, J. R. (2022). Say her name: The socialization of Black women in graduate school. *Journal of Student Affairs Research and Practice*, 1–4. https://doi.org/10.1080/19496591.2022.2042006

Kulp, A. M., Wolf-Wendel, L. E., & Smith, D. G. (2019). The possibility of promotion: How race and gender predict promotion clarity for associate professors. *Teachers College Record, 121*(5), 1–28.

Mathews, K. R. (2014). *Perspectives on mid-career faculty and advice for supporting them*. The Collaborative on Academic Careers in Higher Education.

Misra, J., Lundquist, J. H., Holmes, E., & Agiomavritis, S. (2011). The ivory ceiling of service work. *Academe, 97*(1), 22–26.

Neumann, A., Terosky, A. L., & Schell, J. (2006). Agents of learning: Strategies for assuming agency, for learning, in tenured faculty careers. In S. J. Bracken, J. K. Allen, & D. R. Dean (Eds.), *The balancing act: Gendered perspectives in faculty roles and work lives* (pp. 91–120). Stylus Publishing.

O'Meara, K., Terosky, A. L., & Neumann, A. (2008). *Faculty careers and work lives: A professional growth perspective* (ASHE Higher Education Report no. 34(3)). Jossey-Bass.

O'Meara, K. A., Beise, E., Culpepper, D., Misra, J., & Jaeger, A. (2020). Faculty work activity dashboards: A strategy to increase transparency. *Change: The Magazine of Higher Learning, 52*(3), 34–42.

Perez, R. (2021). Work-life (re)negotiation for mid-career faculty. *New Directions for Higher Education*. https://doi.org/10.1002/he.20400

Shahjahan, R. A. (2020). On being for others: Time and shame in the neoliberal academy. *Journal of Education Policy, 35*(6), 785–811. https://doi.org/10.1080/02680939.2019.1629027

Shavers, M. C., & Moore, J. L., III. (2014). The double-edged sword: Coping and resiliency strategies of African American women enrolled in doctoral programs at predominately white institutions. *Frontiers: A Journal of Women Studies, 35*(3), 15. https://doi.org/10.5250/fronjwomestud.35.3.0015

Terosky, A. L., O'Meara, K., & Campbell, C. M. (2014). Enabling possibility: Women associate professors' sense of agency in career advancement. *Journal of Diversity in Higher Education, 7*(1), 58–76.

Williams, J. C. (1989). Deconstructing gender. *Michigan Law Review, 87,* 797–843.

Section 2

Institutional Programming

Laura Gail Lunsford

Universities have existed for hundreds of years, with the University of Bologna, established in 1088, recognized as being among the oldest universities in continuous operation. Yet faculty (or academic) development only began to be professionalized as a practice in the 1970s and to be studied in the 1990s (Sutherland, 2018). Thus, institutional programming to support faculty development is a relatively new aspect of some of society's oldest organizational structures. Faculty development, which has heretofore largely focused on new tenure-track faculty members, is beginning to apply to faculty at mid- and late-career stages. Austin and Sorcinelli (2013) forecasted this trend. The examples presented in this section show that their other predictions were also correct: faculty development is now more varied, is offered at different institutional types, is delivered in multiple modalities, and engages in partnerships with other campus units, such as instructional technology, assessment, and student affairs.

The chapters in this section highlight how institutional programming can support mid-career faculty development. Two of the chapters feature the creation, or re-envisioning, of faculty development centers at a small liberal arts college (Chapter 7) and at a community college (Chapter 10). Chapters 6 and 9 present programs that support teaching faculty, reflecting a new focus on non–tenure-track faculty members. Institutionalizing better mentorship of faculty at mid-career is a feature of Chapters 8 and 9. These two chapters describe different approaches to enhancing a mentorship culture on campuses.

In sum, these chapters make the point that there is not a "one-size-fits-all" approach to faculty development, as Austin and Sorcinelli (2013) noted. The programming described in this section highlights the effectiveness of cohort programs and of programs that allow faculty members to choose from a portfolio of offerings. These chapters present initiatives that envision a more holistic approach to faculty development and that value and leverage partnerships with other campus units and faculty experts. The pandemic perhaps accelerated a trend to offering programming in

DOI: 10.4324/9781003428626-8

multiple modalities, as the technology has improved along with faculty members' skill in using it. Two chapters describe programming that is available through teleconference software.

In Chapter 6, Hastings presents two tools, a Program Implementation Guide and a Project Plan Template, for faculty development at Texas State University. The tools rely on Lave and Wenger's theory of situated learning (1991) and engage both tenure-track and non–tenure-track faculty members. The programming is focused on engaging faculty members to envision what is next in their career. Their aim is to reduce the isolation experienced by many faculty members and to promote a sense of equality between TT and NTT faculty members by bringing them together. Future programming is planned that advances more holistic approaches, addressing topics like increasing well-being and reducing compassion fatigue.

In Chapter 7, Drinkwater describes a Scheduling Tool to simplify how faculty developers can add professional development programming to an existing Center for Teaching and Learning. Wise resource use is of interest to all institutions. This chapter discusses how Agnes Scott College, a small liberal arts college, leveraged existing resources to create a predictable set of offerings for mid-career faculty members.

Chapter 8 features two tools related to a university initiative to enhance a mentoring culture on campus. Both a Mentoring Institute Agenda and a Mentoring Institute Evaluation can enrich a culture of mentoring among faculty members. Wojton and Mumpower provide the rationale, methods, and tools for developing a networked mentoring initiative to support mid-career faculty. This approach recognizes the diverse needs of mid-career faculty members, who may be better served by a networked mentoring approach. Wojton and Mumpower's assessment data reveals high satisfaction rates among participants, a growth mindset toward adopting a networked approach to mentoring on campus, and concrete plans for managing their networks.

Mentoring at mid-career is also a feature of Chapter 9. Dahlheimer and colleagues present two tools, an application form and a program of activities, for faculty developers to replicate a year-long, mid-career mentoring program for teaching faculty. The monthly meetings are the heart of this program, which aims to help mid-career faculty members discover and cultivate their sense of purpose, consider their professional evolution and goals, explore their interests in pedagogical and curricular innovation, and develop their leadership potential within their organization.

In Chapter 10, Strickland-Davis describes the creation of a new teaching and learning center at a community college. She presents a tool with seven faculty competencies that can be used to guide development and programming for teaching faculty at mid-career. This chapter highlights the importance of aligning faculty programming with institutional goals and strategic plans.

Programming for faculty members at mid-career is relatively new. This section highlights a cross-section of institutions that see such investments as critical to maintaining an effective faculty workforce during the mid-career period. Effective faculty development takes considerable time and resources to plan and deliver. Thus, attention to sustainability should be a top consideration for faculty developers. The strategies posited by the Alignment Framework for Faculty Development are useful in situating mid-career faculty programming as part of institutional priorities (Baker et al., 2017). This framework points to the role of the faculty developer as a bridge between faculty needs, departmental policies and aims, institutional policies (e.g., tenure and promotion), and institutional strategies and goals.

Sometimes, faculty developers are adept at identifying faculty needs but fail to connect programming with institutional priorities. Such efforts are less likely to be sustained, especially if there is a change in leadership. Conversely, there are times when institutions provide mid-career faculty programming, and leaders wonder why no one attends. This problem is also an alignment problem, as faculty members may not view that programming as meeting their needs. The idea of alignment is critical in advancing mid-career faculty support as a matter of practice and to advance the field.

References

Austin, A. E., & Sorcinelli, M. D. (2013). The future of faculty development: Where are we going? *New Directions for Teaching and Learning*, 2013(133), 85–97.

Baker, V. L., Pifer, M. J., & Lunsford, L. G. (2017). Faculty development in liberal arts colleges: A look at divisional trends, preferences, and needs. *Higher Education Research & Development*, 37(7), 1336–1351.

Lave, J., & Wenger, E. (1991). *Situated learning: Legitimate peripheral participation*. Cambridge University Press.

Sutherland, K. A. (2018). Holistic academic development: Is it time to think more broadly about the academic development project? *International Journal for Academic Development*, 23(4), 261–273.

Chapter 6

What's Next? Charting Your Path

A Personal Career Goal Development Program for Mid-Career Faculty

Candace Hastings

Overview

What's Next? Charting Your Path is a university-sponsored cohort program supporting tenured and non–tenure-track (NTT) mid-career faculty as they pursue career development goals within a community of practice. Through a competitive self-nomination application process, a faculty member proposes an idea for a specific career development project intended to lead to a career outcome or goal achievement. Faculty members work on their project plans throughout the semester and attend four monthly sessions on topics such as building mentor networks and project planning, where they share and reflect as a group. At the end of the program, faculty members submit their plans and receive a $500 stipend for attending the program sessions and $1,000 toward full or cost-share funding support for their projects. This chapter provides an overview of the program and includes two tools: a Program Implementation Guide and a Project Plan Template.

Program Focus

What's Next focuses on the success of tenured and non–tenure-track mid-career faculty with seven or more years of full-time service at Texas State University (TXST), a large public university with approximately 38,000 students and 1,500 full-time faculty. The program was designed by the director of faculty development, the associate provost, and three members of the Faculty Development Advisory Committee. The program's initial aim was to support associate professors as they pursued promotion; however, when the program was implemented post-pandemic, the scope was broadened to include all mid-career faculty, including full professors and NTT faculty. The program was piloted in spring 2022 with 13 faculty members.

DOI: 10.4324/9781003428626-9

Although in its initial design, the program focused on supporting all genders, it was intended to emphasize the needs of women faculty, who may have been disproportionately disadvantaged by the pandemic. Squazzoni et al. (2020) found that during the early days of the pandemic, fewer manuscripts were submitted by women than by men. These researchers posited that the pandemic may continue to affect women's research productivity in the years to come, given that many faculty members had new or additional caregiving duties and health challenges that adversely influenced their ability to engage in research.

The rationale for an emphasis on mid-career came from research findings showing that mid-career faculty bear more service responsibility than faculty at other stages that may interfere with pursuing research or other career goals. Further, service work often falls disproportionately on women and faculty of color. Misra et al. (2021) found that white women perceived gender disparities in faculty workloads, as women were assigned heavier workloads than their male colleagues. In addition, women faculty of color reported their labor was not recognized in faculty rewards systems, particularly invisible labor spent mentoring students and doing diversity work. The pandemic exacerbated these ongoing invisible labor issues, as faculty with intersecting identities performed more emotional labor in supporting students during the pandemic (Berheide et al., 2022).

In creating a program to support mid-career faculty, we wanted to provide well-deserved recognition of their work, work that often is ignored at the university level. Bozeman and Gaughan's (2011) study found that faculty career satisfaction is predicated on awareness and appreciation of one's work and contributions. We wanted to create a program that celebrated and formally recognized mid-career faculty for their overall contributions to the university.

Needed Skill

It was important to help faculty members develop skills they could use at any juncture of their career to plan next steps or to explore career development opportunities. Therefore, we identified four common skill sets that were tied to project plan deliverables: (a) designing a project; (b) building a mentor network; (c) developing a project plan; and (d) creating a budget. The deliverables provided accountability and structure; however, the broader intended outcomes were general career growth and skills development. Session speakers provided expertise and instruction on developing skills. Individual written reflections and community discussion were embedded in the sessions as participants internalized and shared lessons learned through successes and struggles.

Rationale

Baker et al. (2019) assert that future academic leaders will come from mid-career faculty ranks, and as such, mid-career faculty members need intentional, targeted programming to prepare them to become effective leaders. The goal of the What's Next program was to encourage faculty members to examine their professional development priorities and to support them in the next step of their career development, which may include academic leadership roles.

In using community of practice as a frame for the program, we were able to connect faculty members from across disciplines, roles, and campus locations to help strengthen bonds among faculty. Faculty members often do not have the opportunity to develop meaningful relationships with faculty members outside their disciplines. However, skilled academic leaders need to know how to leverage the power of community, particularly in building support networks. Engaging with peers in a community of practice strengthens the expertise of all participants as they learn from each other.

Equity and Inclusion Considerations

O'Meara et al. (2018) assert that faculty seek legitimacy in their careers through a sense of belongingness. Belongingness comprises being included and valued. However, their case study found that women, historically underrepresented faculty populations, and NTT faculty felt excluded and dismissed by colleagues. In addition, NTT faculty perceived their accomplishments, including awards and accolades, as being seen as less important than the accomplishments of tenure-track faculty.

Faculty members from historically underrepresented populations often face barriers in reaching their career goals. In particular, the work of faculty of color is often devalued if their research agendas focus on their own communities, and they face disproportionately heavier service loads. In addition, faculty of color often do not receive mentoring from senior faculty because of lack of representation at the senior faculty level (Stanley, 2006). Wolfe and Freeman (2013) recommend using formalized programs to increase equitable access to senior leadership. Many competitive career development awards and programs use a top-down nomination process, which can disadvantage faculty members from underrepresented populations. Therefore, in the What's Next program, we used a self-nomination process and routed the self-nomination form to the department chairs and deans for informational purposes.

Kezar's (2013) study of departmental cultures found that professional development opportunities for NTT faculty are sparse and often dependent on the culture of their departments. Therefore, opening the program up to faculty with seven or more years of full-time service to the university provided *all* mid-career faculty with the autonomy to choose their own path to career fulfilment.

NTT faculty members do not always feel equally valued in their departments (O'Meara et al., 2018). As Kezar and Sam (2011) note, the few studies on NTT faculty often assume a deficit stance that negatively stereotypes their capabilities. Even the common moniker *non–tenure-track* minimizes their status and importance at the university. The decision for us to include NTT faculty in the program was based on the need to recognize publicly the contributions of NTT faculty work, to support their career development, and to empower them by giving them an equal voice in the program.

Theoretical or Conceptual Grounding

The What's Next? Charting Your Path program was designed using Lave and Wenger's (1991) theory of situated learning and legitimate peripheral participation. According to this theory, less-experienced members of the mid-career community (newcomers) would engage with experienced members (old-timers) in experiential learning social networks. Rooted in social process, newcomers develop expertise as a result of engaging with old-timers in a particular sociocultural context, in this case, mid-career development.

At mid-career, faculty members are experts in their respective disciplines, often fulfilling the role of expert or old-timer as perceived by junior faculty and students. However, in this program, faculty members needed mentor support as they explored next steps in their own career development. Creating a network of mentors is situated learning and is in and of itself an act of career self-advocacy (Arredondo et al., 2022). Having strong mentor networks also increases overall job satisfaction, particularly for mid-career faculty (Lunsford et al., 2018).

Creating a learning community cohort fit the frame and tenets of situated learning, where participants could act as newcomers and experts simultaneously. Community discussions took place in each session and served as sense-making conversations. Members of the advisory committee, most of whom were full professors and associate deans, offered stories and advice based on their own experiences.

In situated learning, the development process is an integral part of learning. Deliverables were embedded to track progress and provide practical applications of the learning sessions. However, situated learning is about learning, not teaching, and learning comes from engagement. As Lave and Wenger (1991) assert, "Learners, as peripheral participants, can develop a view of what the whole enterprise is about, and what there is to be learned. Learning itself is an improvised practice: A learning curriculum unfolds in opportunities for engagement in practice" (p. 93).

Tools

In this section, I present two tools: a Program Implementation Guide and a Project Plan Template. Included in the Project Plan Template is an example project plan compiled by Rachel, a senior lecturer in biology, one of the participants. Rachel created two new courses and developed a study-abroad program in London for pre-health students.

Program Implementation Guide

To generate interest in the program, we brought in faculty mid-career expert Vicki Baker to conduct a career development workshop that was open to all faculty. This workshop was followed with the program announcement and pre-cohort activities. Figure 6.1 outlines the pre-programming process that occurred in the fall before the spring that the What's Next cohort began working on their plans.

Participants completed a self-nomination form, which was reviewed by advisory committee members and scored using a Likert scale rubric in Qualtrics. Both the questions and the scoring criteria are listed next.

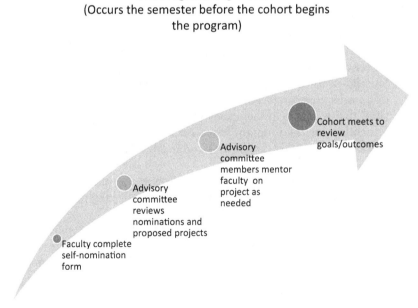

Pre-Programming Process
(Occurs the semester before the cohort begins the program)

Faculty complete self-nomination form

Advisory committee reviews nominations and proposed projects

Advisory committee members mentor faculty on project as needed

Cohort meets to review goals/outcomes

Figure 6.1 **Pre-Programming Process**

**Self-Nomination Form for What's Next?
Charting Your Path**

1. What are your current career development goals? (Include at least one short-term and one long-term goal.)
2. Briefly describe a project (research/creative activities, teaching/learning, leadership) that would help you achieve that goal. How could participating in Charting Your Path help you accomplish that goal or goals?
3. Briefly describe any previous work that shows your commitment to the project and/or goal. (Attach a brief CV highlighting that previous work.)
4. How could your project support and take action on a university, college, or department goal or initiative?
5. What are anticipated disseminated/communicated outcomes of the project, including, but not limited to, presentation, workshop, publication, performance, community action?
6. Is there anything else you would like us to know about your motivation or desire to participate in this program or project?

**Likert Scale Rating Rubric (1 – Strongly Disagree –
5 Strongly Agree)**

1. Suitability for the program based on years of service.
2. Suitability for the program based on current short-term/long-term career development goals.
3. Suitability for the program based on the applicant's description of a project (research/creative activities, teaching/learning, leadership) that would help them achieve their career goals.
4. Suitability for the program based on the description of previous work that shows the applicant's commitment to the project and/or goal.
5. Suitability for the program based on how the applicant's project supports and acts on a university, college, or department goal or initiative.
6. Suitability for the program based on anticipated disseminated/communicated outcomes of the project, including, but not limited to, presentation, workshop, publication, performance, community action.
7. Suitability for the program based on applicant's need, motivation, or desire to participate in this program or project.

Session Topics and Presentations

Participants attended four two-hour in-person sessions, held monthly throughout the spring semester. Sessions included expert-led instruction, self-reflections, and small-group/large-group discussions. Session topics were:

- **Creating a Mentor Network:** Participants received information on creating a mentor network and were required to identify and meet with at least two mentors.
- **Developing a Project Plan and Timeline:** Participants set goals and outcomes and tied those outcomes to institutional priorities, timelines, and resources.
- **Pitching a Plan Workshop:** Participants shared their project plans in revolving pairs in a "speed project sharing" session and filled out a preliminary plan template.
- **Finding Resources and Disseminating Outcomes:** Participants created a budget for their projects.

Participants were given up to eight weeks after the final meeting to turn in their project plans for funding. Table 6.1 shows a template we provided to participants as a suggested plan format.

Table 6.1 Project Plan Template

Overview/Career Development Goals
Describe the career development goal (s) you are addressing in the What's Next program.
What is your broad timeline for reaching those goals?
Project Activity Description
Describe your project activity.
How does your project help you reach your career goal(s)?
How does your project align with department, college, university, or research strategic plans?
Mentor Map/List
List mentors and their roles (or make a mentor map).
How have you engaged with your mentors?
What insights/advice have you gained from your mentors?
Make note of any additional mentors you need to seek for your project and/or career development.
Project Resources
What non-monetary resources will you need to complete your project?
What monetary resources will you need to complete your project?
Do you have future resource needs as you move beyond this project?
Project Deliverable
How will you disseminate the outcome of your project? *Possibilities: Conference presentation, article, writing group, faculty development workshop, academic community, etc.*

Excerpts from Rachel's final study-abroad project plan are included in the box that follows as an example:

Rachel's Project Plan

Overview

I have been teaching in a traditional classroom setting for more than a decade. I often experiment with new ways of teaching and regularly look for new ideas and strategies. To stretch my teaching in more innovative ways, my next goal is to develop a study-abroad program. This will allow me to branch out from the traditional classroom and campus setting and engage students in new ways and in new places.

I am so excited to start by taking pre-health students to London, England, and to teach two brand-new courses: History of Medicine and Explorations in Physiology. I am further excited to see how this program can grow in size and scope, leading to more and deeper faculty collaborations and enrichment possibilities for students.

Timeline

- Feasibility Proposal due April 2022 (*completed*)
- Scouting trip in early August 2022
- Final Program Proposal due September 2022
- New courses entered into CIM in September 2022
- First run of program with students in June 2023
- Continuous run of program annually each June

Project Activity to Date

When developing this study-abroad project, I started with research on the types of programs that already existed at Texas State University and looked for where we weren't meeting student needs. I met with our pre-health advisor to confirm my findings and ensure that a program for pre-health students would be valuable and fit in with their degree plans, verifying they would have financial aid access for the program and that it would increase their competitiveness post-graduation. I then decided on the courses (History of Medicine and Explorations in Physiology) and researched the best place in the world to teach them, taking advantage of historical events, key discoveries, existing museums, and current researchers. This led to the selection of London, England, as the ideal place.

Once I chose the place, I met with several faculty running their own programs for advice and tips. I then met with the Education Abroad office on campus to learn how to get started, what forms were needed, how to approach Program Providers for quotes, which provider to pair with, how to develop a budget, etc.

I worked with our Curriculum Committee Chair to get special topics courses and permanent CRNs for the courses.

Strategic Plan Alignment

My study-abroad project will achieve the following listed goals at the department, college, and university levels.

Biology Department

- "Support & improve science education . . ."
- "Encourage and support faculty to . . . explore new approaches to teaching . . ."
- "Evaluate, improve, & optimize undergraduate curricula . . ."
- "Maintain our reputation for practice-oriented, hands-on learning by continuing to support laboratory & field courses"

College of Science and Engineering

- "The college is committed to nurturing the talents of young scientists by immersing students in a robust curriculum and applied learning experiences . . ."

University

- "Promote the success of all students – Enhance student retention & graduation rates through . . . engagement opportunities"
- "Offer high quality academic & educational programming – Develop new nationally & internationally competitive academic programs that meet economic & cultural needs of the state & nation"

Mentorship

Note: Rachel listed 12 external and university mentors in the plan in the following areas:

- Advice on starting and running a study-abroad program

- Advice on new course content and feasibility
- Advice on technicalities, such as where students should stay and how to get around London
- Encouragement and motivation

Project Resources Still Needed

Monetary: I have never been to London, and it is important that I scout out the stops I am planning to ensure they are appropriate and develop full lesson plans for each of them. This scouting trip will cost around $3,000. (Flights are ~$1,500, a budget hotel near the city center is ~$1,250 for five nights total, a public transportation pass for the London tube is ~$60 for six days total, and the museum entry fees are ~$30 total.)

I am requesting funds to cover the scouting trip from the What's Next Program, the College of Science and Engineering, and the Department of Biology.

Project Deliverables

This project will have five main outcomes:

1. New knowledge of teaching methodologies and engagement with students outside the traditional classroom
2. Development of a strong study-abroad course in physiology and medicine, helping students learn, grow, and submit more competitive applications to medical schools, dental schools, and other graduate programs
3. Enrichment of three of my courses – Human Physiology, Vertebrate Physiology, and Biology of Sex and Reproduction – which all have significant physiology and medicine components and enroll more than 500 students each year
4. Increased collaboration and cohesion among faculty teaching pre-health majors (biology, biochemistry, nursing, radiation therapy, respiratory therapy, medical humanities, etc.) as we grow the program to include more faculty and class options each summer
5. The sharing of my new knowledge and tips with others about how to develop and teach a study-abroad program, potentially even through university workshops or conference presentations

POST-PROGRAM ACTIVITIES AND OUTCOMES

All participants attended the sessions and completed their plans, and most of them completed their projects throughout the following year. One faculty member brought together data scientists from across campus for an interdisciplinary symposium. Several faculty members developed new study-abroad programs. Another was awarded a prestigious NEH grant based on their archival work. Some were able to complete research stalled by the pandemic. Others wrote grants or created mentoring programs. Two faculty participants left the university in pursuit of their personal career goals. Although it was difficult to lose such valuable faculty members, the fact that they were able to use the program to pursue their career passions beyond the context of the university confirmed that we had delivered on our intentions.

Several participants reflected on the impact of the program on their professional lives:

- As this project has blossomed, I found even more exciting benefits, such as the potential for increased collaboration among colleagues.
- I might not have found the step I needed, but I found the way to possibly make it happen. I truly enjoyed meeting all of the peers on the faculty as well as administrative side, connecting with mentors, getting the courage to support others and allow my institution to support me.
- The program helped me to develop a more strategic approach to my professional growth. The workshops and coaching sessions provided practical advice on networking, role advancement, and "branding myself" as a thought leader. I was able to create a stronger personal brand and learned how to effectively communicate my strengths and achievements when formulating my next steps.

Lessons Learned

During our pilot year, we evaluated what went well and what changes need to be made in future iterations of the program. The cohort model worked well, as did the balance between individual plans and collective informational, support, and sharing sessions. In addition, bringing tenured and NTT faculty together provided a space in which all voices were valued equally.

As we listened to participant discussions about career and personal challenges, we realized we need to provide strategies for maintaining personal well-being, such as establishing space and boundaries as a practice of self-advocacy to prevent compassion fatigue (Cordaro, 2020). We will provide additional tools for career self-advocacy and promote and acknowledge participants' contributions to elevate the visibility of their work.

Conclusion

Supporting faculty in mid-career is a fundamental responsibility of the university community. Too often, mid-career faculty are left alone to navigate systems rooted in tacit expectations and social norms. Future iterations of our personal career goal development program will continue to answer Baker and Manning's (2021) call to provide support for TXST mid-career faculty as they explore the question "What's Next?"

References

Arredondo, P., Miville, M. L., Capodilupo, C. M., & Vera, T. (2022). "Be strong!" The role of self-advocacy. In *Women and the challenge of STEM professions: Thriving in a chilly climate* (pp. 83–86). Springer.

Baker, V. L., Lunsford, L. G., & Pifer, M. J. (2019). Patching up the "leaking leadership pipeline": Fostering mid-career faculty succession management. *Research in Higher Education*, 60(6), 823–843.

Baker, V. L., & Manning, C. E. (2021). A mid-career faculty agenda: A review of four decades of research and practice. *Higher Education: Handbook of Theory and Research*, 36, 419–484.

Berheide, C. W., Carpenter, M. A., & Cotter, D. A. (2022). Teaching college in the time of COVID-19: Gender and race differences in faculty emotional labor. *Sex Roles*, 86(7), 441–455.

Bozeman, B., & Gaughan, M. (2011). Job satisfaction among university faculty: Individual, work, and institutional determinants. *The Journal of Higher Education*, 82(2), 154–186.

Cordaro, M. (2020). Pouring from an empty cup: The case for compassion fatigue in higher education. *Building Healthy Academic Communities Journal*, 4(2), 17–28.

Kezar, A. (2013). Departmental cultures and non-tenure-track faculty: Willingness, capacity, and opportunity to perform at four-year institutions. *The Journal of Higher Education*, 84(2), 153–188.

Kezar, A., & Sam, C. (2011). Understanding non-tenure track faculty: New assumptions and theories for conceptualizing behavior. *American Behavioral Scientist*, 55(11), 1419–1442. https://doi.org/10.1177/0002764211408879

Lave, J., & Wenger, E. (1991). *Situated learning: Legitimate peripheral participation*. Cambridge University Press.

Lunsford, L., Baker, V., & Pifer, M. (2018). Faculty mentoring faculty: Career stages, relationship quality, and job satisfaction. *International Journal of Mentoring and Coaching in Education*, 7(2), 139–154.

Misra, J., Kuvaeva, A., O'Meara, K., Culpepper, D. K., & Jaeger, A. (2021). Gendered and racialized perceptions of faculty workloads. *Gender & Society*, 35(3), 358–394.

O'Meara, K., Templeton, L., & Nyunt, G. (2018). Earning professional legitimacy: Challenges faced by women, underrepresented minority, and non-tenure-track faculty. *Teachers College Record*, 120(12), 1–38.

Squazzoni, F., Bravo, G., Grimaldo, F., Garcia-Costa, D., Farjam, M., & Mehmani, B. (2020). Only second-class tickets for women in the COVID-19 race. A study on manuscript submissions and reviews in 2329 Elsevier journals. Preprint at SSRN. https://doi.org/10.2139/ssrn.3712813

Stanley, C. A. (2006). Coloring the academic landscape: Faculty of color breaking the silence in predominantly white colleges and universities. *American Educational Research Journal, 4*(43), 701–736.

Wolfe, B., & Freeman, S., Jr. (2013). A case for administrators of color: Insights and policy implications for higher education's predominantly White institutions. *EJEP: eJournal of Education Policy.* https://in.nau.edu/wp-content/uploads/sites/135/2018/08/WolfeandFreeman-ek.pdf

Chapter 7

Supporting Faculty at Small Liberal Arts Colleges Across the Career Span

Megan Drinkwater

Overview

Small liberal arts colleges (SLACs) place increasing demands on small numbers of faculty members, making it challenging for mid-career faculty to advance to full professor or to otherwise plan for how they would like their careers to unfold. While this "busy-ness" can apply to faculty members at all ranks, for those at mid-career it is especially challenging. In addition to the need to stay abreast of best practices for excellence in teaching and to publish peer-reviewed research, mid-career faculty often have significant administrative duties that support their institutions in innovating and thriving. Fostering close relationships with students through formal and informal advising, career planning, and so forth are often additional "invisible" service obligations that, no matter how rewarding, attenuate faculty resources. These competing pulls on faculty time are often magnified for faculty from underrepresented groups, who are too often asked to do more than their colleagues in the name of representation and are among the too-few faculty members to whom students from similar backgrounds look for mentoring. For mid-career faculty, whether it's pedagogical innovations, research agendas, administrative skill growth, or promotion to full professor status, the competing demands of the job can seem overwhelming.

One tool for helping mid-career colleagues map and execute a plan is a schedule of professional development opportunities that use multiple modalities, leverage the interests and strengths of colleagues, and include the celebration of successes. Such a framework makes it easier for faculty to "opt in" without the fear of missing out if they are focused on other important tasks. This chapter describes the rationale and content of a Scheduling Tool for faculty developers.

Program Focus

The aim of the program was creating a central locus for professional development to provide structure for faculty members looking for support

DOI: 10.4324/9781003428626-10

beyond improving their teaching. This was a new experiment for our institution. The newly envisioned center, focused on teaching, learning, and faculty development, just completed its second year. Thus, this chapter is forward looking, providing a series of proposed next steps whose success is, of course, unproven. The key point for these proposed next steps is that they involve a scheduling tool with a predictable, stable format that provides iterative opportunities for planning and growth and that draws on and celebrates colleagues' existing strengths.

In the first year of the Center for Teaching, Learning, and Professional Development (CTL-PD), we offered a broad range of programming. In the second year, we made more targeted investments in areas that seemed of greatest interest and initiated new faculty conversations that considered the entire faculty career span. In year three, under new leadership, we hope to continue to solidify the structure, launch a more targeted cohort mentoring program for new faculty, and pilot a cohort-based peer mentoring program for mid-career faculty. A key to the success of these changes will be letting faculty know what to expect and when so that they can incorporate development opportunities into their normal workflow.

Needed Skills

The goal of the CTL-PD is to provide holistic professional development support for mid-career faculty members. I define mid-career as associate professors or those relatively newly promoted to full professor. Recognizing, validating, and supporting the range of individual faculty interests beyond the critical area of teaching seemed key to reaching dedicated faculty "where they were."

Among the missing links for our mid-career faculty members was professional development support for long-term career planning. What this meant for us was assessing the broad array of faculty responsibilities so that we could support those that would have the greatest influence on increasing faculty members' morale and sense of purpose.

The goal for a fulfilling faculty career is not simply achieving tenure and promotion but crafting a meaningful process of growth and reinvigoration. The aim is also to model a growth mindset (Dweck, 2015) for our students as opposed to one focused solely on specific goals and benchmarks. Recognizing the individual and changing interests of faculty members is key to meeting broader institutional needs, whether in terms of faculty governance and service, research achievement and the institutional reputation profile, or breadth and excellence of teaching with meaningful innovation. In the bigger picture, ensuring faculty satisfaction is an investment in the institution, because happy faculty are more likely to remain dedicated to the institution, providing continuity for students and the academic program alike while remaining open to reinvention and reinvigoration. Key to this effort is providing opportunities for growth at their home institution rather than requiring faculty with shifting interests to look elsewhere.

Rationale

For our institution, the development of a new Strategic Plan provided a connection point for transformation while our COACHE survey results provided the theoretical framework, which highlighted the need for more targeted mid-career support around specific areas like ill-defined roles, service creep, and innovation fatigue. The survey results informed choices about areas to target, such as competing workplace demands, different service opportunities and their impacts, and workshops highlighting teaching successes in support of institutional innovation initiatives.

At Agnes Scott College, there had long been a Center for Teaching and Learning (CTL), directed by a faculty member as a small part of their workload and compensated by one course-release. The CTL's focus was almost exclusively on student learning. There was little support for other aspects of faculty development, e.g., research, work–life balance, and – most relevant for this collection – career-span support beyond achieving tenure. The idea to provide faculty professional development more broadly emerged from our analysis of 2020 results from the Collaborative on Academic Careers in Higher Education (COACHE) faculty job satisfaction survey. Of particular relevance was the identification of what we refer to as "unhappy associates." This finding was not an alarm bell loudly ringing but a gentle hum that warranted attention and investment. As we were moving into the development of a new strategic plan, the idea was formulated to address faculty work satisfaction in part through broadening the scope of the CTL and renaming it the Center for Teaching, Learning, and Professional Development.

Equity and Inclusion Considerations

In planning and execution of faculty development, it is critical to include the perspectives of DEI-focused stakeholders to create programming for all faculty members that foregrounds an equity focus. For example, we offered a recommendation-writing workshop focusing on eliminating unconscious biases. Such a focus helped to ensure that faculty of color can "see themselves" at the institution through a dedicated focus on providing a more broadly representative curriculum that moves beyond traditional canons. Inclusive mentoring communities or affinity groups can be an effective way to provide support for underrepresented faculty. The National Center for

Faculty Diversity and Development is an excellent resource, and Academic Impressions, to which my institution has a membership, provides a range of professional development workshops and webinars focused on equity and inclusion.

Conceptual Grounding

This chapter introduces a Scheduling Tool that provides predictable scheduling and incorporates multiple ways of reaching and supporting colleagues, builds on the strengths of faculty colleagues, assesses their needs across the institution and the career span, and is adaptable to changing needs. In what follows, I provide a brief discussion of each of these aspects before sharing the specific tool and framework.

Multiple Modalities

In 2021–22, because of the pandemic, we started the semester online, and thus our programming was almost exclusively online. A preference for virtual meetings continued into the spring of 2022, with an emphasis on returning to in-person toward the end of the semester and in the fall of 2022. Choosing modes based on the content of the presentation continued to be important. For example, virtual workshops made the most sense for sessions focusing on how to use our online advising system to support student success; they worked best when participants all had easy access to the system, so this meant that a virtual format was ideal. A conversation about changes to our US history curriculum to make it more broadly representative and inclusive of our extremely diverse student body, on the other hand, was a good fit for an in-person meeting. Similarly, monthly lunches for new faculty worked best in person, while our reading group could be more flexible depending on people's inclinations and schedules. Meeting faculty where they are, and in modes of delivery that match the content, is critical to participation and buy-in.

Leveraging Partnerships

Leveraging partnerships permitted the CTL-PD to support faculty research and writing through a pre-existing program rather than having to invent something new. For example, a Write-On-Site program was run by faculty members at our college. As the CTL expanded into the CTL-PD, the founders of this writing group reached out about a possible affiliation. The program continues with the support of faculty members not formally affiliated with the CTL-PD, with financial support for lunches provided by the CTL-PD.

Similar partnerships are possible with individual faculty members. For example, at end-of-term sessions, we have invited faculty to share "Good News in Teaching" based on a relevant theme each semester. We have found this activity to be a morale-boosting, thought-provoking way to leverage the excellent work of colleagues without requiring additional work from the CTL-PD director. Another example of a partnership was when faculty interest in ChatGPT and AI led to a faculty-led workshop, arranged and financially supported by the CTL-PD in the form of a small stipend for the facilitator and gift cards for participants. These examples of using the framework of the CTL-PD to celebrate faculty accomplishments and harness the interests and skills of colleagues is an important part of sharing the rewards of our work rather than solely dwelling on its demands. It is especially relevant for those at mid-career, as their time in service has typically enabled them to rack up successes and expertise that colleagues may not know about. Using the CTL-PD as a forum for these accomplishments shines a light on their value to the institution and helps maintain morale through a positive feedback loop.

Assessing Needs

In its first year, the CTL-PD took the approach of casting a broad net to assess faculty interests and needs. It held a two-hour workshop in August focusing on pedagogy, specifically accessible education, and hour-long conversations throughout the semester on a range of topics (using our new course management system, library support for students, advising, building community in virtual classes, etc.) aimed at piquing faculty interests. Opening the spring term with a short workshop led by an outside facilitator, Cate Denial, on the pedagogy of kindness allowed us to start the term thinking about where both we and our students were in relation to the ongoing pandemic and its impact on our teaching. From that start, the semester moved forward with a range of activities, conversations, and short workshops.

Adapting and Changing Focus

At mid-year, we chose to focus on an element that had not received attention, namely stepping back to reflect on short- and long-term individual and institutional goals. Providing a framework for consistent discussions and iterative goal setting and progress evaluation was a top priority. At the end of the fall semester, we invited Vicki Baker, a co-editor of this collection and faculty member at a peer institution, to run a virtual workshop titled Preparing for What's Next in Your Career.[1] While Prof. Baker's expertise was critical to the initial offering of this workshop, directors of centers similar to ours could adapt it for their campus's needs. Ideally, an opportunity for this kind of conversation should be provided yearly so that faculty members can take advantage of this kind of structured reflection when they are ready and motivated to do so.

Tool

The Scheduling Tool presents a predictable and iterative calendar of events that enables busy faculty members to engage in faculty development. To ensure predictability, it is helpful to create a set schedule of events. This change to providing a set of events in advance has facilitated faculty development at our institution. The content of core four offerings is presented next. A schedule is provided that relates programming to the academic calendar (see Table 7.1).

Excellence in Teaching

Start the academic year with a workshop on pedagogy. This programming harnesses faculty's chief focus: excellence in teaching. This offering may take a specific focus that is most relevant and timely on your campus. One year, we focused on accessible education best practices coming out of the pandemic, led by Aimi Hamraie, and another year, we focused on

Table 7.1 Scheduling Tool

Timing	Professional Development Activity
Start of the Fall Term	Excellence in Teaching. Workshop on pedagogy to re-engage faculty and focus on the most central element of our work, serving students through the academic program.
Monthly during Fall Term	Topic of choice most relevant to your institution at the given time.
End of Fall Term	Pedagogy Round-Up. Workshop on teaching successes, whether connected specifically to the pedagogy workshop from August or programming from the previous year.
Start of Spring Term	Workshop on faculty needs, e.g., kindness, burnout, time management, goal setting.
Monthly during Spring Term	Topic of choice most relevant to your institution at the given time.
Spring Term	Survey faculty to assess interests and needs for the coming year.
End of Spring Term	Good News Wrap-up. Workshop on teaching successes, with a focus on summer renewal and rededication.

leveraging global learning and digital proficiency skills with a workshop on collaborative online international learning.

Pedagogy Roundup

Offer an end-of-the-semester session on a forward- or backward-looking pedagogy. Forward-looking refers to initiating new projects, while backward-looking refers to reporting on how new pedagogical initiatives worked in practice. Two examples of sessions we have offered are a two-day workshop on problem- and project-based learning (PBL) and a loop-closing opportunity for faculty to share assignments they developed as a result of the PBL workshop from the previous year.

Professional Development/Career Planning

Mid-year is a time to focus on professional development more broadly, with a focus on balance and setting reasonable, thoughtful goals for the spring term. For example, we concluded a fall semester with a workshop on career planning (see earlier) and started a spring semester with a workshop on the pedagogy of kindness with Cate Denial. Another session addressed burnout for faculty and staff, with Rebecca Pope-Ruark (2022) leading a short workshop for all academic affairs faculty and staff. For each of these opportunities, the concerns of mid-career and late-career colleagues were at the forefront, as those longest in service at the institution seemed to be the hardest hit by the concurrence of the pandemic and the increased demands of their career stage.

Good News Wrap-Up

Ending the year by reflecting on teaching success and/or looking ahead along the career path provides both a sense of positive closure and an opportunity to get re-energized about summer plans. This approach can be a good way to highlight moments of pride among our colleagues, permitting faculty to share experiences or assignments that worked particularly well in terms of student engagement. A broad call for participation can also help identify potential partners who could lead a conversation or run a future workshop, ideally with a stipend attached. Our institution was facing a wave of retirements in a three-year period, and thus, we invited some faculty emeriti in Spring 2022 to discuss how they planned for their retirement, what they were doing now, and what they might have done differently as they made this significant life transition. Zoom made virtual offerings easier and more convenient, especially for those no longer teaching on campus. The goal of this session was twofold: to acknowledge how deeply ingrained the identity of an academic can be and to demonstrate that faculty are valued at our institution throughout their lives, not merely when they are with us in the classroom or on campus.

Consistency with Variety

Throughout the year, provide consistent (in our case, monthly) sessions on a wide range of topics: pedagogy and accessible education, student advising, examples of departmental support of institutional initiatives (such as assessments that support preparedness for professional success), and even visits to campus facilities (in our case, a new maker space, during which ideas were generated on how to make use of it in various classes). We settled on a "third Thursday" model, during an open block when classes do not usually meet. While there are inevitably conflicts, choosing a consistent time when colleagues do not teach means that faculty know when events will be offered that could be of interest to them and will thus, in theory, be able to plan around them.

Lessons Learned

There are three points to consider when adding professional development activities to a center with a portfolio of offerings only on teaching and learning. First, develop a consistent plan of offerings and publicize it. The goal is for the offerings to be viewed as part of the institution's culture. Provide visibility for the program by obtaining support from the dean or chief academic officer. For example, these individuals can be asked to include language that introduces the importance of ongoing professional development in initial appointment letters.

Second, carefully assess your resource needs (e.g., course release time, funding, staffing, subject matter expertise, a dedicated meeting space), and have open conversations about what they are and how they will impact your work. A key part of this effort may be to define how much attention should be given to the role of director and what that means in terms of goals and expectations. The director should invest in their own professional development and embrace opportunities for networking, including reaching out to those in similar roles at similar institutions.

Third, a coalition of centers for teaching, learning, and professional development may create a powerful shared resource, especially in terms of mentoring networks and workshops, given the ubiquity of virtual meeting platforms. At SLACs, these centers are, of necessity, very small, often including only one director whose work in that role makes up only a portion of their overall responsibilities. Building a cohort or collaborative of peers to discuss this kind of work can only strengthen our offerings to our faculty.

Looking ahead, consistent mentorship programming is an aspect of regular, predictable support for mid-career faculty that needs attention, and it will hopefully be addressed by future CTL-PD directors at Agnes Scott. A useful starting point for this process would be to consider mentoring needs throughout a faculty career. David Keil's (2019) *Developing Faculty Mentoring Programs* is a resource that points to best practices, including cohort mentoring. The National Center for Faculty Diversity and Development's mentoring map is another helpful guide, illustrating how mentoring can and should extend beyond the institution. As we face both a wave of retirements and unprecedented numbers of new hires, structuring a mentoring program that can take faculty from hiring to tenure and beyond will be critical to supporting colleagues throughout their careers. Making explicit the career-span focus of the professional development aspects of our CTL-PD, from the onboarding of new faculty through the transition to retirement, reminds mid-career faculty members that their development is viewed as important to institutional success.

Conclusion

In this chapter, I have shared a Scheduling Tool to support faculty development that invites busy mid-career faculty members whose time is subject to competing interests to take advantage of a series of programs they can opt in to when their schedule permits. A particular benefit of consistent scheduling is that it can reduce anxiety about missing an opportunity that will only come around once. Reassurance that there will be multiple options to learn new strategies for time management, up-to-date teaching practices, and career planning can reduce the feeling, all too common among mid-career academics, that they are being borne along without agency. The sample schedule provided in Table 7.1 is easily adaptable to the rhythm of any institution's semester or trimester.

Note

1. https://www.leadmentordevelop.com/

References

Dweck, C. (2015). Carol Dweck revisits the growth mindset. *Education Week, 35*(5), 20–24.

Keil, D. (2019). *Developing faculty mentoring programs: A comprehensive handbook*. Academic Impressions.

Pope-Ruark, R. (2022). *Unraveling faculty burnout: Pathways to reckoning and renewal*. Johns Hopkins University Press.

Websites and Other Resources

Academic Impressions. Professional development for higher education with a broad range of programming from which to choose; subscription service. www.academicimpressions.com/

The Agile Academic, Rebecca Pope-Ruark. https://theagileacademic.com/

An excellent resource for underrepresented faculty in particular; membership service, although many free resources, including their mentoring map, are available on their website. Mentoring Map: www.facultydiversity.org/ncfddmentormap

Collaborative on Academic Careers in Higher Education (COACHE). https://coache.gse.harvard.edu/

Collaborative Online International Learning. https://coil.suny.edu/professional-development/

Denial, C. https://catherinedenial.org/

Hamraie, A. https://aimihamraie.com/

Lead Mentor Develop: Advancing Careers and Organizations. Vicki L. Baker and Laura Gail Lunsford. www.leadmentordevelop.com/

National Center for Faculty Diversity and Development. Rigorous extensive survey that addresses many aspects of faculty work; participation is paid at a flat fee depending on institution size plus a dollar amount per faculty FTE. Website, *www.facultydiversity.org/*

Chapter 8

Assessing and Supporting the Needs of Mid-Career Faculty

A Networked Mentoring Approach

Jennifer Wojton and Lori Mumpower

Overview

This chapter provides a rationale, methods, and practical tools for developing a networked mentoring initiative to support mid-career faculty. The featured tools are the Mentoring Institute Agenda and Mentoring Institute Evaluation Instrument. Networked mentoring, or the assumption that a mentee needs a number of mentors for support, upends the traditional notion of one mentor to one mentee. Given the diverse needs of mid-career faculty members, a networked mentoring approach may better serve them. In response to these mentoring needs, the authors developed and facilitated an annual two-day Mentoring Institute to encourage the adoption of a networked mentoring approach for mentees, mentors, and department leaders. Evaluation of the institute reveals high satisfaction rates among participants, a growth mindset aimed at adopting a networked approach to mentoring on campus, and concrete plans for managing attendees' networks.

Program Focus

The Mentoring Institute began in 2022 at Embry-Riddle Aeronautical University (ERAU), a private, STEM-focused university that serves over 6,600 undergraduate students and over 725 graduate students (as of spring 2023 enrollment). In 2021, the campus employed over 342 full-time and 106 part-time faculty (ERAU, n.d., p. 25).

In 2020, the authors conducted interviews with campus chairpersons to achieve several goals. We mapped the range and scope of mentoring practices across departments and colleges and identified what needs department chairs had for mentoring and what challenges they experienced supporting faculty mentoring efforts across career stages. Mentoring efforts across departments and colleges varied, from non-existent to

DOI: 10.4324/9781003428626-11

informal to fully structured programs. Three points became clear from these interviews:

- Mentoring was mostly perceived as having a top-down, hierarchical structure, with senior faculty mentoring early-career faculty.
- Most department chairs did not have a support system for the development of mentoring skills and lacked tools for assessing the effectiveness of mentoring relationships, even though they unilaterally agreed that mentoring is critical.
- Mentoring efforts were primarily focused on new faculty, often leaving mid- and late-career faculty without formal mentoring.

To better support the work of mentors and experiences of mentees across all career levels on ERAU's Daytona Beach campus, a committee of faculty and staff was charged by the Provost, and supported by our Center for Teaching and Learning Excellence (CTLE), with creating a campus mentoring program. A Faculty Mentoring Coordinator was selected to lead the efforts of the committee and partner with the CTLE on delivering mentoring programming and support. The committee was tasked with accomplishing the following: (a) providing resources, (b) setting expectations for effective mentoring, (c) facilitating university processes that would acknowledge and reward the labor of mentors and mentees, and (d) placing particular focus on representation and visibility for underrepresented groups on our campus.

Scholars have expanded the hierarchical model of mentoring to a networked model (Sorcinelli & Yun, 2007; Chesler & Chesler, 2002; Kram & Ragins, 2008). A networked mentoring approach is one "in which one mentee draws on multiple mentors and resources to obtain input into many issues of the academic or professional career" (Montgomery & Page, 2018, pp. 3–4). Given the complex needs of mid-career faculty, the authors determined that shifting the culture of mentoring at ERAU away from a top-down, hierarchical approach and toward a networked approach would better serve them (Wojton et al., 2022).

As a vehicle for promoting a networked mentoring approach on campus, the authors developed a Mentoring Institute, a two-day conference that faculty mentors and mentees could apply to attend. Mentors and mentees were awarded a $500 stipend if they documented an action plan at the end of the institute (Wojton & Mumpower, 2021). The institute featured faculty, administrators, and CTLE staff on campus who had some expertise in mentoring or who were in fields related to mentoring. While developed initially as a tool to support new faculty and their mentors, the institute quickly shifted its emphasis to supporting mid-career faculty.

The focus of this chapter is to describe the Mentoring Institute's tools and to detail the ways in which mid-career faculty mentees and mentors, in particular, responded to and benefited from these tools.

Needed Skill

Three needs drove the development of the Mentoring Institute. First, department chair interviews identified a lack of knowledge about how to best support mid-career faculty. Second, a lack of training and support for mentors revealed a need for communicating best practices for intentional mentoring. Third, there was a cross-campus need to support underrepresented faculty at all career stages. These needs led the authors to develop programming for both mid-career mentors and mentees that would scaffold learning for attendees on a networked model. The Mentoring Institute began by introducing faculty to evidence-based practices supporting networked mentoring. Individual sessions further engaged faculty in activities and discussions leading to the development and maintenance of their mid-career networks.

Rationale

ERAU has long identified the need to support faculty mentoring to cultivate a campus culture that values professional development. Pre-COVID, an institutional survey identified gaps in mentoring support, including for mid-career faculty members. Research has shown that "a mentoring culture sustains a continuum of expectation, which in turn creates standards and consistency of good mentoring practice. A mentoring culture is a powerful mechanism for achieving cultural alignment" (Zachary, 2005, p. X). This cultural alignment can enhance job satisfaction and help in retaining talented professionals (Zachary, 2005, p. 5). Retention is a motivator for our institution's administrators when considering faculty programming. Because everyone is invested in this same goal, CTLE's partnership with faculty and connection to administrators created the perfect opportunity to initiate mentoring support and to connect with interested faculty who would ultimately drive programming. These relationships have been critical to the success of the initiatives.

Equity and Inclusion Considerations

STEM faculty are "predominantly male and White or Asian" (Jones et al., 2018, p. 40), and "only 10.1% of STEM faculty is from underrepresented minorities," according to a National Science Foundation-funded study from the Association of Public and Land-Grant Universities (qtd. in

Stewart, 2020). Ethnographic data from 2020 revealed that instructional staff on the ERAU-Dayton Beach campus were 74% white. A networked mentoring approach could provide more support for underrepresented faculty. A networked model does not limit mentees to a one-to-one hierarchical pairing that may or may not lead to a sense of belonging given the potential for identity differences.

The Mentoring Institute encourages identity-informed mentoring, which capitalizes on the wealth of shared cultural capital that informs every aspect of one's work life (Hsieh & Nguyen, 2020). Identity-informed mentoring starts from a shared assumption that diverse perspectives stemming from different aspects of one's identity inform both faculty practices and needs. Therefore, mid-career faculty should consider finding mentors who understand this approach and can acknowledge/accommodate those practices and needs. A networked approach validates the experiences and perspectives of underrepresented faculty members with the goal of minimizing social isolation, facilitating academic enculturation, and promoting job retention and satisfaction (Hsieh & Nguyen, 2020). Identity-informed mentoring is best accomplished with a networked mentoring approach so that underrepresented groups are not disproportionately called upon to serve as mentors, a situation that a one-to-one model can often bring about.

A deeper awareness of diversity, equity, and inclusion issues and how they impact mentoring networks/relationships can be of particular importance for mid-career faculty who are trying to position themselves for leadership roles. Understanding how to advocate for one's own needs begins with early-career mentoring education, but the need to understand the needs of others becomes central to mid-career faculty members as they navigate opportunities afforded tenured faculty to mentor others and even to shape mentoring practices at their institution. For example, department chairs are often mid-career faculty who are likely to be tasked with shaping mentoring practices within departments. Providing opportunities for mid-career faculty to deepen their appreciation for and understanding of how intentional, identity-informed mentoring practices can benefit not only them but also others is a critical aspect of the Mentoring Institute.

Theoretical Grounding

Our hope for a networked approach to mentoring was that mentees would be empowered at the mid-career level to advocate for themselves and their mentoring needs, which often go undetected since they differ from the well-defined needs and supportive scaffolding and processes that often structure mentoring for early-career faculty who are working toward tenure. Rockquemore (2012) explains that mid-career faculty members often "struggle to adjust their approach, learn new skills, and develop the networks that will lead to the post-tenure pathway they truly desire." Acknowledging this reality, the Mentoring Institute's sessions would begin the critical and practical work of developing a mentee-driven system (rather than a hierarchical system) in which mid-career faculty would identify their needs and preferences (a bottom-up instead of a top-down approach). Furthermore, Rockquemore states that "it's far more effective to talk about specific needs than it is to use the word 'mentoring' as a slush bucket for all . . . needs." Because the needs of mid-career faculty members differ from those of faculty members just entering the academy, the Mentoring Institute focused on developing ways to assess one's own needs and to advocate for support rather than relying on the tacit notion that securing tenure is the ultimate and only goal of mentoring in a university setting. For example, mid-career faculty members could share the resources we provided to them with their chairpersons to advocate for new practices within their departments that might better meet their needs. Finally, mid-career faculty members might leverage their participation in the Mentoring Institute to gain recognition for their outstanding work as mentors. The Mentoring Institute allowed us the opportunity to champion the networked model and frame mentorship in a way that would appeal to mentors, mentees, and campus leadership alike.

Our 2020 department chairperson interviews revealed that a reconfiguration from hierarchical to networked mentoring was necessary to meet the needs of a diverse and complex configuration of departments across campus. For example, one department had a disproportionate ratio of mid-career faculty at the associate professor rank, with only four full professors and sixteen associate professors. In other departments, many senior faculty are close to retirement with fewer mid-career faculty members. A networked approach also allows a person of color, a member of the LGBTQIA+ community, a person with a disability, or a member of another underrepresented community in a department to connect with other similar individuals on campus for their mutual benefit. Networked mentoring capitalizes on the unique characteristics of each department, while mitigating the challenges that their structural differences pose, in pursuit of a universal system of mentoring for all mid-career faculty members.

Tools

We feature two tools in this chapter, a Mentoring Institute Agenda and a Mentoring Institute Evaluation Instrument.

The Mentoring Institute Agenda scaffolds learning for faculty who may be used to a hierarchical model of mentoring (see Table 8.1). Agenda items were culled from the previously mentioned interviews with department chairpersons.

Table 8.1 Faculty Mentoring Institute Agenda

Faculty Research Panel
This panel provides an opportunity to ask questions about how to build
   and maintain mentoring relationships that enable productive research
   partnerships and how to capitalize on mentoring opportunities when not
   directly engaged in research with a colleague.

Identifying Needs and Building Your Network
Attendees will explore how to identify professional needs and networking
   goals and will discuss ways to connect with others in their professional
   communities. Using concrete tools, participants will create a strategic plan
   and share next steps that will help them in their mentoring journey.

Building Effective Mentoring Relationships
This session will focus on some practical strategies for maintaining mentoring
   relationships that serve the needs and meet the expectations of both
   parties. We will discuss challenges to authentically connecting with
   mentoring partners and process some strategies for mitigating those
   challenges.

Qualities of Effective Mentors
This interactive session will have mentors working in groups to examine
   the effective qualities of mentors. Utilizing Kram's mentor role theory
   as a framework, the mentors will develop a mentoring guidebook with
   actionable functions that mentors can use to support their mentees.

**Providing and Receiving Honest and Effective Feedback: Engaging in
Difficult Conversations**
Directed at mentors and mentees, this session will emphasize the importance
   of achieving an honest and transparent mentor/mentee relationship through
   effective verbal and non-verbal communication. Participants will consider
   specific, common scenarios in which both providing and receiving feedback can
   be challenging and will strategize about effective strategies for communication.

The Social Dynamics of Mentoring
This session will focus on understanding and optimizing social dynamics
   related to mentoring, including topics such as the differences between
   mentoring and coaching, awareness of personal bias in mentoring, and
   mentor strengths and strategic value in the mentoring relationship.

Creating Your Mentoring Action Plan
The culmination of the Mentoring Institute experience, this short closing
   session will lead participants to reflect on what they have learned and
   introduce participants to the artifact they will need to submit.

We use programming to connect faculty members to more intentional,
concrete mentoring efforts on campus and to create a recognizable "brand"
on campus. The Mentoring Institute draws on faculty expertise already on
campus to reduce costs and increase the sustainability of programming.
Furthermore, the Mentoring Institute can be offered each year to new faculty with the same or similar programming while rotating through different
topics for mid-career faculty. We also plan to draw on external mentoring
experts to facilitate future Mentoring Institute sessions and themes.

We collaborate with each presenter, specifying both the topic and target audience. For example, we asked a long-time, well-respected department chair who is also a communications scholar to talk about how to have crucial but challenging conversations with mentors/mentees. We emphasized in our request that presenters choose practical/workshop approaches to sessions rather than deliver lectures. This approach leads to more dynamic sessions. All resources are made available to participants during the institute but are also published on the internal website for campus access as an initial resource library. Resources include reference/reading lists for each session, links to any practical tools/documents (implicit bias test, relationship agreement forms, communication preference checklists, building a network worksheet, etc.).

The following agenda is from our inaugural Mentoring Institute in May 2022. Topics were chosen based on three factors: (1) interviews with chairpersons, which revealed the need for the development of particular skills for mid-career faculty, (2) speakers' experience/expertise, and (3) the need to empower mid-career faculty to identify and advocate for their own mentoring needs as well as to assert the need for recognition for their mentoring efforts.

Our Mentoring Institute Evaluation Instrument was developed to assess the short- and long-term impact of the institute on participants. We deployed a pre- and post-survey for all participants and required the submission of a mentoring action plan for those participants who wished to receive the $500 stipend. The pre- and post-surveys were created with two types of alignment in mind. Surveys should:

- ask questions that reflect engagement with some aspect of the campus's mentoring mission.
- assess the level of confidence that attendees had in the skills on which presenters focused.

The pre-survey also collected demographic data. The two most critical questions reflect the aforementioned alignment. Question 1 (see Table 8.2) assesses the need for improvement in areas of mentoring on campus. Question 2 (see Table 8.2) assesses the participant's level of confidence in particular aspects of mentoring relationships, reflecting the topics covered in the Mentoring Institute sessions.

The post-survey, in addition to asking typical questions to gauge attendees' interest in other types of support/programming, also asked them to report on their level of confidence in the same areas as the pre-survey. Our expectation was that confidence in each area would increase based on exposure to evidence-based practices presented in sessions. Results, however, reflected a decrease in confidence in some areas (see Table 8.3).

Table 8.2 Pre-Survey

1. Rate the level of improvement you would recommend regarding the following aspects of mentoring in your department or on campus.[*]
   a. Recognizing and rewarding mentoring activities
   b. Compatibility of mentor to mentee assignments, or vice versa
   c. Identification of mentors beyond the one that is assigned by the department chair
   d. Setting expectations for mentoring activities/relationships
   e. Documenting mentoring activities: i.e., setting and tracking goals, action plans, and schedules (outside of required 1st- and 3rd-year review requirements)
   f. Communication among faculty mentors/mentees regarding strategies for improving mentoring
   g. Availability of resources related to mentoring
   h. Representation of mentors from diverse backgrounds and experiences

2. How confident are you in your ability to effectively navigate the following aspects of mentoring relationships?[**]
   a. Building effective mentoring relationships
   b. Providing honest and effective feedback
   c. Receiving honest and effective feedback
   d. Identifying personal biases in mentoring relationships
   e. Creating a mentoring action plan
   f. Determining actionable steps to support mentees
   g. Documenting mentoring activities
   h. Building a mentoring network

Notes: [*]Response Options: No improvement, Some Improvement, Much Improvement
[**]Response Options: Not Confident, Slightly Confident, Fairly Confident, Completely Confident

Table 8.3 Results of Pre- and Post-Survey Mentoring Level of Confidence

Mentoring Behaviors	Complete Confidence in Mentoring Behaviors		Average Rating	
	Pre-survey	Post-survey	Pre-survey	Post-survey
Receiving honest and effective feedback	63.6%	26.7%	3.6	3.2
Providing honest and effective feedback	54.5%	26.7%	3.5	3.1
Building effective mentoring relationships	45.5%	26.7%	3.5	3.2
Identifying personal biases in mentoring relationships	18.2%	13.3%	2.9	2.9
Creating a mentoring action plan	18.2%	6.7%	2.6	2.8

Most notable was a dip in confidence in mentoring behaviors: receiving honest feedback, providing honest feedback, and building effective mentoring relationships. The decline in confidence in these areas suggests that mentors, once presented with research and guidance on mentoring behaviors, recognized their lack of experience and expertise. We view these results as a positive acknowledgment by mentors that they have more to learn than they had initially anticipated. This result aligns with the goal of our inaugural event: to enhance professional development by introducing evidence-based practices connected to impactful mentoring behaviors. Reflection artifacts (see Figure 8.1) submitted by participants support this analysis. One mentor's comment was revealing:

As a mentor, I realize the degree to which [my mentee] needs support. I was beginning to feel that I should be giving her more time, energy, and so forth in my position as mentor. What the mentoring institute taught me was that no mentor can fulfill all roles for a mentee. In fact, it is better for the mentee to have many mentors who are addressing the various needs. This insight helped me immensely, as I am now relieved of my perception that I needed to be "a miracle worker/mentor" for her. Further, I plan to discuss the mentor network with her, not only to give her insight into proactively building her own support network, but also for me to learn more about any gaps for which I can make suggestions on how to fill those gaps.

The relief expressed in this quote was echoed in a number of artifacts. Figure 8.1 is the prompt used to solicit reflections and action plans from participants.

Mentoring Institute Artifact: Mentoring Action Plan

For those working on building their network:

Create a 1-2 page reflection/action plan that addresses the following prompts:

   1. GOALS– Describe at least three of your professional goals, consider short and long term goals.

   2. NETWORK– Analyze your network: Who can help you fill the roles that you need to support your three professional goals? What gaps exist? Who can help you make the connections you need to develop your network of mentors?

   3. ACTION– What steps will you take to initiate/maintain productive mentoring relationships?

Figure 8.1 Mentoring Institute Artifact: Mentoring Action Plan

Lessons Learned

Through the introduction of a Mentoring Institute, the authors were able to disrupt a hierarchical approach to mentoring on campus with networked mentoring to better support mid-career faculty. This change was achieved by implementing the tool of a Mentoring Institute Agenda, which encouraged development of a networked mentoring plan for both mentors and mentees. While these efforts have proven successful in moving mid-career faculty from intention to action with regard to mentoring, three lessons emerged:

1. Mid-career faculty members are both in need of guidance regarding critical mentoring behaviors and ready to work on that aspect of their professional development.
2. More work with male mid-career faculty members is needed. Despite ERAU's faculty demographics, in which about 60% of our professors are male, attendees were disproportionately female (about 60%). While this result is unsurprising considering the substantial and compelling research showing that women in academia are called to service more often than their male colleagues, we hope to consider ways to improve participation among our male colleagues.
3. The institute had unequal representation among departments/colleges, with the College of Arts and Sciences being most involved and the College of Engineering being least involved. This data gives us an opportunity to focus on specific departments and solicit greater participation from them in the future.

Conclusion

By planning and analyzing assessments of our programming (pre- and post-survey and artifacts), we have been better able to describe our success to administrators and to continue toward our goals of sustainable programming related to the development of intentional mentoring practices and network mentoring for mid-career faculty members.

Programmatic work in mentoring is generative. By reaching out and connecting with faculty via programming designed to facilitate a network mentoring approach, the authors will be better able to assess faculty needs and programmatic goals. As Broughton et al. (2019) explain succinctly in their research about the necessity for intentionality in mentoring, the work of mentoring itself is also generative, creating opportunities for mentors and mentees:

As mentors identify their strengths and weaknesses, improve their cultural competency and interpersonal skills, and implement effective strategies, mentees reap the benefits of their mentors' studied efforts. The implementation of intentional mentoring strategies is not intended to force a "one-size-fits-all" approach on mentorship, but rather a series of actions that provide an inviting space for all mentees to discover the joy of navigating their professional path, while simultaneously enabling them to unearth their own creativity and intelligence.

(pp. 319–320)

This "unearthing" is a worthy goal that aligns directly with the goals of academic institutions. Our goal for initiatives related to mentoring will include avoiding a "one-size-fits-all" approach and continuing to focus on creating an inclusive space for individuals to develop mentoring competencies and to better understand their and others' mentoring needs.

References

Broughton, R. S., Plaisime, M. V., & Green Parker, M. C. (2019). Mentorship: The necessity of intentionality. *American Journal of Orthopsychiatry, 89*(3), 317–320.

Chesler, N. C., & Chesler, M. A. (2002). Gender-informed mentoring strategies for women engineering scholars: On establishing a caring community. *Journal of Engineering Education, 92*, 49–55.

ERAU. (n.d.). *Common data set 2020–2021.* Institutional Research. Retrieved June 7, 2023, from http://ir.erau.edu/Publications/CDS/PDF/CDS_2020-2021%20_DB_v2.pdf

Hsieh, B., & Nguyen, H. T. (2020). Identity-informed mentoring to support acculturation of female faculty of color in Higher Education: An Asian American Female Mentoring Relationship Case Study. *Journal of Diversity in Higher Education., 13*(2), 169–180. https://doi.org/10.1037/dhe0000118

Jones, J., Williams, A., Whitaker, S., Yingling, S., Inkelas, K., & Gates, J. (2018). Call to action: Data, diversity, and STEM education. *Change: The Magazine of Higher Learning, 50*(2), 40–47. https://doi.org/ 10.1080/00091383.2018.1483176

Kram, K. E., & Ragins, B. R. (2008). The landscape of mentoring in the 21st century. In K. E. Kram & B. R. Ragins (Eds.), *The handbook of mentoring at work* (pp. 659–689). SAGE.

Montgomery, B. L., & Page, S. C. (2018). *Mentoring beyond hierarchies: Multimentor systems and models.* Commissioned Paper for National Academies of Sciences, Engineering, and Medicine Committee on Effective Mentoring in STEMM.

Rockquemore, K. A. (2012). A new model of mentoring. *Inside Higher Ed.* www.insidehighered.com/advice/2013/07/22/essay-calling-senior-faculty-embrace-new-style-mentoring

Sorcinelli, M. D., & Yun, J. (2007, November–December). From mentor to mentoring networks: Mentoring in the new academy. *Change*, 58–61.

Stewart, P. (2020). Achieving diversity in STEM faculty requires systemic change, says report. *Diverse Issues in Higher Education.* www.diverseeducation.com/stem/

article/15107243/achieving-diversity-in-stem-faculty-requires-systemic-change-says-report

Wojton, J., Cornejo-Happel, C., & McKee, J. (2022). *The chronicle of mentoring and coaching. "A mentee-driven approach to creating a culture of faculty-to-faculty network mentoring."* University of New Mexico.

Wojton, J., & Mumpower, L. (2021). *The chronicle of mentoring and coaching. "Current practices in a STEM university: A networked mentoring approach."* University of New Mexico.

Zachary, L. (2005). *Creating a mentoring culture: The organization's guide.* Wiley.

Chapter 9

Supporting Teaching-Track Faculty at Mid-Career

*Seema Dahlheimer, Kia Lilly Caldwell,
Amy A. Eyler, and Lori Markson*

Overview

At Washington University in St. Louis, a midsized Midwestern private research university, we identified a need for mid-career mentoring for all faculty members. This chapter focuses on an important subset of mid-career faculty: our teaching faculty. Approximately one-third of our university's faculty are full-time non–tenure-track, on either the teaching track, the research track, or the practice track. We describe these faculty by track rather than as "non–tenure-track" to highlight their professional value rather than defining this group by what they lack. In this chapter, we use the term *teaching faculty* to refer to full-time, non–tenure-track faculty on the teaching track.

In the 2022–2023 academic year, the provost's office launched a program called the Mid-Career Mentoring Program for both tenure-track and teaching faculty, with separate sessions tailored for teaching faculty. This program was a two-semester, cohort-based program with a kickoff session, two Zoom meetings, and six in-person meetings during the academic year. These elements allowed for collaboration and conversations between teaching faculty and tenure-track faculty, as well as breakout sessions tailored to helping mid-career teaching faculty from different disciplines develop in their careers and build community with each other. Thus, faculty in different tracks were not segregated from each other but instead had a space to discuss their unique needs and careers with others in shared career trajectories. Allowing for tenure-track and teaching faculty to mingle and form connections is strategic, as this structure promotes a sense of inclusion for teaching faculty.

Program Focus

Needed Skills

Full-time mid-career teaching faculty had a need for a program that: (a) fosters inclusion for teaching faculty among tenure-track faculty,

DOI: 10.4324/9781003428626-12

(b) offers a chance for teaching faculty to connect with each other and support each other across disciplines, and (c) helps teaching faculty navigate the hidden norms and expectations of career advancement at our university.

Many colleges and universities have well-developed programs for teaching faculty, including pedagogical learning communities, teaching-focused orientations, information on classroom management and educational technology, and other introductions to teaching and learning. Similarly, our university offers such workshops and events through our Center for Teaching and Learning. Additionally, some of our schools and departments offer orientations specifically for teaching faculty. These efforts focus on pedagogy rather than inclusion and networking, and the lack of programming to promote inclusion aligns with Kezar's (2012a) observation that at many institutions, "no mentoring process is offered to help [non–tenure-track faculty] adjust and learn formal and informal rules" (pp. 4–5). Efforts to support and retain these faculty members at mid-career have been scattered. Policies outlining career advancement are often unclear or absent, and teaching faculty may be ineligible for or unaware of opportunities for advancement, such as leadership opportunities, that are available to tenured faculty (Waltman et al., 2012). Structures such as mentorship programs tailored to the needs of teaching faculty can promote job satisfaction and career advancement (de Saxe Zerden et al., 2015; Kezar, 2012a; Waltman et al., 2012). While some institutions might consider adapting the supports for tenure-track or research faculty members to address the needs of teaching faculty, programs tailored to mid-career teaching faculty members can help these faculty members discover and cultivate their sense of purpose, consider their professional evolution and goals, explore their interests in pedagogical and curricular innovation, and develop their leadership potential within their organizations.

Rationale

Non–tenure-track teaching faculty constitute an increasing number of faculty members at colleges and universities across the United States. Teaching faculty teach and develop our curricula, are the face of the faculty to undergraduate students and first-year graduate students, and are integral to achieving the mission in our departments and schools. Haviland et al. (2020) have tracked this shift over the last five decades. In 1969, 22% of faculty members in the United States were not on the tenure track (including part-time faculty). By 2015, 70% of faculty members in the United States were not on the tenure track (including part-time and full-time faculty members). They estimated that in 2013, full-time, non–tenure-track faculty constituted more than 24% of the full-time faculty workforce at research universities such as ours and somewhere in the 20% to 25% range for universities and colleges in the United States (Haviland et al., 2020). Our university's percentage is higher than the national average, with one-third of our full-time faculty members (on the non-medical campus) being non–tenure-track. Kezar (2012b) argues for "a new imperative for change" (p. 7) that fosters inclusion and belonging among teaching faculty, noting that this kind of inclusion would also benefit students. Haviland et al. (2020) advance the idea that universities and colleges should intentionally foster personal and professional development, collegiality, and social interactions among all faculty members. They write:

> Much of faculty work is social; beyond hallway conversations, faculty interact around academic governance and collaborate on teaching and research, for instance. In the healthy departments we studied, the interactions, knowing, and relationships that developed among faculty contributed to and grew from both personal and professional respect that was foundational to collegiality for [non–tenure-track faculty]. These relationships allowed [non–tenure-track faculty] and [tenure-track faculty] to know one another as people, develop appreciation for each other's expertise, and establish a sense of trust and team.
>
> (pp. 86–87)

Although Kezar (2012b) and Haviland et al. (2020) are arguing for greater inclusivity for both part-time and full-time non–tenure-track faculty and faculty on all tracks (teaching, research, and practice), these tenets serve us well in considering ways to support full-time teaching faculty.

Equity and Inclusion Considerations

Our program was not designed to be solely about career advancement but rather was meant to center inclusion and belonging. We aimed to provide chances for teaching faculty and tenure-track faculty to build community with each other but also to break out into conversations that are specific to the needs of their group, to create a sense of belonging for teaching faculty. Thus, we created a mentoring program that (a) is cohort based, (b) encourages teaching and tenure-track faculty members to interact with each other in a meaningful context, (c) creates a network of teaching faculty to support each other, and (d) helps teaching faculty navigate and problem-solve issues around the hidden norms and expectations for career advancement on the teaching track at our university.

Recruiting a diverse group of applicants was important to us. Thus, we advertised the program through multiple channels: official channels such as the vice provost for faculty affairs and diversity's website and newsletter, and informal channels such as emails from affinity and job-related groups including the Association for Women Faculty and the Association for Teaching, Research, and Practice Faculty. We selected a diverse group of participants from the applicant pool. Participants spanned a range of ages; included both teaching and tenure-track faculty members; represented a range of disciplines and schools; and were of different races, ethnicities, national origins, backgrounds, genders, and sexual orientations. This diversity allowed for the development of informal and organic mentoring relationships, creativity, and dynamic discussions; with such a range of people from different backgrounds, participants were able to find people they connected well with.

Theoretical Grounding

The structure of Building Your Institutional Profile – the teaching faculty cohort of the Mid-Career Mentoring Program – is conceptually grounded in the work of Goerisch et al. (2019) and Banasik and Dean (2016), who explore mentoring programs for non–tenure-track faculty. Although much of the literature on mentoring non–tenure-track faculty members focuses on part-time faculty members (e.g., Franczyk, 2014; Luna, 2018), full-time teaching faculty members have a defined career path, opportunities for upward mobility, opportunities for leadership and service at the university, and other benefits that may not apply to part-time faculty members. In considering mentoring programs specific to the needs of non–tenure-track faculty, Goerisch et al. (2019) build upon "the concept of power mentoring, which emphasizes mentoring networks rather than individual relationships" (p. 1739). Banasik and Dean (2016), similarly, suggest cohort-based faculty learning communities for teaching faculty.

We chose a cohort-based structure for teaching faculty members to emphasize building a network of connections, creating a sense of community among teaching faculty members, and fostering a sense of inclusion and belonging. Rather than assigning a single faculty member to a single mentor – where personalities might clash or where participants might not reap the full benefits of connecting with a larger group – the Mid-Career Mentoring Program encouraged a looser and more organic set of relationships.

Tools

We describe two tools used in the Mid-Career Mentoring program: (a) the application form and (b) the program activities – including a keynote speech, special sessions, and monthly meetings.

Tool 1: Application Form

The Mid-Career Mentoring Program had four cohorts for different faculty tracks at mid-career. While three were tailored to tenure-track faculty, one was tailored to teaching faculty members. The cohort Building Your Institutional Profile was open to teaching faculty only and is the focus of this chapter. For our 2022–23 program, the teaching faculty cohort Building Your Institutional Profile had six participants.

Building Your Institutional Profile

Target audience: Teaching faculty

In order to be promoted, teaching faculty must craft institutional profiles that extend beyond a record of superior and innovative teaching. This cohort will serve as a space of support and mentorship for crafting a strategic plan for teaching faculty to move toward promotion.

Tool 1 is a template for the application form, including the descriptions of all four cohorts, and is provided as an online resource. This application form can be adapted for your institution and your unique circumstances.

If you're interested in a form for this, check out e-resource 9.1

Tool 2: Programming

The Mid-Career Mentoring Program offered an in-person kickoff meeting with a keynote speaker, two optional Zoom meetings with the same keynote speaker, and monthly in-person gatherings, each with a unique agenda. See Table 9.1.

Kickoff meeting: For this inaugural meeting of the Mid-Career Mentoring Program, we invited a keynote speaker, Vicki Baker from Albion College (who is also an editor of this volume). We gathered on a Friday morning and met into the midafternoon, and this event included both breakfast and lunch. For your institutional context, budget, and needs, you may choose a keynote speaker from your institution, or you may choose to bring in someone external. Having a kickoff event such as this one brought energy and excitement to the program while giving participants a chance to get to know each other.

Optional Zoom meetings during winter break: To keep the momentum going over winter break, we invited our keynote speaker to do two one-hour Zoom meetings. These workshops centered on being strategic about service and crafting your narrative. We chose, given the speaker's expertise, to focus these sessions on issues surrounding women faculty members only. At your institution, you may identify needs specific to your faculty. These Zoom workshops may be facilitated by an external guest facilitator, a guest from inside your institution, or one of the facilitators of the program.

Six monthly meetings: The monthly meetings were the heart of this program. They allowed each cohort to build mentoring relationships in an organic and sustained way. The series of monthly meetings is the star of the program.

Timing: We held these meetings over lunchtime on Fridays, 11:30 a.m. to 1:00 p.m. This timing was strategic: by providing lunch and taking just an hour and a half, the meetings were designed to respect the participants' time and encourage the development of ongoing relationships (as opposed to having less frequent half-day meetings). Additionally, many faculty members do not teach on Fridays, making it an ideal choice.

Structure: We began each meeting with lunch and a presentation for the whole group on a topic of interest, for about 30 minutes. For the remaining hour, we continued our lunch – perhaps taking seconds of the food or refilling our coffee cups – while moving each cohort into either different areas of a large room or smaller rooms. Each cohort then had an hour to discuss issues unique to their own context and to build community. The same facilitators led these sessions each month, which helped make the facilitator part of this mentoring community. For the teaching faculty cohort, we intentionally chose a non–tenure-track teaching faculty member as the facilitator.

Topics: In 2022–23, we held meetings on the topics listed in Table 9.1. We designed the sessions to include information and discussions that the participants could not get elsewhere – access to guest speakers and high-level administrators, for example, but also discussions and community-building with faculty members from other parts of campus. We also were cognizant that "mid-career" is a wide range, and there would be participants from both the early and later ends of that range. The descriptions and reflections here are specific to the teaching faculty cohort – Building Your Institutional Profile.

Logistical and Budgetary Considerations

Administrative support from the provost office's staff was critical in handling logistics such as:

- Booking a large room and breakout rooms for the in-person sessions
- Ordering and setting up lunches (and breakfast for the kickoff)
- Handling the logistics of a guest speaker on campus
- Setting up Zoom registration and links for the Zoom sessions

Table 9.1 Monthly Meetings

Session	Description of Session for Teaching Faculty: Building Your Institutional Profile Cohort
Aligning Your Values with Your Work **Pre-work:** • Read Chapter 1 of *Charting Your Path to Full* (optional) **Online resources:** • Presentation talking points for the facilitator If you're interested in a handout or presentation for this, check out e-resource 9.2	After a presentation on finding joy and purpose in our work, the teaching faculty cohort, Building Your Institutional Profile, gathered in a breakout room and got to know each other. While the presentation provided guiding questions about finding purpose in your work, the cohort's conversation trended more toward community building. The participants started an email chain so that everyone could stay in touch and connect with each other outside of the program.
Cultivating Multiple Mentors (and Sponsors) **Pre-work:** • Read Chapter 6 of *Charting Your Path to Full* (optional) • Mentoring map available at www.facultydiversity.org/ncfddmentormap **Online resources:** • Discussion questions to hand out to participants If you're interested in a handout or presentation for this, check out e-resource 9.3	After a presentation on mentorship and sponsorship, the teaching faculty cohort sat at one side of the large classroom where this session was held. We took some time to fill out our mentoring maps; though this was assigned as pre-work, most had not done it. The group discussed the difficulties of building connections outside their departments and schools. Group members offered to connect each other with colleagues and friends and tried to bridge some of the gaps between our university's various silos.
Planning your promotion timeline **Pre-work:** • Bring an up-to-date copy of your CV • Find the promotion timeline for your school (if it's available)	The cohort facilitator brought handouts of the official promotion information and requirements for each participant's school. We discussed best practices on CV and teaching statements, university resources to help develop these items, the group's frustrations with the process, and some potential hidden expectations for promotion to different levels. The cohort volunteered to observe each other's classes for promotion files, and some of the senior lecturers provided advice for the lecturers.

Session	Description of Session for Teaching Faculty: Building Your Institutional Profile Cohort
Time Management and Service **Pre-work:** • None **Online resources:** • Presentation talking points for the facilitator If you're interested in a handout or presentation for this, check out e-resource 9.4	As this session was not very well attended – particularly by teaching faculty – the presenter combined the cohorts. This setup allowed for a rich discussion among different groups, but as the discussion progressed naturally into research concerns, the teaching faculty expressed that they felt a bit alienated and that they did not have much to contribute. A lesson learned from this session is that, even if the cohorts are very small on a particular day, breaking out into cohorts would still be valuable and perhaps preferable.
Lunch with the Leaders *(Teaching Faculty Only)* **Pre-work:** • If you would like to ask questions anonymously, submit them ahead of time via online survey • Bring questions you may want to ask in person	This panel included faculty advancement leaders from different schools to discuss and answer questions about promotion to teaching professor – the highest promotion on the teaching track. Providing participants access to leadership in an intimate and unstructured setting allowed people to both ask questions and gain access to the kind of two-way communication we hope for, where administration and faculty learn from each other.
Amplifying and (Re)Branding, followed by a closing reception **Pre-work:** • None	After meeting in the larger group with faculty and administrative panelists to answer questions about branding and rebranding, we broke into cohorts and discussed the difficulties of reaching out in new directions, especially for those who have been at the institution for a longer period of time. At the closing reception, held at an on-campus pub, the cohorts easily and collegially mingled with each other rather than staying apart. The closing reception had an air of festivity, brought about in part by the change of location.

- Sending the participants reminders, campus maps, and pre-work materials
- Setting up and sending out survey links for pre-work and for collecting feedback after the sessions
- Providing name tags for each session's participants
- Organizing the closing reception

The costs associated with this program were as follows:

- Speaker fee for our keynote speaker for both the kickoff and the two Zoom sessions
- Premium on-campus conference rooms (rather than traditional classrooms) for meetings
- Monthly lunches, one breakfast, and snacks and drinks for the closing reception
- Administrative support for coordinating these items and handling communications with participants

If your unit or institution has more budgetary constraints, this program could be adapted as a brown-bag lunch series rather than one in which meals are provided and could also have an internal speaker as a keynote speaker, thereby mitigating speaker fees and food costs. However, having lunches provided gives participants a strong incentive to attend every month, and having a keynote speaker from outside the institution provides added value.

Lessons Learned

From this program and from participant surveys, we learned four lessons: (a) the importance of mentoring networks, (b) the effectiveness of having cohort-based time during each of the six monthly meetings, (c) the challenges of finding topics that appeal to all participants, and (d) the opportunity to include more special topical sessions in the future.

First, faculty feedback indicated that they found the more organic and natural development of relationships in this program to be more helpful than being assigned a one-on-one mentor. This finding echoes work done by Goerisch et al. (2019) and Banasik and Dean (2016), who advocate for learning communities and mentoring networks rather than more rigid one-on-one relationships. Teaching faculty members appreciated the topics and the time, especially the time they had in breakout rooms with their cohort.

Second, there were times – especially in the session when we combined teaching faculty and tenure-track faculty for the entire time – when teaching faculty felt alienated or felt like they could not contribute to the conversation. Moving forward, we plan to stick to breaking out into cohorts for at least half of the session, even if attendance is low.

Third, there are challenges in crafting content and choosing speakers that resonate with all of the participants. For example, one teaching faculty member skipped the session on promotion because he already had his promotion packet ready to submit in the upcoming cycle. As another example, two teaching faculty members who had chosen the New Directions cohort had already been promoted to teaching professor and therefore could not benefit from many of the questions that the university leaders answered specific to promotion to that position during the leadership panel.

Fourth, in the future, we plan to keep the same structure but include smaller get-togethers that are not cohort based. For example, a session focused on refining CVs or a teaching philosophy statement might attract faculty members from both the teaching track and the tenure track. A session focused on writing articles for publication or conference presentations might attract both teaching faculty doing pedagogical research and tenure-track faculty.

Conclusion

This inaugural Mid-Career Mentoring program has served teaching faculty members' needs in many ways and created a strong network of faculty members to support each other across campus units. The teaching faculty cohort, in particular, has coalesced and come up with innovative ideas, such as observing each other's teaching. Allowing time for different cohorts to mix has created a sense of inclusion for teaching faculty among their tenure-track peers; giving each cohort time in breakout rooms has allowed for rich and in-depth discussions and created a strong sense of community. It was particularly valuable to teaching faculty to have the opportunity to ask questions of leaders at an intimate lunch, because at an institution like ours, having that kind of access is unusual. We hope that the multi-way communication between leadership and teaching faculty can help break down barriers, inspire leadership to clarify and hone policies with an eye toward equity, and reduce gatekeeping at multiple levels – from the university level to the school level to the department level.

References

Banasik, M. D., & Dean, J. L. (2016). Non-tenure track faculty and learning communities: Bridging the divide to enhance teaching quality. *Innovative Higher Education*, *41*, 333–342.

de Saxe Zerden, L., Ilinitch, T. L., Carlston, R., Knutson, D., Blesdoe, B. E., & Howard, M. O. (2015). Social work faculty development: An exploratory study of non-tenure-track women faculty. *Journal of Social Work Education*, *51*(4), 738–753.

Franczyk, A. (2014, April). How to mentor non-tenure-track faculty: Principles and underpinnings of a program in place in post-secondary education. *Journal of the World Universities Forum*, 6(4).

Goerisch, D., Basiliere, J., Rosener, A., McKee, K., Hunt, J., & Parker, T. M. (2019). Mentoring with: Reimagining mentoring across the university. *Gender, Place & Culture*, 26(12), 1740–1758.

Haviland, D., Alleman, N. F., Allen, C. C., & Jacobs, J. (2020). *Inclusive collegiality and non-tenure-track faculty: Engaging all faculty as colleagues to promote healthy departments and institutions*. Stylus Publishing.

Kezar, A. (2012a). *Embracing non-tenure track faculty: Changing campuses for the new faculty majority*. Routledge.

Kezar, A. (2012b). Spanning the great divide between tenure-track and non-tenure-track faculty. *Change: The Magazine of Higher Learning*, 44(6), 6–13.

Luna, G. (2018). Making visible our invisible faculty: Mentoring for contingent online faculty. *Journal of Higher Education Theory & Practice*, 18(2).

Waltman, J., Bergom, I., Hollenshead, C., Miller, J., & August, L. (2012). Factors contributing to job satisfaction and dissatisfaction among non-tenure-track faculty. *The Journal of Higher Education*, 83(3), 411–434.

Chapter 10

Meeting Them Where They Are

Supporting the Professional Learning Needs of Community College Educators

Shantell Strickland-Davis

Overview

Through a strategic planning process, Central Piedmont Community College's president, Dr. Deitemeyer, its executive cabinet, and its academic affairs leaders recognized a need to be more intentional about supporting faculty members in becoming effective, student success–focused teachers. "Training" faculty through "one and done" solutions was not the right approach for us. There needed to be planned and purposeful programming aligned with institutional goals and efforts for student success. We agreed with Smorynski's statement that "if the fundamentals for success are put into place and practiced consistently, then faculty development will be successful both in terms of institutional impact and faculty career satisfaction" (2015, p. 12).

A generous gift from the Wilton and Mary W. Parr family, in response to a need in Central Piedmont Community College's strategic goals, enabled the creation of the Parr Center for Teaching and Learning Excellence (CTLE). The Parr CTLE is a place where faculty learning, collaboration, and innovation contribute to the college's vision of being student champions, catalysts for opportunity, and exceptional providers of learning experiences. We saw the value of a teaching center that could help achieve the vision of transforming lives into a reality. This chapter focuses on the creation of the Parr CTLE, a proven faculty development strategy, that continues to meet the most critical needs of all Central Piedmont educators, especially mid-career faculty.

The context for our center is that it is located at a community college in Charlotte, North Carolina. Central Piedmont serves 43,000 college-credit and 12,500 continuing-education students annually (2023). Students have over 55 professional pathways to pursue at eight campuses or learning centers in Mecklenburg County. Almost 300 full-time faculty and about 1,000 adjunct faculty members are employed at Central Piedmont. Our faculty members are not classified as tenured based on years of service; however, we recognize faculty members' service milestones (new, mid-career, and

DOI: 10.4324/9781003428626-13

senior) across their career journey. For the purposes of this chapter, we define mid-career faculty members as those who have been teaching at the college for 5 to 15 years.

Program Focus

Prior to the opening of our center, our college's faculty development department mainly targeted and supported new and less experienced faculty (0–5 years). Common services from the department included orientations to teaching, learning communities focused on the art of teaching, and workshops meant to provide foundational approaches to student learning. The department had little input from faculty members about their specific needs and tended to operate in a silo, oftentimes missing opportunities to drive institutional change and innovation. Central Piedmont's president, executive cabinet, and academic affairs leaders recognized that we needed a change and that a well-designed and well-operated teaching center to provide mission-aligned professional learning might be a solution to encourage more faculty members to adopt and implement culturally responsive and effective teaching practices.

Central Piedmont's shared values statements guided our decisions. The Parr CTLE encompasses these institutional values in every practice, policy, and program we facilitate in our faculty development programming. These values are:

- Student-centered: We commit to students and their learning through intentionally designed faculty learning, development, engagement, and motivation.
- Collaborative: We model and use effective collaboration and the power of partnerships, both internally and externally, as a priority effort of the Parr CTLE.
- Excellent: We strive for excellence in faculty support and development by recognizing opportunities for teaching and learning excellence, solving problems and issues in educational development, and facilitating innovative programming to serve our faculty and college stakeholders.
- Accountable: We demonstrate and uphold integrity, transparency, and the effective use of our resources by assessing our programming and practices and using data to inform our decision making.
- Equitable: We believe all learners (students and faculty alike) have the potential to succeed, and we provide opportunities for all faculty to engage with inclusive pedagogical practices and critical reflection in support of student-focused pathways to achievement.
- Courageous: We acknowledge our strengths and weaknesses continuously and confront all challenges with intentionality.

Since opening in the fall of 2020, Central Piedmont's Parr CTLE has been able to provide targeted services, programs, and resources in the holistic support of faculty and teaching staff, instituting our vision of engaging and inspiring faculty across all career stages and teaching modalities. The research, planning, and implementation of our center proved successful because of the contributions of an organized, strong cross-functional action team (comprising faculty, academic leaders, student affairs representatives, and faculty development specialists), supportive and resourceful executive cabinet members, and a robust partnership with Achieving the Dream. This cross-functional action team worked for approximately 18 months to learn about teaching centers nationally, including how they were funded, the resources provided, and their vision for faculty success. It is important to note that there were limited teaching centers in community colleges during this research phase; the action team also included centers at the university level to create a robust plan of the "possibilities."

Needed Skills

Sorcinelli wrote that "teaching centers often occupy a unique place in the structure of an institution because their mission is to address the interests and needs for the entire academic community in support of the education that students receive" (2002, p. 11). A key purpose of many centers of teaching and learning is to be responsive to institutional goals and priorities and to work in collaboration with faculty and academic units, guided by their missions, goals, and practices (Lieberman, 2018). Our vision for the design of a new center was guided by a number of key resources, including practitioners like Dr. Mary Deane Sorcinelli (author, researcher, and Senior Fellow in the Institute for Teaching Excellence and Faculty Development at the University of Massachusetts) as well as Achieving the Dream's Good Practice Principles and Four Cornerstones of Excellence and the American Council on Education, which, in collaboration with the POD network, developed a Center for Teaching and Learning (CTL) Matrix (2017). Additionally, we held faculty focus groups and asked for feedback from faculty in the form of a needs assessment survey. Survey results revealed a variety of perspectives; a mid-career faculty member shared that "with such a diverse group of students from different cultural, social, economic, and educational backgrounds, it [would be] helpful to have a center devoted to developing clear strategies for optimally engaging students from these different backgrounds in the classroom, especially ideas for improving what I have always done."

Through the work of our center, we know that the promotion of good teaching will lead to meaningful learning. We have been intentional about providing our faculty with the mission-aligned support they need to foster learning for our diverse group of students from different cultural, social, economic, and educational backgrounds. These efforts begin with the inclusion of our faculty competencies to frame the work we do. All programs, events, workshops, and instructional resources are aligned with at least one faculty competency: pedagogical content knowledge, feedback and assessment, inclusive pedagogy, curriculum alignment, classroom climate, instructional strategies, and faculty engagement.

Rationale

With the higher education landscape constantly evolving, faculty members need to engage with well-designed faculty development opportunities to serve a diversity of students. In contrast to their university peers at research institutions with a teaching emphasis, community college faculty are expected to spend much of their time teaching students and focused on student learning. Community college faculty often begin their tenure with little to no training in teaching pedagogy and, in particular, training in supporting a wide diversity of students. Finley and Kinslow (2016) inform us:

> Even with the challenges of students' varying backgrounds, teaching at a community college can be immensely rewarding because of one's ability to help make a genuine difference in the lives of students. Some of our students never thought they would have the chance to pursue higher education, or they came from countries where only the privileged could enter a university. I have received thank-you notes from students who were grateful for the chance to learn. Watching students get excited about learning and encouraging them to continue their education makes teaching worthwhile.
>
> (p. 10)

Our faculty competencies frame the work of our center but also provide faculty members with a clear road map of the skills they need to be successful in the classroom. Competencies are inclusive of both the core teaching skills needed for student learning and the soft skills needed to be an effective, reflective, equity-minded educator. Hamblin wrote, "Teachers [need] to think critically about their own understanding of what it means to be a community college teacher" (2015, p. 32). With this point in mind, the Parr CTLE incorporates research-based strategies for student success, assesses needs directly by engaging with our faculty and their leaders, integrates our faculty competencies and key indicators in all of our programs, and uses student voices to drive offerings.

Equity and Inclusion Considerations

At Central Piedmont, we believe all individuals have the potential to succeed, and we provide student-focused pathways to achievement. Equity is a shared value of all Central Piedmont educators, and we strive to make equity a priority by developing, curating, facilitating, and coordinating identity-conscious professional learning opportunities for faculty. Our Equity-Mindset Framework is a curriculum to support faculty and staff educators with critical reflection, awareness, and exploration; inclusive and culturally responsive teaching practices; and evidence-based curriculum development. The curriculum is designed to help our educators see the challenges faced by our students and provides a safe space for them to learn, explore, and share in an environment that fosters trust, openness, and respect. The Parr CTLE faculty and staff members partner with other departments under our organizational learning umbrella in the facilitation of the teaching and learning curriculum of the framework.

There are two main learning tracks to support faculty and staff educators at all skill levels: (1) foundational and (2) specialized. The foundational track includes professional learning around data literacy, emotional intelligence, implicit bias, and an examination of racism and privilege. The specialized track includes professional learning in culturally responsive teaching, inclusive teaching best practices, student support, and inclusive leadership. Our Equity-Mindset Framework of programs includes and encourages participation from all Central Piedmont educators, regardless of the seat they sit in.

Conceptual Grounding

Professional learning and development for faculty members provides support and guidance regarding best practices in classroom management, student engagement, and instructional strategies. Gyurko et al. (2016) note that "faculty professional development has long been understood as central to improving teacher satisfaction, classroom instruction, and student achievement (p. 7)" and promotes faculty responsibility for continuous, career-long growth through theory, research, and professional collaboration with colleagues (Altany, 2012). Faculty development connects faculty across disciplines and career stages, creating a pedagogical community and opportunity for creative innovation. Faculty members need to engage with well-designed faculty development opportunities to serve as change agents when implementing new educational tactics, programs, and policies (Hanover Research, 2014).

Historically, community colleges have served local communities regarding workforce and social needs, such as business and industry training and promoting cultural appreciation for the arts and humanities. Today, the role of the community college has evolved to also prepare students to be productive members of today's workforce, walking the tightrope between pre-professional subjects, the liberal arts and sciences, and practical applications of their acquired knowledge and the technical skills needed to be successful in the 21st century (Hainline et al., 2010). With this shift, community college faculty have also experienced a shift in focus from simply access to student access and success. There is an expectation that community college faculty will teach a more diverse group of students while also juggling challenges related to student enrollment, progress, and completion. Given this shift in responsibility for student learning and success, community college faculty need to be sufficiently prepared. They may have expertise or experience within their specific subject area or field but may not have pedagogical teaching experience. That is, they may not have teaching credentials or have participated in professional development related to the art of teaching and learning (Illian, 2008), and thus may be unprepared to appropriately design and facilitate instruction that addresses this diverse student body.

Planning for, developing, and growing our teaching center have been dependent on evidence-based frameworks, resources, and nationally recognized communities of practice. Our center's design was guided by two key resources: the Center for Teaching and Learning Matrix (2017) (CTL Matrix) and a partnership with Achieving the Dream.

The CTL Matrix was used by our college as a tool to guide our center's development, practice, and assessment. Using the matrix as a resource, we created Parr CTLE objectives for

- Ensuring effective leadership, management, and resources
- Building stakeholders by listening to all perspectives
- Developing a mission, guiding principles, clear goals, and assessment procedures
- Offering a range of programmatic opportunities, leading with our strengths
- Creating collaborative systems of support
- Providing measures of engagement, recognition, and rewards

Achieving the Dream, an organization that champions community colleges across the country, provided us with expert coaching, impactful professional learning, and access to a peer network to support the development of our center. We were fortunate to partner with Jonathan Iuzzini, director of teaching and learning at Achieving the Dream, in strategizing and planning for the strong implementation of a well-designed and thoughtful hub for faculty success, our Parr CTLE. As we worked with Achieving the Dream to develop these objectives, specifically when developing our guiding principles, our faculty competencies were created to serve as a foundation for all faculty supports.

Tool

All faculty face professional challenges and have unique needs that must be met to be successful in the classroom. However, research has shown that these needs differ across career stages (Seldin, 2017; Gappa & Austin, 2010). For example, mid-career teachers indicate that professional development experiences are most satisfying when they support role shifts, build a strong rapport with students, and highlight significant successes (Huberman, 1989). Because we want our faculty to have a clear understanding of those behaviors needed to achieve teaching excellence, we established a set of seven faculty competencies (see Figure 10.1).

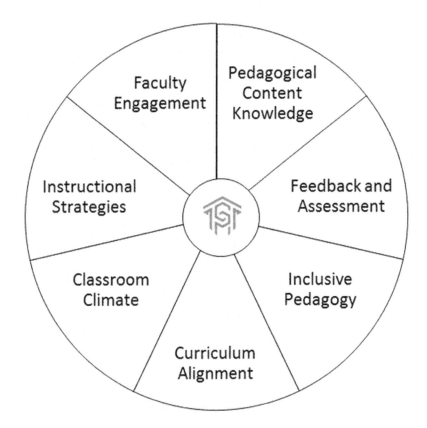

Figure 10.1 Faculty Competencies

The Central Piedmont faculty competencies were created during the research phase of planning for our center. The research team spent roughly four months consulting with other colleges, evaluating relevant literature, documenting our expectations for faculty effectiveness, and reviewing websites of US-based university and community college teaching centers to gauge those skills and competencies needed for faculty success. Valencia College, an award-winning community college serving central Florida, shared a faculty competency model that we learned from and used as a foundation for our work. Through robust discussions, facilitated working sessions, and faculty input/feedback, the team came to a consensus about our seven faculty competencies and those skills needed for teaching success at Central Piedmont. In addition to the inspiration one might gain from external research, we recommend that community colleges looking to develop faculty competencies consider the needs associated with the institution's strategic goals, student success outcomes, and assessment practices for gauging faculty effectiveness.

Every Parr CTLE program or workshop is aligned with one or more faculty competencies; however, faculty are reminded to view teaching excellence as a developmental process integrating time, experience, reflection, and goal-setting (Table 10.1).

Table 10.1 Central Piedmont CC Faculty Competencies with Targeted Programming

Faculty Competencies	Programming to Include Workshops and Resources
Classroom Climate	Professional learning and workshops for upholding internal policies and procedures (i.e., attendance, safety, ADA standards, initiatives, Student Code of Conduct, etc.); support for and faculty partnerships with college resources (e.g., counseling, Single Stop, and Care Team)
Curriculum Alignment	Professional learning and workshops for developing and selecting appropriate learning objectives/outcomes, lesson planning, and scaffolding at the course and program levels; translating course descriptions into meaningful, day-to-day classroom instruction; using teaching practices like "backward" design for outcomes alignment
Faculty Engagement	Professional learning and faculty engagement programming that promotes community involvement, self-care, and wellness; programs that facilitate partnerships and connections between faculty and the community (internal and external; locally, nationally, globally)

Faculty Competencies	Programming to Include Workshops and Resources
Feedback and Assessment	Professional learning, workshops, and support on developing authentic assessments, meaningful and scaffolded feedback, and assessment techniques; collaborations for the application of authentic assessment; the use of institutional and classroom data to inform reflective improvement for the instructor, course, program, and college
Inclusive Pedagogy	Professional learning and workshops to implement the appropriate application of information concerning local and national issues of social and economic inequality; understand barriers students face in college; engage a diverse student population; undertake reflection practices for continuous improvement
Instructional Strategies	Professional learning, development, and workshops for adoption of best practices in teaching and learning; active learning strategies and teaching to multiple learning modalities ("learning styles"); professional learning and development aimed at using the learning management system and engaging technological tools for in-person and online teaching
Pedagogical Content Knowledge	Support for maintaining professional licensure; attending conferences and external training; assistance with identifying and securing grants; assistance with and support for faculty-led research, publications of articles/books; participation in faculty development days and conference-like events; guidance with completing the faculty titles application/portfolio

Lessons Learned

Founding an effective and respected teaching center requires dedication, perseverance, and resourcefulness. Community colleges interested in opening a teaching center should consider the voice of the faculty in all decisions, from brainstorming through implementation. Faculty needs should be considered, particularly the institution's unique needs with respect to faculty tenure. Examining how the teaching center will serve staff educators is also important. We realized through our research that most teaching centers are led by faculty members, either on release/reassign time or through a long-term contract.

Our college realigned and merged efforts from our faculty development and online learning areas to scale the work of our center. These areas were operated by staff members who teach one or two classes per year (versus full-time faculty). We recognized quickly that some faculty did not appreciate the experiences and insight of teaching staff the same way they did that of a full-time faculty member. We learned that faculty members hold a high regard for their peers who can speak to their daily experiences with students, faculty administrative responsibilities, committees, and so forth. As a staff-led center, we have been purposeful about ensuring that the faculty voice is front and center and resonates throughout our work. To balance our unique organizational structure, the Parr CTLE employs Faculty Fellows, recruits faculty to lead CTLE committees, and facilitates a faculty-led CTLE advisory board.

Conclusion

Community colleges have a unique purpose in higher education, serving as an avenue for individual social mobility (Cohen et al., 2014); innovation; and providing a pathway for career readiness and entry into four-year colleges and universities. Community college faculty are responsible for student success and retention; this begins with effective course design, inclusive teaching practices, and confidence in their ability to teach their subject matter in their respective discipline, trade, or industry. Teaching centers provide faculty with the opportunity to "ponder new teaching approaches and experiment with new formats" (Lieberman, 2018, para 4) but are also positioned to facilitate campuswide change and ultimately improve classroom experiences for all students.

Central Piedmont's faculty serve as drivers of instructional methodologies, assessment strategies, and technology integration to help our students learn. Our Parr Center for Teaching and Learning Excellence prides itself on being responsive to institutional priorities and initiatives. We provide our faculty with the support and resources they need to utilize inclusive, evidence-based instructional practices, embrace professional learning for continuous improvement, and engage as active learners in an empowering and supportive academic community. Though in operation only a few years, the Parr CTLE is a place where faculty learning, collaboration, and innovation contribute to the college's vision of being champions of students, catalysts for opportunity, and exceptional providers of learning experiences.

References

Altany, A. (2012). Professional faculty development: The necessary fourth leg. *Faculty Focus*. www.facultyfocus.com/articles/faculty-development/professional-faculty-development-the-necessary-fourth-leg/

A Center for Teaching and Learning Matrix. (2017). *American Council of Education and POD Network*. https://podnetwork.org/resources/center-for-teaching-and-learning-matrix/

Cohen, A. M., Brawer, F. B., & Kisker, C. B. (2014). *The American community college* (6th ed.). Jossey-Bass.

Finley, D., & Kinslow, S. (2016). Faculty talk about teaching at the community college. *Oxford Handbooks Online.* https://doi.org/10.1093/oxfordhb/97801 99935291.013.47

Gappa, J. M., & Austin, A. E. (2010). Rethinking academic traditions for twenty-first-century faculty. *AAUP Journal of Academic Freedom, 1,* 1–20. www.aaup. org/sites/default/files/Gappa-Austin.pdf

Gyurko, J., MacCormack, P., Bless, M., & Jodl, J. (2016). *Why colleges and universities need to invest in quality teaching more than ever.* Report of the Association of College and University Educators. http://acue.org/wp-content/ uploads/2016/05/WhitePaper-201611114-Web.pdf

Hainline, L., Gaines, M., Feather, C., Padilla, E., & Terry, E. (2010). Changing students, faculty, and institutions in the twenty-first century. *AAC&U – Peer Review, 12*(3). www.aacu.org/publications-research/periodicals/changing-students-faculty-andinstitutions-twenty-first-century

Hamblin, C. (2015). *How Arizona community college teachers go about learning to teach* [Doctoral Dissertation, Utah State University]. http://digitalcommons. usu.edu/cgi/viewcontent.cgi?article=5330&context=etd

Hanover Research. (2014). *Best practices in faculty development. Report of the Academy Administration Practice.* www.hanoverresearch.com/insights-blog/ 3-trends-in-higher-education-faculty-development/

Huberman, M. (1989). The professional life cycle of teachers. *Teachers College Record, 91,* 3157.

Illian, P. P. (2008). *Creating passion in the classroom: Using professional development to create behavioral changes in adjunct college faculty* [Doctoral Dissertation]. http://proxy.lib.odu.edu/login?url=https://search-proquest-com.proxy.lib.odu. edu/docview/250764951?accountid=12967

Lieberman, M. (2018). Centers of the pedagogical universe. *Inside Digital Learning.* www.insidehighered.com/digital-learning/article/2018/02/28/centers-teaching-and-learning-serve-hub-improving-teaching

Seldin, P. (2017). Tailoring faculty development programs to faculty career stages. *To Improve the Academy, 24*(1), 137–146. https://doi.org/10.1002/j. 2334-4822.2006.tb00455.x02/j.2334-4822.2006.tb00455.x

Smorynski, H. (2015). Making faculty development an institutional value and professional practice. In *Faculty development: A resource collection for academic leaders* (pp. 10–13). Magna Publications.

Sorcinelli, M. D. (2002). *Ten principles of good practice in creating and sustaining teaching and learning centers.* http://citeseerx.ist.psu.edu/viewdoc/download? doi=10.1.1.821.363&rep=rep1&type=pdf

Section 3

Consortial and Professional Association Programming

Vicki L. Baker

Introduction

As Adam Grant, organizational psychologist at Wharton and *New York Times* best-selling author, said, "If we create networks with the sole intention of getting something, we won't succeed. We can't pursue the benefits of networks; the benefits ensue from investments in meaningful activities and relationships" (2023). This quote aptly characterizes the tools and collective efforts of the contributors featured in Section 3, Consortial and Professional Association Programming. Despite best intentions, investments and related support aimed at mid-career faculty across the academy are lagging behind those provided to early-career colleagues (Baker & Manning, 2021). Yet there is a recognition of the power of mid-career faculty and the need to strategically invest in their growth and development (Texter & Lennox Terrion, 2022). To counter the lack of institutional resources, the chapters in this section illustrate how consortia (e.g., associations of two or more individuals, organizations, or institutions participating in a common activity) and professional associations can and should foster discipline-based communities and targeted resources aimed at mid-career faculty. As a collection of knowledge and practice, the tools in Section 3 highlight the power of intentionality, capacity-building, and shared values in service to supporting mid-career faculty and leaders as they navigate this stage of life and career: a win-win for the faculty and their institutions. In the following paragraphs, I briefly highlight each chapter and how its featured tools contribute to critical knowledge and practice at mid-career.

The work of Boyd and colleagues illustrates the power of faculty developers and institutional leaders coming together to advance mid-career faculty scholarship and practice at the consortial level. Chapter 11 introduces the potential of multi-campus faculty learning communities (FLCs) designed to support the psychological safety and visibility of mid-career faculty participants employed at member institutions from the Associated Colleges of the South (ACS). The benefits of FLCs are

DOI: 10.4324/9781003428626-14

twofold: (1) promoting faculty engagement and peer support between campuses, and (2) enabling faculty to feel seen and heard in a community in which psychological safety and visibility are foundational values supporting faculty growth and learning. The authors offer guidance from their experiences designing and facilitating FLCs on their respective campuses. Moreover, readers hear about the power of FLCs from the mid-career faculty participants as well as the faculty developers who sought to support the faculty employed at their institutions.

Fueled by the need to address a problem that permeated the academy during the pandemic – faculty who lacked the skills and knowledge to respond to technological advances and needs in teaching and learning – an international effort in Türkiye undertaken to fill this gap is featured in Chapter 12. Elçi and colleagues were integral in fostering a voluntary faculty professional development network initiative, the YÖMEGA Higher Education Professional Development Network. Rooted in social network theory, YÖMEGA represents members from diverse institutions and disciplinary areas and with various academic titles via a virtual speaker series on topics that span diverse areas of teaching and learning. Inspired to enable skill development across the various areas of the faculty career (e.g., teaching, learning, scholarship), participants learn how to build a faculty professional development–focused network that serves as a model of diversity and inclusivity aimed at embracing both global developments and cultural differences.

Inspired by a charge communicated by Dr. Karen Stout, CEO of Achieving the Dream, leaders from the Belk Center for Community College Leadership and Research strategically invested in the professional development and learning of community college faculty in the state of North Carolina. Colclough and Deal, the authors of Chapter 13, feature faculty development efforts happening in community colleges via the North Carolina Teaching and Learning Hubs. The Hubs (e.g., 58 community colleges, 100 counties, and 22 workforce development zones) support full- and part-time faculty and staff educators as they seek to build equity into learning and student success. The Hubs are dedicated to creating complementary opportunities for educators to learn, implement, and assess evidence-based strategies that have been associated with increased equitable student success outcomes across disciplines. Readers learn about how the Hubs enabled the delivery of evidence-based professional learning directly to faculty and staff educators across North Carolina and how the Hubs provided support for building capacity via colleges' teaching and learning centers, spaces where supplemental support is a necessary investment in ensuring equitable student success.

Although not all industry practices are suitable for the academy, Chapter 14 features one such tool that has the potential to support strategic career advancement at mid-career: the SWOT analysis (Strengths, Weaknesses, Opportunities, Threats). Heasley and Baker walk readers through a professional association-level effort supported by the Association for the Study of Higher Education (ASHE), along with the Council for the Advancement of Higher Education Programs (CAHEP), which strives to strengthen the community of mid-career scholars and practitioners who are members of ASHE. In response to calls for more professional development aimed at mid-career, CAHEP created a Mid-Career Faculty Workshop chair position and began offering a mid-career faculty workshop as part of its professional development programming. This chapter features a session from the mid-career faculty workshop that helps participants uncover their future academic trajectory, via a SWOT analysis, which is in alignment with personal strengths and opportunities.

As I reflect on the knowledge gleaned from this collection of chapters, I highlight three main takeaways. First, investing in a community that extends beyond one's home institution is invaluable to navigating mid-career. The literature is clear: the mid-career stage is isolating (Canale et al., 2013). This reality, coupled with the limited resources aimed at this career stage, means that mid-career faculty and leaders are in need of guidance, mentorship, and peer support. The efforts featured in this section provide readers with a road map for how to begin building a mid-career community at the consortial and professional association levels. Second, the chapter contributors illustrate what is possible when like-inspired individuals come together to invest in the growth and development of others, even with few to no financial resources available for doing so. All the chapter contributors have "day jobs" on their respective campuses in which career development and advancement is perhaps only a small portion of their work portfolios. Yet collectively, their efforts illustrate what is possible when working collaboratively for a greater good. Third, there is an anecdotal connection between investments in faculty development and student success and institutional effectiveness. As we continue to navigate an evolving academy, we must ensure that our faculty have the needed skills, resources, and tools to be successful as they seek to advance in their careers and as they support student learning, growth, and development. Investing in mid-career faculty and leaders is a wise choice.

References

Baker, V. L., & Manning, C. E. N. (2021). A mid-career faculty agenda: A review of four decades of research and practice. *Higher Education: Handbook of Theory and Research, 36*, 419–484.

Canale, A. M., Herdklotz, C., & Wild, L. (2013). Mid-career faculty support: The middle years of the academic profession. *Faculty Career Development Services, the Wallace Center, Rochester Institute of Technology, 10*, 1–9.

Grant, A. (2023). *Top 35 Adam Grant quotes.* https://quotefancy.com/adam-grant-quotes

Texter, L. A., & Lennox Terrion, J. (2022, May 2). The Care and feeding of mid-career faculty: Professional development across the career life cycle. *Academic Leader.* www.academic-leader.com/topics/faculty-development/the-care-and-feeding-of-mid-career-faculty-professional-development-across-the-career-life-cycle/

Chapter 11

Leveraging a Consortial Approach for Mid-Career Faculty Learning Communities

Diane E. Boyd, Nancy L. Chick, Linda M. Boland, and Katherine A. Troyer

Overview

Research on higher education faculty reveals a well-documented "mid-career malaise," the phenomenon of tenured associate professors – especially those in rank for more than six years – experiencing low satisfaction resulting from increased service obligations, the relative lack of support for research or creative work and other forms of professional growth, the disconnect between professional goals and a greater sense of purpose, increased expectations for leadership without leadership development, and unclear expectations for promotion to full professor (Matthews, 2014; Baker & Manning, 2021). To address these known challenges, as well as the emergent threats of burnout and disengagement due to the COVID-19 global pandemic, we designed and facilitated a Mid-Career Advancement Pathways Program (MAPP) for the Associated Colleges of the South (ACS), a consortium of sixteen liberal arts colleges and universities from twelve states. MAPP invited applications from ACS associate professors and enrolled 38 participants from 14 institutions. Program goals were to:

1. Support mid-career colleagues in crafting viable professional development plans predicated on joy.
2. Cultivate collegial support and a sense of belonging during this often-neglected career stage.
3. Expand participant peer-mentorship networks.

Drawing from the literature on mid-career faculty, we developed a program intended to invite participants to interrogate the relationships between their work values, their lived experiences, and their developing plans for the future. For some, this might provide a path to full professorship, but our programmatic goal was broader than this single achievement. To achieve the program's goals, participants met in virtual workshops and faculty learning communities (FLCs) and completed individual offline exercises

DOI: 10.4324/9781003428626-15

that guided them through relevant reflection and planning. The consortial context attracted a diverse group of mid-career faculty and facilitators, resulting in synergies and insights that exceeded the program's initial goals.

Program Focus

This chapter features one component of MAPP, its signature initiative of faculty learning communities (FLCs), or groups of faculty members who regularly gather for ongoing conversation and connection throughout the program. Because MAPP was a consortium-sponsored program, we were able to assign colleagues from the same campus to different FLCs; we knew this would be beneficial, but we didn't anticipate how profoundly it would affect participants' experiences. This structure, complemented by some key facilitation strategies, helped us promote participants' psychological visibility and safety by making them feel seen as individuals and safe to open up to themselves and to the group. As a result, FLC members quickly grew willing to address the hard questions facing mid-career faculty.

Needed Skills

Milton Cox identifies 10 qualities necessary for FLCs: safety and trust, openness, respect, responsiveness, collaboration, relevance, challenge, enjoyment, esprit de corps, and empowerment (2004, pp. 18–19). In our FLCs, participants also needed to bring or develop specific dispositions. First, because FLCs require that participants grow in community, our participants must be open to talking with others not only about their logistical goals but also their values, joys, and other affective dimensions of their work lives. This FLC is a productive space for mid-career faculty unaccustomed to opportunities for developing these abilities. Further, our participants must be willing to think beyond practicalities. To illustrate, our participants report on learning to navigate pathways to the next promotion and being more productive but, even more significantly, on improving their engagement, job satisfaction, and connectedness.

Rationale

Because mid-career faculty face multifaceted and largely unspoken challenges, many conceptualize their experiences as idiosyncratic, and many assume fault of some kind. As Maggie Berg and Barbara K. Seeber experienced when they began critiquing the stressors plaguing faculty, this kind of thinking can "appear self-indulgent" and can even be met with calls to "stop whining" (Berg & Seeber, 2013, p. 3). Our participants expressed feeling unsafe when asked to respond to questions like "What do I want? What do I need? And how can I get there?" on their campuses, because career trajectory conversations there were focused on meeting requirements for promotion to full professor, and their responses might be interpreted as indicating disinterest in supporting the institutional mission or, worse, a lack of professional purpose.

Equity and Inclusion Considerations

Mid-career challenges include inequitable service burdens and hidden labor for women faculty and faculty from underrepresented groups in the academy (O'Meara et al., 2022). In addition, access to effective mentors who can support diverse faculty at this critical career stage is often lacking. Small colleges, known for their relational strengths and small department sizes, can be challenging settings for these faculty, who may feel simultaneously isolated in their academic niches and surveilled because "everybody knows their name." Multi-campus FLCs offer these faculty a sense of community with commonalities and yet appropriate distance, freeing them from judgment from their campus colleagues and a potential stereotype threat that might inhibit the kinds of authenticity and risk-taking needed at this stage of their careers (Verschelden, 2017, p. 40).

Theoretical Grounding

Reframing the trajectory of a career post-tenure is a vulnerable endeavor. Not all mid-career faculty share the same goals, though, so they need spaces that prioritize psychological safety, or "a shared belief that the team is safe for interpersonal risk taking" (Edmondson, 1999, p. 354). We facilitators planned our FLCs with that priority top of mind. From beginning to end, we focused on uncovering the various needs of mid-career faculty and creating trust by acknowledging the vulnerabilities inherent in articulating one's needs. This design supported participants' risk-taking in the form of honest exploration of what they want in the many years remaining in their careers (Kvernenes et al., 2021, p. 881).

Tool

Cox describes faculty learning communities as cohorts designed to "address the teaching, learning, and developmental needs of an important group of faculty or staff that has been particularly affected by the isolation, fragmentation, stress, neglect, or chilly climate in the academy" (2004, p. 8). One strength of classical FLC formation is a group-guided dynamic that flattens power differentials rather than centering on any one person – especially the facilitator – as an expert. Facilitators can operationalize this approach by sharing experiences of "not knowing" or making mistakes and, most importantly, by deferring to participants' experiences as the focus of conversations. These facilitation goals aligned with our FLCs' focus on exploring participants' specific challenges and hopes as mid-career faculty.

Designing Our FLCs

L. Dee Fink's modified backward design process to support significant learning experiences (2013) proved a core resource for planning our specific type of FLCs – namely, multi-campus FLCs that support participants' feelings of psychological safety and visibility. We envisioned this process as similar to the title of Fink's book, *Creating Significant Learning Experiences*, and we drew from the steps he describes to "Build Strong Primary Components" (p. 74). Table 11.1 outlines his steps, the prompts we adapted, and the design outcomes for each step. This outline can be used to develop similar FLCs in other contexts, and consulting Fink's book for additional prompts can support additional design considerations beyond those we offer in what follows.

This design process led us to some key but simple touchpoints in our FLCs that supported our overarching goals: the program application, the specific types of interactions we facilitated, and our communications sent after each FLC meeting.

Table 11.1 Guide for Designing Multi-Campus FLCs That Promote Psychological Visibility and Safety

Design Steps	Design Prompts	Design Outcomes
Situational Factors	• How many faculty apply, and how many can we accept? • How many facilitators are available? • When will the FLC meet, and how often? • How will the FLC meet (e.g., on which virtual platform)? • What are the shared and divergent experiences of participants? • What are their goals and expectations?	Responses will shape the number, size, schedule, and platform of FLC, as well as participants' specific goals.

Design Steps	Design Prompts	Design Outcomes
Goals	• How do the FLC goals of psychological visibility and safety align with participants' stated goals? • Given the above goals, what should the FLC "learning environment" look like? • What are the key ideas and types of information participants need to support these goals? • What kinds of thinking are necessary to meet these goals? • What connections (similarities and interactions) do participants need to make to meet these goals? • What do participants need to learn about themselves and each other?	Responses will shape selection of topics (e.g., difficult conversations, finding time to write, handling high service load) and how psychological safety and visibility can be integrated into addressing those topics.
Feedback and Assessments	• How will we know participants have met our goals? • How will we know participants have met their goals? • What will participants produce as evidence of meeting these goals? • How will participants know what goals they have met? • What resources do we need to gauge impact?	Responses will inform assessment instrument, such as a post-FLC survey.
Activities	• What offline activities and virtual discussions will support FLC and participant goals? • What resources do facilitators need to provide support and feedback to participants?	Responses will aid the development of specific activities and discussion prompts and identification of needed resources.
Integration of Components	• How do all components – goals, assessments, and activities – align? • What's missing? • What and where can we modify to amplify integration?	Response will inform review of FLC design plan and suggest additional needs before implementation

Key Application Questions

In addition to posing basic demographic questions and asking about career goals, our program application asked two questions that emphasized caring and that primed participants for the kinds of thinking the FLC would ask of them:

- "What brings you joy in your professional work?"
- "What brings you joy outside of your professional work?"

Like the first chapter in Vicki Baker's *Charting Your Path to Full* (2020), titled "What Is Your Joy?" we wanted to signal the importance of joyful work as a key to successful career progress. Applicants thus learned that, in these FLCs, their quality of life – at work and beyond work – matters most. This framework proved to be a powerful and necessary lens for guiding participants to grapple with when, why, and even if they wanted to seek promotion, leadership roles, and other opportunities often expected of mid-career faculty. This openness to all possibilities may be one reason one of our participants described the FLC as "the first time in a long time that someone has taken the time to design a program that is aimed at someone like me. Middle of my career, unsure of [the] next step."

Facilitating Cross-Campus Interactions

Informed by the application numbers and responses, we formed three FLCs (one focused on leadership and two on scholarship) with 10 to 12 participants each. We had correctly anticipated that some participants would feel a sense of discomfort, guilt, and even self-indulgence for talking about what brings them joy, what challenges them most, and what they genuinely hope for for the next stages of their careers, so our priority (and our advantage as part of a consortium) was to distribute faculty from the same campus across different FLCs. When this distribution wasn't possible, we would assign same-campus FLC participants to different breakout groups, which was the site for the most vulnerable group work. As one participant confessed, "Anyone you're going to talk to about this [on your own campus] will eventually evaluate you, so, do I want to admit I'm unhappy or [that I] want something else?" This attention to group structure is essential to support participants' honest reflections, vulnerable dialogues, and shared problem-solving.

Session Structure

With this group structure, each FLC session followed the simple rhythm reflected in Table 11.2.

Table 11.2 Design of Each FLC Session

Step	Participants	Activity	Zoom Logistics
1	Individuals	Think and write in response to a prompt.	Everyone gathers in the main Zoom room, with cameras turned off and sound muted.
2	Pairs or triads	Share, listen to, and discuss each other's responses.	Participants are sent to breakout rooms.
3	Whole FLC	Share experiences, patterns, epiphanies, and/or solutions that emerge in small-group discussion.	Everyone meets in main Zoom room.

With this simple approach of a modified think-pair-share, we foregrounded participant engagement and centered their thoughts, needs, and mutual support as the content of the FLC meetings. The conversations thus flowed from the precise needs of the participants in the room and ultimately focused on the human interactions that characterize academic life and how to capitalize on uplifting collaborations and reduce time- and energy-sucking work. This intentional scaffolding ensured that participants felt seen, heard, and supported by their quickly emerging community that spanned campuses.

Sample Discussion Prompt

The prompts in Step 1 aren't complicated. One that yielded a lively discussion was

> "Reflect for two minutes on your experiences and mental states over the last week. Write down one high and one low to share with a partner in the breakout room."

This simple prompt met two goals. First, it helped participants develop comfort in sharing vulnerability, initially with just one or two colleagues. Second, sharing with someone who listened and potentially experienced something similar reinforced participants' feelings of being seen. One participant expressed gratitude that these discussions "helped normalize my struggles, which helped me be kinder to myself. That was then motivating to make changes."

Post-Session Communication

To reinforce the benefits of the FLC conversations, we composed follow-up messages to consolidate participant recall of the interactions and to sustain their sense of feeling seen and heard. We were intentional with validating language, such as "Thank you for such a thoughtful, real conversation," "We were so inspired by how everyone wrestled with . . . ," and "We've been thinking about our last conversation and are revising our plans for our next session." Although we didn't intentionally use a template to write our messages, analyzing them later surfaced a consistent set of moves outlined in Table 11.3.

FLC Outcomes

According to a post-FLC survey, participants were grateful for the time to think strategically about their careers. For instance, 90 percent agreed or strongly agreed that they felt motivated to develop a plan for their next career phase that was guided by "intentionally ma[king] choices to focus my career in ways that are personally meaningful to me." However, the most successful outcome of the program was the sense of psychological safety, which participants attributed explicitly to the multi-campus FLCs. Indeed, 93 percent strongly agreed or agreed that the FLCs were the most effective component of the MAPP program. As one participant explained, "The consortium model is really vital to find shared voices, concerns, and experiences, when at our home institutions we might feel like the odd one out." Others described these virtual gatherings as providing "a place free of judgment and full of vulnerability and respect" and "space, time, and intellectual resources to engage in prioritizing and planning."

Table 11.3 Structure of Facilitator Communications After FLC Meetings

Move	Description
Extend Grateful Greeting	Express gratitude for time and investments in the conversation.
Acknowledge Challenge	Name what was difficult in the reflection and/or conversation.
Emphasize the Interpersonal	Highlight relationship dynamics during conversation and their impacts both in the short and long term.
Support Application	Share resources to support individual application of insights and/or strategies emerging from discussion.
Reinforce Psychological Visibility and Safety	Conclude with a participant quote from the discussion, demonstrating that their voices were heard and their experiences matter.

Challenges and Benefits

Paradoxically, the goals and activities that were the FLC's strengths – capitalizing on joy, linking that to professional purpose, and cultivating psychological safety – were also areas in which participants initially struggled. Many describe their experiences before the FLC of feeling alone, being uniquely dissatisfied with their circumstances, and feeling unable to voice their dissatisfaction. Some confessed that thinking about what makes them unhappy in their work is the epitome of privilege, and talking about these issues would be a gilded bridge too far. One participant described their inner voice as saying, "You're at the top of your game! You enjoy what you do, and you're good at what you do. This is a dream job, so be grateful."

To respond to this resistance, we regularly addressed participants as "mid-career faculty members"; by explicitly naming them as such, we foregrounded their shared identity and demonstrated that being "a mid-career faculty member" is *a thing*. Our regular references to the experiences shared by the diverse FLC members – across discipline, institution, geographical location, age, gender, race, and more – reminded participants that their concerns are not individual, and in fact, their common experiences are well documented as a problem that deserves attention (Baldwin & Chang, 2006; Mathews, 2014; Monaghan, 2017; Baker et al., 2018). One participant described the program as granting "permission to think about questions I didn't know I needed to ask, like – what is thriving? What do you need?"

Another challenge for participants came when we encouraged them to consider how their career paths aligned with their values – or didn't. In delving into what mattered to them and how that translated into their work (and in completing this inquiry with others at similar stages), some participants discovered that their path forward would be different from what they had previously planned. One participant explained, "This focus on the 'why' or newfound sense of purpose has allowed me to consider and start to pursue a new direction in my scholarship from a traditional academic approach to one that allows me to build new skills that are more rewarding for myself and my community." Some even decided that completing the necessary requirements for promotion to full professor was not for them.

The FLC design and facilitation helped faculty work through these affective barriers and was viewed by many as one of the strongest benefits of participation. The psychological visibility and safety bolstered by the FLC allowed them to take the intellectual and emotional risks needed to become "unstuck," make some decisions, and move forward with making plans. The program became a space in which experimentation was valued as the iterative process to yield "better" answers to the mid-career puzzle.

Lessons Learned

One year after the last meeting of our FLC, we highlight three takeaways for others seeking to establish multi-institutional FLCs. First, financial resources are necessary to support both faculty participants and facilitators. FLCs like ours should be included with other institutionally supported high-impact professional development activities that allow time for vocational and professional reflection, such as sabbaticals and research leaves. A stipend for participants at this critical moment in their careers signals to faculty that their institution values their well-being, their connectedness, and their sense of purpose, all of which support the institution's goal of long-term retention and engagement of their faculty.

Second, we recommend two facilitators per FLC and ensuring post-session debriefs. The emotional labor of supporting faculty in this work is high, and two facilitators should share this load. Debriefs after each FLC session allow facilitators to support each other and to consolidate insights, generate follow-up resources, and maintain a flexible plan that's responsive to specific participants' needs.

Finally, we recommend a logistical necessity: scheduling the FLC meetings at a time when academics typically are available (e.g., Friday afternoons) and communicating those dates and times during the application phase. This preparation ensures that participants can and will commit to the FLCs.

Conclusion

Our FLCs were enriched by engaging faculty across multiple campuses, transcending the complex, potentially fraught relationships that mid-career faculty may have with their own campuses. This structure enables a formative rather than evaluative space for professional development, leading to psychological safety and better outcomes. We acknowledge, though, that not all campuses are part of formal consortia that invite and fund such activities. In lieu of such a membership, some campuses can take advantage of larger institutional systems, such as a (state) university system. More informal communities, such as ones built on institutional proximity, can also leverage the multi-institution approach. Larger institutions may also achieve the consortial effect by engaging faculty from different colleges or departments within the university. Ultimately, the consortial effect can be simulated by ensuring that participants are involved in neither each other's evaluation or daily lives.

Facilitating these FLCs reinforced a lesson the global pandemic highlighted for everyone in higher education: undertaking emotional labor for oneself and for others is necessary and hard work. Those of us in faculty development roles frequently tend to the emotional labor of faculty, but we rarely tend to ourselves. One year later, as we facilitators (the authors of this chapter and two additional team members) reflected on the experience, we had an epiphany: we had become an FLC of our own. Together, we mirrored the work we were doing for faculty participants. Without fully realizing it, we, too, reflected on our common experiences, shared our differing values, had hard conversations about our careers, and ultimately felt seen and heard by colleagues who cared. We had done for each other what we'd designed the FLC to do for mid-career faculty participants. As one of us noted, "We started this project to support faculty, and we also ended up supporting ourselves."

References

Baker, V. L. (2020). *Charting your path to full: A guide for women associate professors*. Rutgers University Press.

Baker, V. L., Lunsford, L. G., Neisler, G., Pifer, M. J., Terosky, A. L., & Sorcinelli, M. D. (2018). *Success after tenure: Supporting mid-career faculty*. Stylus Publishing.

Baker, V. L., & Manning, C. E. (2021). A mid-career faculty agenda: A review of four decades of research and practice. *Higher Education: Handbook of Theory and Research, 36*, 419–484.

Baldwin, R., & Chang, D. (2006). Reinforcing our "keystone" faculty. *Liberal Education, 92*(4), 28–35.

Berg, M., & Seeber, B. K. (2013). The slow professor: Challenging the culture of speed in the academy. *Transformative Dialogues, 6*(3), 1–7. https://td.journals.psu.edu/td/article/view/1307

Cox, M. (2004). Introduction to faculty learning communities. *New Directions for Teaching and Learning, 97*, 5–23.

Edmondson, A. (1999). Psychological safety and learning behavior in work teams. *Administrative Science Quarterly, 44*(2), 350–383.

Fink, L. D. (2013). *Creating significant learning experiences: An integrated approach to designing college courses*. John Wiley & Sons.

Kvernenes, M., Valestrand, E. A., Schei, E., Boudreau, J. D., Ofstad, E. H., & Hokstad, L. M. (2021). Threshold concepts in group-based mentoring and implications for faculty development: A qualitative analysis. *Medical Teacher, 43*(8), 879–883.

Mathews, K. (2014). *Perspectives on midcareer faculty and advice for supporting them*. The Collaborative on Academic Careers in Higher Education.

Monaghan, P. (2017, May 7). Helping professors overcome midcareer malaise. *The Chronicle of Higher Education*. www.chronicle.com/article/helping-professors-overcome-midcareer-malaise/

O'Meara, K., Culpepper, D., Misra, J., & Jaeger, A. (2022). *Equity-minded faculty workloads: What we can and should do now*. American Council on Education. www.acenet.edu/Documents/Equity-Minded-Faculty-Workloads.pdf

Verschelden, C. (2017). *Bandwidth recovery: Helping students reclaim cognitive resources lost to poverty, racism, and social marginalization*. Stylus Publishing.

Chapter 12

YÖMEGA

Empowering Faculty Members in
Türkiye Through a Collaborative
and Sustainable Professional
Development Voluntary Initiative

*Alev Elçi, Begüm Çubukçuoğlu Devran,
and A. Mohammed Abubakar*

Overview

The global environment of higher education is moving toward digital technologies and as such needs a radical transformation both in terms of strategies and related policies. At the center of this transformation process is faculty, particularly mid-career faculty members, who are aware of their changing roles and recognize that this change must be actualized in practice. Faculty professional development (FPD) in teaching and learning started in the 1970s and has gained momentum during this century, with models of FPD evolving over the past several decades. Türkiye, a developing country, is concerned about making qualitative improvements in higher education, not just increasing the quantity of higher education institutions and students. Hence, FPD is essential for the development of efficient uses of digital technologies to support effective teaching and learning.

The COVID-19 pandemic that emerged in early 2020 globally disrupted teaching and learning at all levels of education. In addition to the pandemic, the Ukrainian war, and earthquakes in Türkiye and Syria in 2022 and 2023, compounding the issues brought about by the pandemic. As a collective, higher education must be ready to manage a potential global education crisis that will likely create new interruptions.

Globally, organizations including the United Nations, UNESCO, and OECD are aiming to reduce the effects of possible future educational disruptions to minimize potential learning losses. UNESCO (2003, 2021) came up with a strategy and a path for recovery in educational situations of emergency, crisis, and reconstruction. The Transforming Education Summit Initiative, supported by the United Nations (UN, 2022), situated education at the forefront of the global political agenda. Relatedly, according to an OECD (2021) report, the global crisis has revealed an urgent need for higher education policymakers and institutional leaders to reorganize their traditional education patterns and models. Thus, policymaking for

DOI: 10.4324/9781003428626-16

revolution and development in higher education has become significant. YÖMEGA is answering this call by serving as a holistic FPD umbrella organization that embraces faculty members, researchers, staff from teaching and learning and distance education centers, members of NGOs (nongovernmental organizations), and stakeholders in the education industry.

Program Focus

YÖMEGA is guided by the understanding that traditional approaches to teaching and learning are insufficient because of changed student profiles, digital technologies, and innovative teaching and learning methods. Digital technologies are both knowledge providers and co-creators, mentors, and assessors of knowledge (Haleem et al., 2022). Mid-career faculty members, given their institutional knowledge and remaining career runway, are the drivers and leaders of educational transformation, and their role as facilitators of learning cannot be denied. Thus, mid-career faculty members must be equipped, via professional development, with the needed skills and competencies that will empower them during this transformational era in higher education.

Needed Skills

The skills and competencies required for the students of the twenty-first century must also be mastered by the faculty members who must teach those skills. Skill development topics have typically encompassed leadership, cognitive, social, and networking skills. Haranaka (2018) expanded the list of required skill sets to also include information, media, and technology literacy; flexibility; initiative; productivity; connectivity; emotional intelligence; and self-responsibility. Since AI technologies (e.g., robotics, chatbots, and smart devices) have become prevalent in common practice, AI competency has emerged as one of the most important twenty-first-century digital skills (Ng et al., 2023). YÖMEGA is dedicated to supporting faculty in fostering and improving the aforementioned skills to cater to today's different models of teaching and learning. The authors are committed to supporting faculty and have published previous related studies together (Elçi et al., 2017; Elçi & Abubakar, 2021; Devran & Elçi, 2020; Kara et al., 2020).

Rationale

Given the absence of a national FPD network for non-formal learning in Türkiye, the authors sought to facilitate peer collaboration and the development of digital skills (Elçi, 2021a) by establishing an FPD network for participants independent of their home institutions. To that end, YÖMEGA was established in December 2020 to support the professional development of faculty members in teaching and learning by (1) embracing digital technologies, (2) sharing knowledge, experiences, and narratives, and (3) discussing diverse views and experiences. The intention was to form a focused interest group that is not connected to but is in collaboration with public and foundational universities, associations, agencies, and policymakers. Later, an executive committee was established. YÖMEGA was initially formed (as Network Google Groups) by inviting faculty developers, faculty members, and administrative staff members from higher education institutions in Türkiye who are interested in FPD.

Equity and Inclusion Considerations

The YÖMEGA initiative aims to enhance the academic and intellectual environment in higher education institutions by providing faculty members with sufficient opportunities to pursue research and to participate in events for FPD. YÖMEGA is and has been very committed to diversity, equity, and inclusion, from its formation to the present day, in terms of the communication, collaboration, and professional development of its members. YÖMEGA relies on the following definitions of diversity, equity, and inclusion, as outlined by Dali et al. (2021), to guide its efforts:

> **Diversity** is understood as a broad concept, including demographic characteristics (e.g., race, ethnicity, body ability, gender identity, etc.); diversity of user communities; diversity of resources and collections; diversity of professional practices; and so on; **Equity** is understood as an organizational (event-related) state whereby everyone is optimally equipped to succeed; and
> **Inclusion** in PDEs is interpreted as a subjective feeling of belonging by participants, accompanied by the recognition that their uniqueness is appreciated.

YÖMEGA was established with the goal of understanding, valuing, and inspiring individual differences, keeping in mind that all faculty members should be granted the same opportunities to flourish in their various roles (teaching, research, service, administration, and leadership). YÖMEGA relies on speakers with diverse backgrounds, both from Türkiye and internationally, who present on topics that are of mutual interest and that are newsworthy. Although YÖMEGA was established for faculty members in Türkiye, interested faculty members from Turkish-speaking countries (e.g., Northern Cyprus and Azerbaijan) are welcome to engage in and attend activities. Also, individuals of all genders, races, ethnicities, and religions can engage with the YÖMEGA group.

Conceptual Grounding

YÖMEGA, conceived as an initiative-based FPD, embraces a holistic and sophisticated approach to supporting members, which includes virtual networking, informal mentoring, non-formal learning, raising awareness, and building community and educational narratives tacitly. This approach moves FPD outside organizational and national boundaries, thus opening it up to a global educational development environment. Of critical importance to this approach is accounting for local and cultural differences. Faculty members as adult learners are encouraged to draw on their prior knowledge and experiences as they relate to the event topic to support knowledge transfer and learning (Lawler & King, 2000). In today's conditions, to be well prepared for the complexity of working environments, Hase and Kenyon (2000) extol the benefits of self-determined learning by faculty – referred to as *heutagogy* rather than andragogy – which also embodies the self-management of learning.

The efforts of YÖMEGA are grounded in the theories of social networks. Social networks facilitate the creation of connections and relationships in virtual environments. Based on social network research, virtual communities provide rich learning, opportunities for communication, and collaborative environments for transferring tacit knowledge (Oguz et al., 2010). Buckley and Nimmon (2020) stated that FPD has evolved from traditional training activities to contemporary models – models in which relationships and networks play an important *mediating role* in the mobilization of knowledge. Moreover, the authors claim that non-formal professional social networks encourage both participation and learning so that FPD can be positioned as a dynamic social enterprise. The emphasized mediating role supports global participation in striving for improvement, with a sense of responsibility to influence events and conditions, and requires a guiding purpose and the ability to take actions to achieve a goal (OECD, 2018; Patrick, 2010). YÖMEGA leverages the influence of social media to cultivate its social communities. The YÖMEGA Talks Series is disseminated over the network via emails and through Facebook, LinkedIn, and X (formerly called Twitter) to generate awareness, while Zoom serves as the virtual communication platform to facilitate all activities.

It is worth mentioning that there are some global *exemplary professional development networks* aimed at improving teaching and learning in higher education, in the form of face-to-face community building in virtual environments. The Professional and Organizational Development (POD) Network in Higher Education, established in 1976, has members mainly in the USA and more than thirty countries (POD Network, 2023). Founded in 1993, the International Consortium for Educational Development (ICED) comprises twenty-eight members, encompassing national and regional organizations as well as networks dedicated to educational and academic advancement (ICED, 2023). YÖMEGA has achieved membership in the prestigious ICED Council, representing the Republic of Türkiye, as of June 2023. Also, going beyond academia, EDUCAUSE is a large community of technology, academic, industry, and university leaders whose aim is digital transformation in higher education (EDUCAUSE, 2023). These role models are guiding YÖMEGA in becoming a pioneering network in Türkiye and possibly beyond, in other Turkish-speaking countries, to support faculty excellence that will benefit both faculty members and their developing countries.

Tool

As universities shifted to online education globally during the pandemic, faculty members needed academic and professional development support to gain experience with online education. Research has revealed that faculty members are eager for personal and professional development (Elçi et al., 2020; Elçi, 2021b). In response, YÖMEGA began organizing virtual events by inviting distinguished guest speakers (alternating between local and international guests) every two weeks.

Next, we provide a sample email shared with invited speakers:

Dear [Guest]

*I hope this email finds you well. I am writing to extend a cordial invitation to you on behalf of the **Higher Education Professional Development Network (YÖMEGA) in Türkiye.***

As the founder of YÖMEGA, a dynamic community comprising 222 esteemed faculty members and researchers hailing from diverse universities across Türkiye, I am thrilled to introduce our unique initiative. Modeled after the renowned Professional Development Network (POD), YÖMEGA has garnered an impressive assembly of professionals, particularly specializing in faculty professional development and academia. Notably, nearly half of our members are esteemed professors, including rectors, vice-rectors, deans, directors of teaching and learning centers, as well as distance education centers, rendering our group a truly exceptional gathering, "a special purpose boutique group."

In alignment with our commitment to fostering knowledge dissemination and intellectual growth, I have inaugurated the academic YÖMEGA Speech Series. This engaging series encompasses a carefully curated selection of talks, encompassing an array of specialized themes, presented by distinguished guest speakers. These insightful discussions, meticulously alternating between local and international luminaries and speakers, held twice a month at intervals of fifteen days. Each session commences with a 30-minute presentation on Zoom, delivered by our esteemed speaker, followed by a vibrant exchange of questions and discussions.

Having meticulously examined your pioneering work and profound areas of expertise, I am truly impressed. It is with great anticipation that I reach out to you, extending an invitation to grace our YÖMEGA audience as a distinguished guest speaker. Your invaluable experiences are poised to ignite a captivating discourse and catalyze a profound knowledge exchange. Should you choose to accept our invitation, we invite you to present a talk centered around faculty development, accentuating the focal points that resonate with your field of expertise.

Your contribution to our YÖMEGA community would undoubtedly enrich our collective intellectual fabric, and your insights have the potential to inspire and resonate deeply with our audience. We are earnestly hopeful that you will consider this invitation and honor us with your presence as a featured speaker.

The organized boutique events (virtual talks/workshops/panels) on Zoom convene network members and facilitate discussion of local and global issues of importance to faculty members and to higher education as a whole. After the events, video recordings are uploaded to the YÖMEGA YouTube channel, accessible to network members. Guests join for approximately 60 minutes; 30 minutes are allotted for topic presentation, followed by Q&A, general discussion, and concluding remarks.

Each YÖMEGA Talks Series has had ten guest speakers. To date, of the fifty invited speakers, 50% were from Türkiye, 50% were from abroad, and all six panelists were from Türkiye. Sixty-two percent of the speakers were women, and 38% of them were men.

Based on the YÖMEGA invited talks between 2020 and 2023, a comprehensive deliverable has resulted from the Talk Series, an edited volume featuring twenty-seven chapters authored by thirty local and global authors along with two forewords by distinguished authors of educational development. The chapters are in both Turkish and English. This volume, *Professional Development of Faculty Members During- and Post-Crisis State*, is the first book published on FPD in Türkiye (Elçi, 2023).

Lessons Learned

Our main aim in establishing YÖMEGA was to convene a collaborative network of TLCs to foster knowledge exchange and achievement sharing. While most of the faculty developers became members of YÖMEGA, there was not adequate communication via the network for members to share their own activities, programs, or experiences. The executive board realized the need to foster a more active FPD initiative via the YÖMEGA Talks Series. In the process of engaging in this work, we learned several important lessons.

Early in the series, reputable faculty development academics/developers were chosen by YÖMEGA as speakers. Later, a needs analysis assessment led to an opportunity for YÖMEGA members to also serve as invited speakers, allowing members to share their expertise with each other. The needs assessment was critical to identifying topics of interest, which guided speaker engagement. The selected topics to date have been closely connected with members' interests, thus encouraging deep reflection and engagement. Table 12.1 summarizes the topics of interest identified by YÖMEGA membership. All but one of the topics have been featured in the invited speaker series as of the writing of this chapter.

Despite the successes realized to date, there have been several challenges. First, a lack of participation has resulted in limited interaction between members and the invited speaker. While members appreciate the

Table 12.1 YÖMEGA Members Needs Analysis

Category	Topics of Interest	Frequency
Planning of Teaching and Learning Process		
	Current trends in higher education	73%
TLC Support Services		
	Organizing activity programs for faculty members	67%
	Efficient faculty mentoring	67%
Using Digital Technologies		
	Teaching online classes	67%
	Teaching practical and lab work	67%
Teaching and Learning Models		
	Online teaching and learning	67%
General Interest Areas		
	Teaching strategies to cope with the teaching and learning needs of new generations	67%
Enhancing Students' Learning		
	Student engagement strategies	60%
Supporting Students' Learning		
	Enhancement of critical thinking	64%
Evaluation and Assessment		
	Learning analytics	64%
Psycho-Social Support Programs		
	Protecting the personal and professional health of faculty members while teaching online	50%

boutique-style events, strategies to increase engagement include introducing a buddy system for junior faculty members, an orientation workshop for new members, and increased role modeling and mentorship (Steinert et al., 2010).

At its founding, YÖMEGA was established as a non-profit network that relies heavily on volunteers to carry the considerable workload. As YÖMEGA grows, professional staff and funding sources will be needed. Hence, YÖMEGA is looking forward to being registered as a non-profit organization.

Conclusion

YÖMEGA seeks to support faculty members and guide policymakers in a national or regional context using the prior experiences of global researchers. The number of supporting centers is expected to increase, and FPD will be a means to an end. YÖMEGA is a non-formal FPD initiative, an alternative to formal FPD, that has allowed its founders and members to foster a supportive network.

The activities undertaken by YÖMEGA aim to enable the skill development of members across various dimensions of faculty development. YÖMEGA is proud that distinguished speakers from abroad and agencies of higher education governing bodies and policymakers in Türkiye (e.g., Higher Education Council [HEC-YÖK], Turkish Higher Education Quality Council [THEQC-YÖKAK], and the Scientific and Technological Research Council of Türkiye [TÜBİTAK]) have contributed to its success to date. The YÖMEGA network is proud to be involved in educational development on a national basis, contributing to faculty members' development personally and professionally.

The authors would like to conclude by mentioning their appreciation to the YÖMEGA board, the invited speakers, the attendee faculty members, and the supporting professors and officials that have facilitated the sustainability of the network.

References

Buckley, H., & Nimmon, L. (2020). Learning in faculty development: The role of social networks. *Academic Medicine*, 95(11S), S20–S27, https://doi.org/10.1097/ACM.0000000000003627

Dali, K., Bell, N., & Valdes, Z. (2021). Learning and change through diversity, equity, and inclusion professional development: Academic librarians' perspectives. *The Journal of Academic Librarianship*, 47(6), 102448. https://doi.org/10.1016/j.acalib.2021.102448

Devran, B. Ç., & Elçi, A. (2020). Traditional versus digital assessment methods: Faculty development. In E. A. Railean (Ed.), *Assessment, testing, and measurement*

strategies in global higher education (pp. 20–34). IGI Global. https://doi.
org/10.4018/978-1-7998-2314-8.ch002

EDUCAUSE. (2023, May 24). *About EDUCAUSE*. www.educause.edu/

Elçi, A. (2021a). Using social media to support online teaching and learning. In M.
Kurt & F. Altınay (Eds.), *Narratives on online education* (pp. 103–109). Pegem
Akademi. www.academia.edu/45155401/Narratives_on_Online_Education

Elçi, A. (2021b). Academics' professional development needs and gains during
COVID-19 distance education emergency transition in Türkiye. *International
Journal of Curriculum and Instruction, 13*(1), 343–358. https://eric.ed.gov/?
id=EJ1285540

Elçi, A. (Ed.). (2023). *Professional development of faculty members during- and
post-crisis state*. Atatürk Üniversitesi Yayınevi. https://ekitap.atauni.edu.tr/index.
php/product/ogretim-elemanlarinin-kriz-sirasi-ve-sonrasinda-mesleki-gelisimi/

Elçi, A., & Abubakar, A.M. (2021). The configurational effects of task-technology
fit, technology-induced engagement and motivation on learning performance
during Covid-19 pandemic: An fsQCA approach. *Education and Information
Technologies, 26*, 7259–7277. https://doi.org/10.1007/s10639-021-10580-6

Elçi, A., Abubakar, A.M., Özgül, N., Vural, M., & Akdeniz, T. (2017, Şubat 4–11).
Öğretim elemanlarının teknoloji ile zenginleştirilmiş öğrenme ortamlarını etkin
kullanımı: Uygulamalı Çalıştay. In *Akademik Bilişim (AB '17)* (pp. 127–130).
https://ab.org.tr/kitap/ab17.pdf

Elçi, A., Yaratan, H., & Abubakar, A. M. (2020). Multidimensional faculty professional development in teaching and learning: Utilizing technology for supporting
students. *International Journal of Technology-Enabled Student Support Services
(IJTESSS), 10*(1), 21–39. http://doi.org/10.4018/IJTESSS.2020010102

Haleem, A., Javaid, M., Mohd Asim Qadri, M. A., & Suman, R. (2022). Understanding the role of digital technologies in education: A review. *Sustainable Operations and Computers, 3*, 275–285. https://doi.org/10.1016/j.susoc.2022.05.004

Haranaka, L. (2018, October 15). *21st Century skills for teachers*. www.rich-
mondshare.com.br/21st-century-skills-for-teachers/

Hase, S., & Kenyon, C. (2000, December). From andragogy to heutagogy. In *ulti-
BASE In-Site*. RMIT.

ICED (2023, May 24). *The international consortium for educational development*.
https://icedonline.net/

Kara, N., Çubukçuoğlu, B., & Elçi, A. (2020). Using social media to support
teaching and learning in higher education: An analysis of personal narratives.
Research in Learning Technology, 28. https://doi.org/10.25304/rlt.v28.2410

Lawler, P. A., & King, K. P. (2000). Refocusing faculty development: The view
from an adult learning perspective. *Adult Education Research Conference*.
http://newprairiepress.org/aerc/2000/papers/4

Ng, D. T. K., Leung, J. K. L., Su, J., Ng, R. C. W., & Chu, S. K. W. (2023). Teachers' AI digital competencies and twenty-first century skills in the post-pandemic
world. *Educational Technology Research and Development, 71*, 137–161.
https://doi.org/10.1007/s11423-023-10203-6

OECD. (2018). *The future of education and skills: OECD learning framework
2030. E2030 Position Paper (05.04.2018).pdf*. oecd.org

OECD. (2021). *The state of higher education: One year into the COVID-19 pandemic*. OECD Publishing. https://doi.org/10.1787/83c41957-en

Oguz, F., Marsh, C. V., & Landis, C. (2010). Collaboration through communities of practice in the digital age. In S. Kurbanoğlu, U. Lepon, P. Erdoğan, Y. Tonta, & N. Uçak, (Eds.), *Technological convergence and social networks in information management. IMCW 2010. Communications in Computer and Information Science, 96*. Springer. https://doi.org/10.1007/978-3-642-16032-5_3

Patrick, W. (2010). *Recognising non-formal and informal learning outcomes, policies and practices: Outcomes, policies and practices* (Vol. 2009, No. 35). OECD Publishing.

POD Network. (2023). *The professional and organizational development (POD) network in higher education*. https://podnetwork.org/

Steinert, Y., Macdonald, M. E., Boillat, M., Elizov, M., Meterissian, S., Razack, S., Ouellet, M. N., & McLeod, P. J. (2010). Faculty development: If you build it, they will come. *Medical Education, 44*(9), 900–907. https://doi.org/10.1111/j.1365-2923.2010.03746.x

UN. (2022, September 16, 17, and 19). *Transforming education, building our future. Transforming education summit*. United Nations. www.un.org/en/transforming-education-summit.

UNESCO. (2003, January 23). *UNESCO education in situations of emergency, crisis and reconstruction: UNESCO strategy* (Working Paper). Division of Policies and Strategies of Education Support to Countries in Crisis and Reconstruction. https://tinyurl.com/2bkafkfx

UNESCO. (2021, January 10). *The state of the global education crisis: A path to recovery. A joint UNESCO, UNICEF, and World Bank Report*. https://tinyurl.com/2p9jzdcw

Chapter 13

Data-Informed Community College Teaching and Learning Hubs in North Carolina

Monique N. Colclough and Sarah A. Deal

Overview

The Belk Center for Community College Leadership and Research holds the annual W. Dallas Herring Lecture, which invites national community college leaders to address emerging and urgent topics in post-secondary education – framing the issue, response, and trajectory for transformational change at community colleges in support of equitable student success. At the 2018 lecture, Dr. Karen Stout, CEO of Achieving the Dream, argued that accomplishing the community college mission of student success could not occur without transformational change through a strategic investment in faculty professional development/professional learning for teaching and learning excellence. Stout identified five components to the investment:

- Introduce and cultivate reflective practice among faculty
- Position centers for teaching and learning and/or teaching and learning centers as a bedrock of college operations/structure
- Honor the diverse experiences and identities of college faculty
- Intentionally and meaningfully seek out investment in adjunct and/or part-time faculty
- Identify teaching and learning investments as central to student readiness/student-centeredness

In response to the 2018 Dallas Herring Lecture, the Belk Center began exploring opportunities for North Carolina's community colleges to collectively work to transform its collaborative efforts for student success outcomes through investments in faculty professional development. This work began with a six-college comprehensive evaluative case study that explored existing teaching and learning work, institutional capacity, and opportunities for statewide faculty development. The six institutions – Durham Technical Community College, Lenoir Community College, Catawba Valley Community College, Wilkes Community College,

DOI: 10.4324/9781003428626-17

Forsyth Technical Community College, and Central Carolina Community College – were selected for geographical diversity, institution size, history with faculty professional development initiatives, and ratio of part-time to full-time faculty.

This chapter features the work pursued through the Belk Center that involved more than 200 full- and part-time community college faculty and staff educators participating in professional development to increase opportunities for educators to implement responsive teaching and advising strategies. The aim of this chapter is to share how the Hubs, led by faculty codirectors, respond to faculty and staff educator requests for faculty-led learning communities of practice and evidence-based, high-impact teaching and advising practices that have been associated with increased equitable student success outcomes.

Program Focus

The Hubs' initial strategy was guided by conversations with more than 200 college faculty staff and administrators, 130 of which were faculty in curriculum and career and technical education (CTE). These conversations revealed six thematic areas of opportunity for faculty and staff engaged in teaching and learning work: (1) culture; (2) leadership; (3) communication; (4) professional development examples; (5) professional development recommendations; and (6) ideal items, like cohort-based professional development for faculty leading work on their campuses; prioritization of course-planning release time; physical campus workspace; and financial support for adjunct faculty professional development. For the purposes of this chapter, we highlight two specific takeaways that furthered the foundation for the development of the North Carolina Teaching and Learning Hubs model: (1) the role and value of faculty is clear and (2) clearly articulated connections among teaching and learning initiatives and existing community college strategic plans are necessary for student success.

The investment in connecting community college strategic plans affirmed the need to understand the comprehensive needs of North Carolina's community college faculty and chief academic officers (CAOs). To further our shared mission of fostering student success across North Carolina, Achieving the Dream and the North Carolina Student Success Center, the latter which is housed within the North Carolina Community College System (NCCCS), joined the Belk Center, drawing on state and national expertise. Project partners introduced a faculty needs self-assessment instrument, which mapped to Achieving the Dream's Four Cornerstone Framework (Eynon & Iuzzini, 2020), for building a culture of teaching and learning excellence and a professional learning assessment instrument for CAOs. This instrument was distributed throughout the NCCCS to all faculty and

CAOs during the 2020–2021 academic year, in partnership with the NCC-CS's Student Success Center, Achieving the Dream, and evaluation team DVP-PRAXIS.

Important findings from this self-assessment included the fact that, among the CAOs, fewer than 45% reported having at least one full-time staff member leading their community college's teaching and learning work, while just over a third support their college's teaching and learning work through faculty release time. The North Carolina Teaching and Learning Hubs were created to build this needed capacity and facilitate connections and support faculty through a comprehensive statewide framework.

Aligned with the focus of this volume, mid-career faculty were the primary audience for and participants in the Teaching and Learning Hubs. As illustrated in Figure 13.1, more than 70% of faculty participating in the Hubs during the inaugural year had over six years of teaching experience (Deal et al., 2023). Hub codirectors – who are peer leaders in professional learning and also mid-career faculty – hypothesized that newer faculty are focused on learning how to prepare their classes and how to do administrative tasks related to a new position. Mid-career faculty may be better positioned to understand what they need to do to improve their teaching and are ready to take advantage of opportunities offered by the Hubs. Colleges also often provide supplemental professional learning for new faculty during employee onboarding.

The first two Hubs were launched in fall 2021. The East Hub, cohosted by Lenoir and Carteret Community Colleges, and the West Hub, cohosted by Catawba Valley and Wilkes Community Colleges, began offering professional learning that reached 522 unique NCCCS employees through 44 Hub-offered opportunities in their inaugural year (Deal et al., 2023). Importantly, the Hubs reached faculty and staff educators at more than half of the state's community colleges. North Carolina's community colleges, like those in many states, are a diverse set of institutions and provide higher education and industry training for the state's most disadvantaged

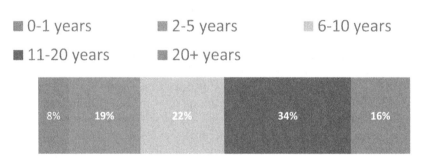

Figure 13.1 Years of Teaching Experience, HUB Faculty

students, including low-income, adult, and minoritized students who may benefit the most from obtaining these credentials (Edgecombe, 2022). While community colleges serve these populations of students, they receive less funding per student, making the Hub-offered supplemental support for teaching and learning a critical investment in equitable student success (Edgecombe, 2022). In fall 2022, the remaining two Hubs launched – the Central Hub, cohosted by Durham Technical and Central Carolina Community Colleges, and the Piedmont Hub, cohosted by Forsyth Technical and Davidson-Davie Community Colleges – and the combined Hubs are now supporting all of North Carolina's community colleges.

Needed Skills

The Hubs provided needed skills for mid-career faculty. In focus groups with faculty, they pointed to personal growth and internal motivation as the primary factors for participating in the Teaching and Learning Hubs (Deal et al. , 2021). These faculty members want to innovate to better support student learning. Having the Hubs to support faculty is particularly important because community college faculty are usually subject matter experts in their fields of study but often have fewer classroom management skills and less knowledge about strategies for being an engaging teacher, designing transparent assignments, and using active learning techniques. Faculty across various roles and disciplines described participating in professional learning as important because it allows them to learn these classroom management and teaching skills to better serve their students (Deal et al., 2021). One faculty member said, "[My reasons for participating in professional learning have] been my own internal motivation. If I didn't have my own motivation, I wouldn't be as effective of a teacher and I think I would be doing my students a disservice by putting me in a classroom without any teaching skills. We also have many low-income students, and through professional learning, I can better understand what supports are available." The Hubs provide professional learning opportunities about specific, in-depth topics that include actionable, practical guidance and support for implementing the new, needed skills.

Rationale

The NCCCS is the third-largest community college system in the country, serving more than 500,000 students throughout the state annually. The system's 58 community colleges are located across 100 counties, from urban and more resourced areas in the Raleigh and Charlotte regions to rural and economically distressed communities ranging from the mountains to the coast (NCCCS, 2022). In 2022, North Carolina was ranked as America's top state for business, yet despite opportunities for economic growth and mobility, there is a gap in the number of workers available to fill jobs (MyFutureNC, 2023). In the years ahead, community colleges will continue to play a vital role in reskilling and upskilling members of the workforce (awarding short-term credentials and degrees) to close the gap between the number of available workers and the number of jobs. For community colleges to best serve their students, support is needed for teaching and learning in classrooms, where students spend the majority of their time, and where underfunded community colleges are least likely to have resources to invest. As outlined by Jaeger (2017) in Figure 13.2 the inclusion of teaching and learning excellence, strategies and scholarship is critical in the faculty pathway to excellence.

The Teaching and Learning Hubs were conceptualized for two purposes: first, to deliver evidence-based professional learning directly to faculty and staff educators across North Carolina, and second, to provide support for building capacity in colleges' own teaching and learning centers, where supplemental support is a critical investment in equitable student success. By taking this statewide approach, the Hubs' reach, where educators and students are concerned, is exponential. In their inaugural year (2021–2022), the East and West Hubs reached 279 faculty and staff instructors, who taught 2,411 courses, ultimately reaching 20,922 students (Deal et al., 2023).

Figure 13.2 Faculty Pathway to Excellence

Equity and Inclusion Considerations

As aligned with the Hubs' focus on equitable student success, Hubs reached 37 instructors of color who taught 312 courses with 2,888 students enrolled. This metric is significant, given that instructors of color are more likely to be new faculty, to teach in continuing education departments, and to be in career and technical programs with a higher population of adult students, students of color, and Pell recipients (Deal et al., 2023). These data point to opportunities for the Hubs to provide needed support to instructors and students who stand to benefit the most and where equitable student success can be achieved.

Hub codirectors have strategically designed professional learning to provide this support for equitable student success. For example, in 2021–2022, opportunities targeting diversity, equity, and inclusion included Equitizing the Syllabus; West Hub Café Active Learning; Asynchronous Course; Going Virtual: Creating Engaging Classes Students Will Love; and Before the First Day Matters Series: Cultivating Regular and Substantive Interactions in Distance Education. In 2022–2023, opportunities included Syllabus Revision: Rethinking our Language, Tone, and Policies; Applying the TILT Framework (Transparency in Learning and Teaching) Tiered Feedback; and QPR – Questions, Persuade, Refer Suicide Prevention, Holistic Student Supports for Faculty and Staff.

Conceptual Grounding

In academic year 2020–2021, full-time and adjunct faculty within the NCCCS were invited to share their interests and experiences around teaching, learning, and faculty professional development using an instrument that maps to Achieving the Dream's framework for building a college culture of teaching and learning (Eynon & Iuzzini, 2020).

Achieving the Dream's framework is a four-point Cornerstone of Excellence that encourages (1) investment in full- and part-time faculty use of evidence-based teaching practices for student learning, (2) cross-college collaboration that links faculty and student services to catalyze student learning and success, (3) opportunities for educators and students to experience active learning in accessible and affirming spaces, and (4) institutions that support faculty and staff educator professional development in practice, policy, and resources.

As outlined in Table 13.1, college-level support after the integration of new instructional approaches decreases for faculty with 6 to 15 years of experience. Faculty in the 16+ year group report increases in support thereafter. For full-time faculty, declines in levels of agreement in the 11- to 15-year group are present, with an increase among more seasoned faculty. This trend persists for part-time faculty, though overall, part-time faculty agree less

Table 13.1 % Agree/Strongly Agree

	< 5 years	6–10 years	11–15 years	16–20 years	> 20 years
Full-time Faculty	58%	55%	46%	54%	55%
Part-time Faculty	55%	48%	45%	49%	45%

than full-time faculty that they have substantial or adequate knowledge of best practices. The report also showed that an area for improvement is colleges providing follow-up support as new instructional approaches are tried.

Tool

Development of Hub Strategy

The four Teaching and Learning Hubs are led by eight faculty codirectors, employed by their respective North Carolina community colleges. Each codirector receives a 50% course release to lead the planning, coordinating, and contextualizing of professional learning activities in each Hub. The codirectors collectively assess faculty professional learning needs in close communication with faculty from the Hubs and with support from the Belk Center, Achieving the Dream, and the North Carolina Student Success Center. Hubs codirectors design and implement effective professional learning practices that support excellence in teaching as well as faculty and staff educator development, which requires that the codirectors engage in comprehensive onboarding and professional learning of their own.

The investment in the Hubs codirectors began with an eight-part summer intensive planning series, which was led by Achieving the Dream in 2021, prior to the East and West Hubs launch. During the series, the codirectors used the Achieving the Dream Teaching and Learning Toolkit (2020) and the American Council on Education (ACE) and POD Network A Center for Teaching and Learning Matrix (Collins-Brown et al., 2018) to identify the purpose of, components of, and national examples of transformational change through professional learning. These tools were used to guide the codirectors in the following areas:

- Short- and long-term goals for Hub development and growth
- Program building – in collaboration with the North Carolina Student Success Center – in response to direct faculty requests from community colleges within each Teaching and Learning Hub, and in pursuit of capacity-building opportunities
- Communication with constituents and college stakeholders
- Operating structures within the Hub

Figure 13.3 Teaching & Learning Hub Co-Director Manual

This professional learning for codirectors was codified in the North Carolina Teaching and Learning Hub Manual (Figure 13.3).

Strategic support for the eight faculty codirectors, averaging 17 years of teaching experience and reflecting mid-career faculty across disciplines, is ongoing; in the inaugural year, support included monthly coaching, planning and strategy sessions for each pair of Hub codirectors, access to professional development resources through North Carolina State University, and monthly meetings to inform the infrastructure of the teaching and learning work.

- Monthly coaching: Topics addressed in these sessions with the NC Student Success Center, the Belk Center, and Achieving the Dream included outreach to peer professional learning leaders at affiliate colleges within each Hub, leveraging the Teaching & Learning toolkit to sustain a college culture of teaching and learning excellence, and using the registration platform to capture relevant participant data and session feedback to be married with the evaluation plan efforts.
- Planning and strategy sessions: Eight sessions were supported and held during the codirectors' onboarding experience, in partnership with Achieving the Dream. The topics addressed included reflecting on the Good Practice Principles from the Teaching & Learning Toolkit, drafting plans for the professional learning offerings for the academic year, and identifying shared work and communications within the Hub as a codirector.
- Professional development resources: Initially offered virtually, because the Hubs were launched during the COVID-19 pandemic, the

codirectors' resources included the Equity in Teaching & Learning Institute led by Achieving the Dream; Dr. Amy Climer's Classroom to Zoom Room, facilitated by the NC Student Success Center; and the ITLC Lilly Online conference. Professional development for the codirectors also incorporated several national resources, including Virginia Tech's Conference on Higher Education Pedagogy.

• Monthly meetings: Led by the Belk Center, these meetings aimed to solidify the infrastructure of the Hubs' work with emphases on communication, best practices for collaboration, and integrating stakeholder feedback.

Codirectors and their community college stakeholders, namely CAOs, also participated in national conferences delivered by the POD Network, ITLC Lilly Online Conference, and professional learning through the Office of Faculty Excellence at NC State. After the inaugural year, codirectors also had opportunities to present at national conferences, including DREAM 2023, hosted by Achieving the Dream, and the 2023 Innovations Conference, hosted by the League for Innovation in the Community College. The Belk Center also convened with community college stakeholders several times throughout the academic year to continue informing the framework for the statewide model.

In spring 2022, faculty participants, who were interviewed during focus groups, shared positive reflections on the opportunities provided by the East and West Hubs, particularly on how they heard about the professional learning activities, the diversity of topics addressed, and the opportunities to connect with other faculty. During the Hubs' second year, the codirectors leveraged feedback with emphases on three areas: (1) that there is a need for additional professional learning that is specific, in-depth, and grounded in practical actionable guidance; (2) that faculty are most likely to implement classroom changes when their learning environment is supportive, engaging, and easy to process; and (3) that faculty are eager to share what they learn with their peers.

Lessons Learned

As with any large-scale initiative that involves diverse stakeholders, this work resulted in critical lessons learned. As we share those lessons and insights, our hope is that the knowledge gleaned provides a road map for others interested in harnessing the power of learning hubs and cross-institution collaborations.

First, the registration numbers shed light on the readiness of faculty and staff educators engaging in a statewide professional learning model, on the malleable and strategic collaboration among North Carolina's partners, and on the impact that catalyzing faculty and staff educators can have on student success. For others interested in scaling student success initiatives, it is critical to remember that students spend the majority of time on community college campuses in the classroom; therefore, the greatest mechanism for impacting students is faculty. The Hubs provide state-level support for high-quality, evidence-based professional learning that many smaller, more rural, and less-well-resourced colleges would not have access to otherwise. By providing this professional learning, the Hubs can increase student reach exponentially. For example, in the inaugural year, when just two of four Hubs were piloting this new statewide model for professional learning, 279 faculty participated in professional learning, and those faculty reached more than 20,000 students through their classes. As the Hubs evolve and expand, the impact on students through faculty will scale substantially, and this level of scale is difficult to reach if not through statewide support.

Second, virtual, in-person, and hybrid formats revealed opportunities for responsive and reflexive professional learning. Unpacking best practices in general, and with an emphasis on instructional challenges that the COVID-19 pandemic initially presented, was critical, as was a focus on post-pandemic recovery challenges, like holistic support for students navigating career and economic changes. Lessons learned include the need to flexibly organize professional learning opportunities that are accessible for full-time and part-time adjunct faculty's teaching schedules, redesigning opportunities with shorter run times to address scheduling and virtual learning–delivery fatigue.

There is still much to be learned about the impact of institutional and system changes in leadership and overall institutional capacity within a statewide framework. There is even more to be learned about the impact of enrollment shifts and budget changes on investment in faculty and staff retention and, by default, the capacity to engage in meaningful and sustainable professional learning. Logistically, the greatest lesson learned by far is the critical nature of communication within and across institutional faculty, staff educators, and leadership stakeholder groups. Institutional leaders are often tasked with connecting institutional expectations – student success metrics and strategic plans to the statewide framework designed to complement existing institutional efforts. Providing them support to make these connections is critical to the success and sustainability of the Hubs and their ability to positively influence student success.

Conclusion

Supporting faculty with evidence-based professional learning is one strategy to achieve transformational change for student success the mission of community colleges. The North Carolina Teaching and Learning Hubs were developed from a desire to support equitable and scalable student success, centering faculty expertise and reflective practice. In North Carolina, the Hubs create a community for colleges of diverse size, geographical location, and resources, driving collaboration with nearby affiliate colleges through the sharing of ideas and strategies. For mid-career faculty who are looking to better support students through enhanced classroom management and teaching strategies, the Hubs provide actionable and relevant content and support. Mid-career faculty are the primary participants in the Teaching and Learning Hubs because they have identified what they need to grow their practice and are internally motivated to do so. The first model of its kind, the Hubs can provide other states and community college systems with a blueprint for supporting equitable student success through the statewide provision of faculty professional learning.

References

Collins-Brown, E., Haras, C., Hurney, C. Iuzzini, J., Magruder, E., Sorcinelli, M., Taylor, S., & Wright, M. (2018). *A center for teaching and learning matrix.* https://podnetwork.org/resources/center-for-teaching-and-learning-matrix/

Deal, S. A., Valentine, J. L., & Price, D. V. (2021). *North Carolina faculty experiences with professional development: Formative feedback memo to inform community college teaching and learning hubs.* DVP-PRAXIS LTD.

Deal, S. A., Valentine, J. L., & Price, D. V. (2023). *The reach of the North Carolina teaching and learning hubs: An inaugural year report.* DVP-PRAXIS LTD.

Edgecombe, N. (2022). *Public funding of community colleges: Policy fact sheet.* Community College Research Center, Teachers College Columbia University.

Eynon, B., & Iuzzini, J. (2020). *ATD teaching and learning toolkit: A research-based guide to building a culture of teaching and learning excellence.* https://achievingthedream.org/teaching-learning-toolkit/

Jaeger, A. J. (2017, September). *Focus on faculty: Loss momentum and the faculty role.* Invited Keynote for Completion by Design North Carolina.

MyFutureNC. (2023). *The state of educational attainment.* www.myfuturenc.org/ourwork/the-state-of-educational-attainment/

NCCCS Dashboards. (2022). *Total headcount: NC Community Colleges.* www.nccommunitycolleges.edu/analytics/dashboards/total-headcount

Chapter 14

Fostering a Mid-Career Community

A Workshop for Personal Focus and Academic Advancement

Chris Heasley and Vicki L. Baker

Overview

In his article "Facing Your Mid-Career Crisis," Setiya (2019) described his mindset as a mid-career faculty member who had a job "doing what I loved" (para 1). Yet he found himself in a cycle of successively completing and replacing projects in a rote manner in what he characterized as a mid-life crisis. His experience, and those of his mid-career faculty peers, caused him to pose a very powerful question: "When is mid-career malaise a signal to change course, as opposed to changing how you think and feel?" (para 24). We argue that in order to answer this question, mid-career faculty need support to engage in intentional career planning and reflection (Baker & Boland, 2023).

The literature is clear: the mid-career stage is challenging, often characterized by expanded roles and responsibilities, often with little (to no) support to meet associated expectations (Baker & Manning, 2021). Simultaneously, mid-career is a time in which opportunities abound to re-envision the next stage; faculty find themselves staring down the question of what's next and how to be more intentional with charting a path forward (Baker, 2020). Although we do not argue all tools or strategies from the business world are applicable in the academy, we do believe a Strengths, Weaknesses, Opportunities, and Threats (SWOT) analysis is particularly apropos for aiding faculty who seek to establish a career road map, one aimed at identifying opportunities for growth and scholarly learning (Baker, 2020; Heasley, 2021, 2022).

In this chapter, we feature a SWOT analysis tool and corresponding reflection prompts from a session featured in the Mid-Career Faculty Workshop and supported by the Association for the Study of Higher Education (ASHE), specifically the Council for the Advancement of Higher Education Programs (CAHEP). In using this tool, mid-career faculty are given an opportunity to discern their past progress and their future aspirations and to determine how they might best navigate their careers.

DOI: 10.4324/9781003428626-18

Program Focus

ASHE is a US-based professional association dedicated to the field of higher education. At present, there are more than 2,100 members, including masters and doctoral students and faculty members as well as practitioners who work in non-university settings, such as governmental agencies, think tanks, and advocacy organizations. For nearly 50 years, ASHE has been a steady presence in higher education through its annual conference, professional development, and contributions to scholarship and practice (Renn, 2020).

The organizational structure of ASHE includes four councils (as of 2019): the Council for the Advancement of Higher Education Programs (CAHEP), the Council for Ethnic Participation, the Council for International Higher Education, and the Council for Public Policy in Higher Education. Through these councils, fundraising, advocacy work, and contributions to the field are realized. Members of ASHE are able to join councils that align with their scholarly and/or practical interests.

CAHEP is home to the mid-career faculty workshop. Originally conceived as a symposium session offered during the pre-conference program in 2018 and 2019, the workshop consisted of a panel of scholar-practitioners focused on the challenges and opportunities faced by mid-career faculty across the academy. Based on interest among CAHEP (and ASHE) members, the decision was made to re-envision the symposium as a pre-conference workshop. The second author of this chapter was nominated and voted in as the first chair of the Mid-Career Faculty Workshop for a three-year term. Several individuals from the original symposiums serve as panelists presently (and are contributors to this volume). The decision to create a workshop focused on mid-career faculty, coupled with a formal leadership position charged with executing the workshop's vision, aligns with ASHE's overall mission to be more intentional about developing members and creating community around critical issues and career stages.

Needed Skills

As mid-career faculty advance in their careers, their need for support and guidance also continues. Yet many lack the tools or strategies to engage in intentional career planning that acknowledges personal and professional career-stage realities. Broadly speaking, our experiences with mid-career faculty reveal that they wrestle with putting thought into and action behind next steps. Additionally, mid-career faculty need support in developing skills that enable them to be more intentional in identifying and understanding their strengths, available resources, and assets. Finally, mid-career faculty need space in which they can be honest about the barriers preventing forward movement toward their personal and academic goals.

To ensure we are meeting the needs of workshop attendees, we administer a pre-workshop survey that includes three prompts:

1. What are your goals/reasons for attending this workshop?
2. What do you hope to gain by participating?
3. My time attending will be worth it if [fill in the blank].

Responses were shared with all panelists as workshop organizers and presenters worked to meet the needs of those registered for the workshop. "I don't know what I need, I just need help and guidance"; "help defining goals other than earning full professor"; "resetting expectations; mentoring for the next steps"; and "honestly, I'm not sure!" are just a few of the comments we received from the workshop's 2023 participants.

Rationale

Although the earning of tenure and promotion, in a system where tenure is present, is one measure of subject matter expertise and competence in one's respective disciplinary field, the need for continued mentoring, professional development, and opportunities for growth and learning do not stop once this milestone is achieved. We agree with Texter and Terrion (2022), who note there are fewer opportunities and resources allocated to support mid-career faculty: resources that are necessary to overcome the obstacles that accompany this career stage. Many mid-career faculty members are unsure of what help they need to move beyond this state of malaise.

Faculty across the academy continue to feel the strain of the global pandemic, and yet such hardships are particularly challenging for mid-career faculty members, who experience disruptions to their scholarly and creative agendas. Others' challenges relate to leadership roles and the need to support peers along their career journey, often at the expense of their own personal health and well-being. SWOT analysis provides these faculty members with a self-reflective experience through which they can develop a strategy to navigate their mid-career journey.

Equity and Inclusion Considerations

Inclusive participant engagement and learning is given intentional consideration in this chapter. Herein, equity and inclusion are met in two ways: through reflective practice and inclusive pedagogy.

Reflective practice, or deep contemplation with regard to thoughts, actions, and behaviors, provides an open framework for learning and exploration. Self-knowledge, a model that brings self and reflection into focus, is a useful practice in moments where "leaders attempt to uncover their vocation of life" (Dufresne et al., 2015, p. 11). Purposely, SWOT analysis and the accompanying exercise described in this chapter allow participants to authentically discern their lived experiences: the personal narratives of their aspirations and their desired career trajectory. A practice of self-knowledge promotes personal accountability, fosters better decision making, and assists in validating suppositions (Callahan, 2013). SWOT also centers DEI work, as participant responses vary based on one's relation to structures of power (e.g., race, gender, SES, etc.). Advantageously, no prerequisites or prior learning are required for full participation. All one needs is time, an open mind, and permission to practice self-reflection.

Inclusive pedagogy provides for equitable and inclusive practices (Hogan & Sathy, 2022). Presenters of SWOT must be cognizant of the audience's physical needs to ensure successful facilitation. We call for intentionally considering the modality of the session and, in accordance, crafting appropriate presentation materials that provide various access points to the content. Auditory learners appreciate questions read aloud, visual learners benefit from reading activity prompts via a handout or PowerPoint slide deck, and kinesthetic learners prefer participation through experiences in actively solving problems. Multi-sensory learning opportunities can be offered in facilitating a SWOT analysis. Whether working on SWOT in a place-based location or in a synchronous online environment, care should be given to ensuring inclusivity of the learning space. Several of the aforementioned considerations can be present in both modalities; however, an online setting may also allow for voice-to-text transcription for hearing-compromised participants. Use of inclusive pedagogical practices ensures that all participants can actively engage with planned learning objectives (Hogan & Sathy, 2022).

Conceptual Grounding

The SWOT analysis and its application in the field of business dates back several decades (Puyt et al., 2023). Today, SWOT analysis is an activity employing a logical chain of reasoning to establish organizational goals. As complex organizations, institutions of higher education utilize goal setting to ensure future growth and success. But developing goals requires intentional focus when working within large structures. Hence, strategic planning is often the vehicle used to create alignment between institutional mission, vision, and goal development (Bryson, 2011; Heasley & Palestini, 2023).

Several strategic planning models exist to assist organizations in drafting their future objectives. Typically, an early step in plan development includes a data-informed assessment of the current state of the organization (Sherlock, 2009). Contemporary practice often centers data-collection efforts in SWOT analysis. As an assessment tool, a SWOT analysis encourages stakeholders to be both reflective about institutional capacity and knowledgeable about environmental considerations (Middaugh, 2010; Sanaghan, 2009). Giving a nod to the intentions of this chapter, a SWOT analysis can be applied beyond its original purpose for organizational planning – but even so, its data collection process remains fairly unchanged.

Explorations of the aforementioned conditions are done through a scripted sequence of guided questions. Here, stakeholders are asked to consider the strengths of the organization in responding to *what makes the organization's work unique among a field of contemporaries?* Exploration of organizational strengths leads to reflection on institutional weaknesses in contemplating *what attributes warrant additional attention, resources, and focus.* After developing an internal profile for the institution, focus is directed to external opportunities in considering *what trends or conditions may positively impact the organization?* In the last phase of SWOT analysis, stakeholders deliberate on organizational threats. This work is guided by answering *what trends or conditions may be negatively impactful to the institution's future?*

As diverse pathways for mid-career faculty are envisioned, we argue a SWOT analysis is a practical, self-reflective tool aiding personal goal setting. With slight modifications in guided questions, a shift from organizational focus to a focus on individual needs can be realized. For example, we can refocus strengths by discerning *what makes a faculty member's teaching, service, scholarship, and/or leadership unique and contributory in their field, department, college, or among scholarly peers?* Such nuanced adjustments to scripted SWOT analysis questions can allow faculty to more successfully navigate the process.

Tool

Guiding participants through a facilitated exercise requires a specific mindset for optimum engagement. In the Mid-Career Faculty Workshop, we offer a primer on SWOT analysis to allow audience members to center their thoughts on the forthcoming activity. We find that reviewing trends in higher education allows one to mindfully consider current and future developments that might be center stage in their personal analysis. The Society for College and University Planning (SCUP) authors an annual *Trends in Higher Education* report, which we use to begin our analysis session. SCUP organizes education trends into five distinct categories using the STEEP framework: social, technology, economic, environmental, and political (Motley, 2022). We provide the STEEP categories and crowdsource examples of trends found within each. An example might include asking participants to share social trends; they might offer "employee burnout" and "student and employee mental health" as two topics for discussion. In leading this activity, participants may get probing questions from facilitators, such as *how might* [a particular trend] *impact their workplace environment, job responsibilities, and/or position within the institution?* We track this activity through at least three or four iterations using a different STEEP trend for each cycle. Participant interest is assessed to determine which STEEP trends we engage. In the aftermath of a 15- to 20-minute discussion on trends in higher education, participants are prepared for a SWOT analysis.

As with many conceptual models, an analysis of strengths, weaknesses, opportunities, and threats is illustrated through a 2 × 2 cross-tabulation table (see Figure 14.1). Displaying SWOT in this way emphasizes the relationships between categories of the model. Specific to the table, strengths are located in the upper-left quadrant. Following in a clockwise direction, we see weaknesses in the upper-right quadrant, threats in the lower-right quadrant, and finally, opportunities in the lower-left quadrant.

Importantly, the location of elements composing a SWOT analysis table allows additional relationships to be inferred. The top row, encompassing both strengths and weaknesses, represents internal characteristics, factors in which the participant has a decided influence (see Figure 14.1). Opportunities and threats, located on the bottom row, represent external considerations, or factors outside the participant's locus of control (Heasley & Palestini, 2023). If the table is presented on a handout during a facilitated session, space should be left available following each square's title to allow participants room to write their reflections.

Each of the four components of SWOT analysis provides unique insights for participants as they respond to guided questions given by the workshop facilitator(s). In the following sections, each SWOT component is discussed in detail, with sample prompts provided.

Strengths (Internal)

The first quadrant of the table gives space for participant *strengths* to be listed. This component acknowledges participant competencies or skills that they have mastered. We ask participants to consider areas of motivating work in which they find joy, as these are likely where they thrive. Tasks at which a participant compares favorably to that of exceptional colleagues and peers is also noted in this section. Facilitator reminders are given to ensure participants are aware that strengths can be found in many functional areas. Some examples include administrative acumen, empathetic leadership, work/life balance, research tenacity, inclusive pedagogical practice, etc. Within the space and time allotted for this portion of the activity, participants are asked to provide as much detail as possible or to specify examples of how they actualize their strengths in practice. Guiding questions for the strengths section of the SWOT analysis are asked in the order provided as follows. The facilitator is ready to progress to the next component in the SWOT table after each question is asked and ample time is given for participant responses.

- What are your strengths?
- What unique capabilities and resources do you possess?
- What do you do better than others?
- What do others perceive as your strengths?

Weaknesses (Internal)

Describing areas of personal and professional *weakness* can trigger feelings of inadequacy, self-doubt, and imperfection (among many other possible emotions). We often approach weakness as an area for improvement, development, and growth. In some cases, a weakness may stem from lack of exposure, access, and opportunity. Using a growth mindset, we frame weaknesses as factors stopping or impeding us from performing at optimum levels, perhaps temporarily (a competency or skill that is not a strength . . . yet). The following questions are used to guide participants through reflective practice regarding weaknesses.

- What are your weaknesses?
- What can you improve given your current situation and abilities?
- What do your colleagues/peers do better than you?
- What can you improve given your current situation and abilities?
- What do others perceive as your weaknesses?

Opportunities (External)

Although all quadrants on the SWOT table are value neutral, *opportunities* are often described as favorable external factors that give a competitive advantage, enhance participant strengths, and/or help one overcome a personal or professional weakness. Opportunities present themselves in experiences outside the workplace. Environmental scanning, a process of systematically surveying the professional landscape, and an awareness of SCUP's STEEP trends help one stay attuned to new opportunities. An example of an opportunity might be emerging programmatic offerings as the result of an institutional merger or acquisition, new federal research grant funding in an area of scholarly interest, or a professional development opportunity to help advance a skill. Following are prompts used to elicit responses for the opportunity quadrant of the SWOT analysis table.

- What trends or conditions may positively impact you?
- What opportunities are available to/for you?
- What institutional/administrative supports are available for your growth?

Threats (External)

Exploring threatening factors completes the SWOT analysis exercise. *Threats* refer to elements, events, or issues that are potentially harmful to the professional vitality of an individual or an organization. As external forces, threats are composed of elements outside the control of participants. Despite the impact a potential threat may have, there are several ways to respond, including ignoring, addressing, or retreating. Preparing for threats requires awareness of their potential dangers as well as preemptive strategies to thwart their impact. The following are questions used to tap into threats.

- What trends or conditions may negatively impact you?
- What are your colleagues/peers doing that may impact you?
- What institutional/administrative supports are lacking for your growth?
- What impacts do your weaknesses have on the threats to you?

Once participants complete their personal SWOT analysis, we like to provide additional strategy questions. These prompts ask participants to consider interactive effects between the four components of SWOT analysis. Sometimes, limited time requires these to be given as takeaways for future contemplation and self-reflection. Strategy categories and aligned questions are provided here:

- Strength-Opportunity Strategy: *Which of your strengths can be used to maximize the opportunities you identified?*
- Strength-Threats Strategy: *How can you use your strengths to minimize the threats you identified?*
- Weakness-Opportunity Strategy: *What action(s) can you take to minimize your weaknesses using the opportunities you identified?*
- Weakness-Threats Strategy: *How can you minimize your weaknesses to avoid the threats you identified?*

The previous group of questions pushes participants beyond single-node component responses. They require acknowledgment of the intersectional complexity inherent in a SWOT analysis. Purposefully, participants conclude this SWOT activity with new knowledge and developed strate-gies for identifying valued competencies and skills, addressing areas for personal and professional growth, advancing potential career opportuni-ties, and considering threats to their success.

Lessons Learned

As a collective, we have facilitated countless mid-career faculty in under-taking a SWOT analysis. Each time, we consistently receive positive feed-back about the utility of the activity and an appreciation for the time given to complete the SWOT, including the guided reflection as a necessary foundation to answering the "what's next?" question plaguing many mid-career faculty members. A fundamental lesson learned is that in order for the tool to be most useful, it must conceptualize learning as intellectual-ized by Neumann (2005), who posits, "Learning, as changed cognition, involves the personal and shared construction of knowledge; it involves coming to know something familiar in different ways, or to know some-thing altogether new, from within one's self and often with others" (p. 65). In defining learning, Neumann (2005) refers to interrelated assertions about it. Within her model, content, the learner, and context matter. The learning process requires individuals "to be exposed to, question, reflect, and re-conceptualize [learning experiences] in ways that build on current understandings and develop new understandings" (Heasley & Terosky, 2020, p. 22). It is within these moments of contemplation that individual-ized and personal learning thrives.

Utilization of goal planning and reflective tools is not a new practice in personal growth, particularly as a career development strategy in the acad-emy. As such, we offer complementary activities that align with SWOT for those who seek to adapt and adopt the SWOT tool and the correspond-ing prompts presented in this chapter. *The Johari Window* (Luft, 1969) and the *Ignatian Perspective on Leadership* (Dufresne et al., 2015) both provide structures that center mindfulness, reflective thought, and human interaction from both an individual and community perspective. These models provide easily applicable insights for all learners. The former relies on exploring what is both known and unknown to self and others (Luft, 1969), whereas the latter is structured to explain the interconnectedness within reflection–action and self–other polarities (Dufresne et al., 2015).

Conclusion

Being mid-career faculty ourselves, we know all too well the challenges and opportunities that surface during this phase of life and career. Tools pro-moting critical thinking, self-knowledge, goal setting, and discerning path trajectories are particularly helpful and apropos for mid-career faculty.

We have firsthand experience in using SWOT analysis to free faculty from a mid-career slump. It is our hope that the SWOT activity outlined in this chapter will help our readership, especially those who identify as mid-career faculty, learn something altogether new that rejuvenates the soul, sparks the mind, and motivates forward momentum.

References

Baker, V. L. (2020). *Charting your path to full: A guide for women associate professors.* Rutgers University Press.

Baker, V. L., & Boland, L. M. (2023). Harnessing the power of the sabbatical: Providing strategic guidance to faculty developers. *Journal of Faculty Development, 37*(3), 48–53.

Baker, V. L., & Manning, C. E. (2021). A mid-career faculty agenda: A review of four decades of research and practice. *Higher Education: Handbook of Theory and Research, 36,* 419–484.

Bryson, J. M. (2011). *Strategic planning for public and nonprofit organizations* (4th ed.). Jossey-Bass/Wiley.

Callahan, R. F. (2013). Professional reflection: The alignment of Ignatian pedagogy principles with Jesuit business school education and business practices. *Journal of Jesuit Business Education, 4,* 25–35.

Dufresne, R. L., Botto, K., & Steele, E. S. (2015). Contributing to an Ignatian perspective on leadership. *Journal of Jesuit Business Education, 6,* 1–19.

Heasley, C. (2021). SWOT analysis at mid-career faculty workshop. Presented at the Council for the Advancement of Higher Education Programs Session at the Annual (Virtual) Meeting of the Association for the Study of Higher Education.

Heasley, C. (2022, April 19–26). SWOT analysis at mid-career faculty workshop. Presented at the Annual Meeting of the American Educational Research Association, San Diego, CA.

Heasley, C., & Palestini, R. (2023). *Untangling leadership: Aligning mind and heart to advance higher education.* Rowman & Littlefield Publishers.

Heasley, C. L., & Terosky, A. L. (2020). Grappling with complexity: Faculty perspectives on the influence of community-engaged teaching on student learning. *Journal of Higher Education Outreach and Engagement, 24*(2), 19–35.

Hogan, K. A., & Sathy, V. (2022). *Inclusive teaching: Strategies for promoting equity in the college classroom.* West Virginia University Press.

Luft, J. (1969). *Of human interaction.* National Press Books.

Middaugh, M. (2010). *Planning and assessment in higher education.* Jossey-Bass.

Motley, A. (2022, Fall). Trends for higher education. *The Society of College and University Planning.* www.scup.org/learning-resources

Neumann, A. (2005). Observations: Taking seriously the topic of learning in studies of faculty work and careers. In E. G. Creamer & L. Lattuca (Eds.), *New directions for teaching and learning: No. 102. Advancing faculty learning through interdisciplinary collaboration* (pp. 63–83). Jossey-Bass.

Puyt, R., Lie, F. B., & Wilderom, C. P. (2023). Origins of SWOT analysis. *Long Range Planning, 56,* 1–24.

Renn, K. A. (2020). Association for the Study of Higher Education (ASHE). In P. N. Teixeira & J. C. Shin (Eds.), *The international encyclopedia of higher education systems and institutions*. Springer. https://doi.org/10.1007/978-94-017-8905-9_206

Sanaghan, P. (2009). *Collaborative strategic planning in higher education*. NACUBO.

Setiya, K. (2019, March–April). Facing your mid-career crisis. *Harvard Business Review*. https://hbr.org/2019/03/facing-your-mid-career-crisis

Sherlock, B. J. (2009). *Integrating planning, assessment, and improvement in higher education*. NACUBO.

Texter, L. A., & Terrion, J. L. (2022, May 2). *The care and feeding of mid-career faculty: Professional development across the career life cycle*. www.academic-leader.com/topics/faculty-development/the-care-and-feeding-of-mid-career-faculty-professional-development-across-the-career-life-cycle/

Section 4

Grant-Funded Initiatives

Vicki L. Baker

As anyone in the academy knows, a diversity of resources is necessary to invest effectively in the career advancement of faculty. Four relevant areas of resources are financial (e.g., operating budget funds, grants), human (e.g., faculty developers, adequate staffing), physical (e.g., community space, meeting space), and intellectual (e.g., access to professional development, "how to" guides). In addition, we need to think more broadly about the types of support faculty want, particularly at mid-career, and the resource investments and (re)allocations that must be made across the four resource areas to support a robust portfolio of faculty development programming. Despite an acknowledgement of and appreciation for the need to provide more robust programming and professional development at mid-career (Baker et al., 2015), institutional leaders continue to grapple with dwindling budgets and employee turnover due to the great resignation (Massa & Conley, 2022). This section provides guidance for thinking creatively about how to secure funds and leverage related resources to support sustainable long-term programs.

Section 4, "Grant-Funded Initiatives," features four efforts across the academy aimed at supporting mid-career professionals. While each program featured was launched with external funds, examples of human, intellectual, and physical resources are on full display. As a collective, the contributions in this section help you, the reader, think about strategies for securing external funding, how to use that funding effectively, and how to sustain the mid-career programming and related resources well after the grant cycle ends.

In Chapter 15, Schepmann and colleagues introduce readers to the power of regional inter-institutional peer alliances and the cultivation of human and intellectual resources as levers for the professional growth and leadership development of mid-career faculty and administrators. Funded by the National Science Foundation, the chapter features the ASCEND Network, which seeks to support mid-career women in STEM fields. ASCEND consists of discipline-specific alliances of mid-career women STEM faculty in

DOI: 10.4324/9781003428626-19

three geographic regions (Northwest, Midwest, and Southeast) from 51 predominantly undergraduate institutions (PUIs); each region also has an administrator alliance to provide leadership support and to facilitate critical conversations between stakeholder groups. Via their featured tool, the Building Peer Alliances to Empower Advancement and Leadership Guide, the authors provide guidance on how to establish an effective peer mentoring program and related career advancement programming that brings together mid-career faculty and administrators. The peer networks created through ASCEND provided faculty participants with a sense of inclusion and empowerment and increased resiliency in the face of challenges. As the authors share in their chapter, "Peer support not only benefits the individual but promotes the collective advancement of groups, which leads to powerful institutional change" (p . XX).

Culpepper, Liu, and O'Meara provide a road map for how to sustain faculty development and career advancement efforts once initial funding has ended. Initially focused on the professional growth of diverse groups of women faculty, Chapter 16 features a National Science Foundation–funded ADVANCE-IT grant, secured in 2010 at the University of Maryland, which expanded to include faculty with varied appointment types. With the support of that funding, the ADVANCE Program for Inclusive Excellence was established to foster cohort-based faculty peer networks for associate professors who identify as women. Culpepper and colleagues present readers with strategies for building an infrastructure of faculty support rooted in social networks (e.g., human resources, intellectual resources), including a sample syllabus for Advancing Together. Informed by multiple years of program evaluation data, they provide insight into the role of peer networks and career advancement while acknowledging the very real challenges faculty and institutional leaders face as they work to invest in career advancement infrastructure.

In Chapter 17, Sun and Pratt spotlight a federally funded program that prepares mid-career United States Army soldiers as future university-level instructors for military science programs. Through taking graduate-level courses on teaching and learning, student development, higher education administration, and organizational change, participating Army soldiers learn and master best practices in equity-oriented teaching and advising. Sun and Pratt provide a detailed description of goals, instructional approaches, and outcome assessments of the University of Louisville/Army Master Educator Course (MEC), a two-semester "boot camp" that can easily be adapted for other audiences across higher educational institutions. The two-phase approach of MEC – a residency, cohort-based foundational experience and an application at the participants' home institutions – serves as a theory-to-practice model that helps improve teaching and student learning among mid-career faculty.

The final chapter in this section offers insight into the role of external funding in supporting mid-career faculty in the humanities. In Chapter 18, Van Duinen shines a light on a critical expectation placed on mid-career faculty: securing external funding to support career advancement. Further, she acknowledges the very real challenge of the limited guidance available to help faculty in the humanities navigate this process. Via critical intellectual resources she has cultivated, including a Scholarship/Project Assessment worksheet and a Grant-Funding Considerations worksheet, Van Duinen walks readers through how these tools have helped her be successful in securing funding to support her and her colleagues' growth and advancement in humanities fields.

As I reflect on the knowledge and insight gleaned from this collection of chapters, I highlight three main takeaways. First, as financial resources become increasingly limited across all institution types, we need to think more broadly about how to leverage the human, physical, and intellectual resources available internally and externally at our respective institutions to support mid-career professional growth and advancement. Each of the chapters featured provides guidance on how to achieve that aim and extols the related benefits to faculty and their institutions.

Second, long-term program sustainability is a critical consideration that all academic leaders grapple with as they engage in resource-allocation decisions. The section contributors offer examples of how to work smarter with available resources in service to the career advancement of those firmly situated in mid-career. As we learn from these chapters, being clear about aims, intended outcomes, and the role of institutional commitment is paramount.

Last, individual agency is powerful: in the face of limited resources and guidance on how to navigate the mid-career stage, section contributors reveal how and in what ways they leveraged their own networks and experiences to better support the next generation of mid-career professionals. The challenges and opportunities they so honestly share are both relatable and inspirational.

References

Baker, V. L., Lunsford, L. G., & Pifer, M. J. (2015). Systems alignment for comprehensive faculty development in liberal arts colleges. *To Improve the Academy*, 34(1–2), 91–116.

Massa, R., & Conley, B. (2022, August 1). The great resignation . . . or the great surrender? *Inside Higher Ed*. www.insidehighered.com/views/2022/08/02/great-resignation%E2%80%94or-great-surrender-opinion

Building Community, Confidence, and Capacity for Advancement and Leadership Through Regional Inter-Institutional Peer Alliances

Hala G. Schepmann, Sarah R. Kirk, Mary Katherine Watson, Victoria L. Turgeon, Maria E. Bertagnolli, Chrystal D. Bruce, Patricia M. Flatt, and Elizabeth S. Roberts-Kirchhoff

Overview

Origin of ASCEND

As with any good origin story, the history of the ASCEND initiative reveals both the intent of those of us involved in developing this program and the underlying need we sought to address. In 2012, five of the authors, all mid-career chemists at different predominantly undergraduate institutions (PUIs), responded to a call to participate in the National Science Foundation (NSF) ADVANCE grant #1107034, ASAP: Advancing the Careers of Women in STEM at Primarily Undergraduate Institutions (McGrath et al., 2019). The inter-institutional, multi-disciplinary ASAP network, spanning early-, mid-, and late-career participants, created a confidential space where brave conversations and broader learning could occur. From 2012 through 2016, our five-member alliance met regularly to provide each other mentoring and peer support, resulting in significant personal growth, individual career advancement, and greater institutional engagement (Bruce et al., 2022a; McGrath et al., 2019). By promoting collaborative sharing of institutional practices and support mechanisms, we were able to realize systemic change within our institutions (Bruce et al., 2022a).

The positive outcomes experienced by those involved in the ASAP program and our own recognition of unmet needs specific to mid-career faculty motivated us to create a multi-regional, inter-institutional peer-mentoring network focused on supporting the advancement of mid-career women STEM faculty: the ASCEND Network (Bruce et al., 2022a). As a rising tide lifts all boats, these alliances are designed to build supportive

DOI: 10.4324/9781003428626-20

communities that promote confidence and empower faculty to be leaders and change agents who drive institutional transformation. This chapter outlines our efforts.

Program Focus

The ASCEND Network consists of discipline-specific alliances of mid-career women STEM faculty in three geographic regions (Northwest, Midwest, and Southeast) from 51 PUIs. Each region also has an administrator alliance, which not only provides supportive leadership but also uses the knowledge gained regarding the challenges and obstacles that faculty face to address systemic barriers at their own institutions.

Our alliances function as peer-mentoring groups. Unlike in hierarchical mentoring, peer mentoring brings together a community of equals, and the advantages are numerous. Every participant has access to multiple mentoring partners since no single individual possesses the knowledge and skills needed to address all facets of an academic career. Additionally, members of the same rank or position report that they find it easier to share information, including challenges that cross work–life boundaries (Angelique et al., 2002). Peer mentoring in small communities of equals facilitates collaboration, career advisement, and strategy sharing to tackle institutional barriers. We seek to facilitate satisfying and successful careers for women in STEM and to improve the academic landscape by creating diverse STEM communities that lead to innovation and creativity.

Needed Skills

Faculty need to be able to contextualize personal and institutional challenges with respect to their own professional advancement in order to create an individualized career plan with well-defined goals and strategies for successfully navigating the obstacles they encounter. Essential professional skills include self-advocacy, collaboration, conflict management, and negotiation. While each person faces unique challenges and opportunities, building a network provides a supportive community that helps one not only persist but also flourish throughout one's career. Furthermore, the ability to locate and access resources instills confidence and encourages advocacy for self and others.

Rationale

Many mid-career women STEM faculty experience barriers to advancement that impact their confidence, lead to frustration and burnout, and result in lower job satisfaction (O'Connell & McKinnon, 2021; Pedersen &

Minnotte, 2017). Commonly encountered obstacles include significant yet undervalued service commitments; unclear promotion policies; insufficient support for professional development activities; and a sense of isolation. These challenges are exacerbated at PUIs where faculty have high teaching and advising loads and are often the sole expert in their field. As a result, some mid-career faculty delay standing for promotion or applying for leadership positions, while others leave academia altogether (Xu, 2008; National Science Foundation, 2019). Peer mentoring within departments and institutions has been shown to alleviate gaps in support and provide an effective framework for promoting faculty development and leadership training (Thomas et al., 2014; Elrod et al., 2023). Furthermore, the coupling of a collaborative community with the development and implementation of supportive policies and procedures can lead to positive and sustainable institutional changes that create a culture of equity and inclusion.

Equity and Inclusion Considerations

While we use peer-mentoring networks to advance the professional and leadership development of women faculty, we also believe they are valuable in supporting marginalized or isolated groups across disciplinary boundaries in academia by promoting a sense of community, alleviating isolation, and thwarting burnout. The ASCEND Network members are at PUIs, which have specific challenges that may differ from those at other types of institutions. The PUIs are often located in rural areas with minimal racial and ethnic diversity; there are fewer colleagues to turn to for support and guidance; and faculty are tasked with a broad and demanding range of responsibilities, including high teaching, advising, and service loads – leaving little time and support to advance their scholarship, a necessity for promotion to full professor. Early indicators show that ASCEND faculty fellows are benefitting from the support received through the program (Bruce et al., 2022b).

Tool

Although we are all at PUIs, we firmly believe that inter-institutional alliances are valuable for faculty at all institution types. Creating and supporting peer-mentoring groups is a significant undertaking, one that could be organized by professional societies or institutional leaders who have resources to connect faculty across multiple institutions. While there are tools for all readers in this chapter and in the eResources, the primary audience is institutional and professional society leaders looking to build capacity and develop leadership. In the following section we share a guide (Table 15.1) for others who seek to foster peer-to-peer mentoring networks.

Table 15.1 Building Peer Alliances to Empower Advancement and Leadership Guide

	Build Network	Create Community	Promote Advancement	Expand Network
Aims	1. Recruit participants with common goals and assemble alliances 2. Facilitate engagement	1. Develop an inclusive, supportive, trusting culture	1. Support peer mentoring 2. Guide individualized plan development 3. Promote skill development 4. Deliver multi-alliance meetings	1. Encourage network development
Needed resources	1. Application with specific selection criteria 2. Participant meeting time and location constraints	1. Community of Trust Agreement; community-building activities	1. Common goals; regular meeting times 2. Framework with assessment and action components 3. Skill development that aligns with goals 4. Relationship building and professional development opportunities	1. Network opportunities to connect with faculty and administrators from other institutions
Critical considerations	1. Ascertain applicants' diverse priorities and needs 2. Establish expectations of participants; set meeting times	1. Ensure confidential environments that facilitate open dialogue	1. Understand that needs are not static; requires communication and a variety of resources 2. Provide healthy accountability and check-in 3. Provide variety of opportunities for developing and practicing skills 4. Create space for engagement, action, and reflection	1. Network development needs to be a value-add, with provision of diversity of skills and resources that support advancement and job satisfaction

A. Building a Network

Recruiting Participants and Assembling Alliances

Mid-career faculty juggle many competing demands on their time. To draw a large enough group to create inter-institutional peer networks with four to five members in each alliance, it is necessary to cast a wide net, actively recruit participants, and highlight the value of such a group for both individuals and institutions. For the ASCEND project, the call was sent to provosts, deans, department chairs, individual faculty, and professional societies and associations (see eResources).

To assemble an alliance, it is best to have specific selection criteria when developing the participant application (see eResources). The ASCEND project asked for academic discipline, years in rank, time in position, motivation for participating, and existing institutional support. Recognizing the role that intersectionality plays in barriers to career advancement, we invited applicants to identify whether they were from a minoritized background with prompts related to gender, race, ethnicity, disability status, economic status, first-generation status, foreign-born and foreign-trained status, and sexual orientation. The application process allowed faculty applicants an opportunity to describe their intersectional identities, reflect on events that have influenced their professional progress, assess their readiness for promotion, identify support needed to advance their career, consider their interest in pursuing leadership positions, and identify institutional changes they desire to effect.

Facilitating in-Person Meetings

In-person interactions are an important complement to other program components. The significant physical separation and three-hour time zone difference were challenges the original ASAP alliance participants faced. As a result, the ASCEND project focused on specific geographic regions, ensuring that faculty in each group were within one or two time zones and a reasonable driving distance or short flight from one another. This decision provides significant cost and time savings, increasing the likelihood and frequency of in-person interactions, and strengthens regional connections and collaborations. ASCEND participants identify the in-person meeting as the most valuable component of the project, and we strongly recommend considering how alliance members will be able to meet in person annually.

B. Creating a Supportive, Trusting Community

Inter-institutional groups provide confidential environments that facilitate open dialogue so that participants can discuss individual and institutional

challenges and receive candid feedback while benefiting from policy sharing that empowers participants to enact change on their campuses (Cree-
Green et al., 2020; McBride et al., 2017; Thomas et al., 2014). Therefore,
it is necessary to create a supportive, trusting, joyful community culture
in which participants listen to one another, share successes, and trust that
what is shared will be held in confidence.

Within the ASCEND network, we set the tone by drafting a Community
of Trust Agreement that was informed by participant input (see eResources).
Our agreement included a brief mission statement and articulated commitments related to approaches and behaviors that cultivate spaces "where all
are welcomed and experience a true sense of belonging." In writing it, we
were mindful of its language, intent, and impact, and, as a living document,
it served as the cornerstone for each meeting and evolved over time.

Creating an inclusive culture requires social awareness and mindfulness
of current events. We purposefully built a space where every person could
safely share their whole selves, take risks, find support to overcome barriers, and celebrate joys. Reminding participants that they are more than
their job titles encourages authenticity as groups tackle sensitive topics,
including work/life alignment, charting one's leadership journey, and the
impact of unforeseen circumstances on personal and professional goals.

Beyond an explicit Community of Trust agreement, we also recommend providing prompts that encourage participants to get to know each
other better and to continually share both their professional and personal
pursuits, challenges, and accomplishments. We also collectively celebrate
accomplishments by posting updates in our monthly newsletter.

C. Designing Structures to Promote Advancement

A primary goal of the ASCEND program is to support the career advancement of mid-career faculty. However, the activities and programming
described herein can be easily tailored to meet readers' specific objectives
for their networks. We designed a multi-component project framework to
provide consistent, readily accessible support and programming with the
flexibility required to address our participants' developing needs. Key components included virtual monthly alliance meetings, individualized career
planning, virtual professional development workshops, and multi-alliance
meetings (see eResources). Importantly, community-building activities
were incorporated into each meeting to enhance participants' capacity to
do the hard work required to realize their career advancement goals.

Identifying and Meeting Participant Needs

Understandably, all the resources needed to construct such a framework
cannot be fully ascertained at the outset of a program. Therefore, being

nimble and responsive to changing priorities and challenges is required for program organizers to effectively advance participants' goals. Identifying needed resources and their sources are two different objectives. The first requires communication, whereas the second requires collective knowledge of what exists, as well as a mindset to create new resources.

To identify the resources needed, we combined information from the initial survey used to select our participants with one developed and administered by our external consultant, Education Development Center. Collectively, this provided a detailed understanding of our participants, which helped us develop programming to inspire and support them. Armed with this information, we inventoried the skill set within our steering committee and determined which external resources were needed. The diversity of our committee's personal and professional experiences, combined with our disciplinary and institutional connections, provided a breadth of resources.

Regular Alliance Meetings

Since a blended mentoring approach is expected to sustain relationships, virtual monthly alliance meetings were intentionally designed to incorporate both formal and informal elements. To support formal mentoring, the steering committee provided guidelines, resources, and monthly discussion prompts. However, as participants' preferences and needs varied with regard to meeting structure, alliances were encouraged to function autonomously to address their members' specific challenges and needs and to use their time in a manner that would benefit them best. As a means to ensure timely and relevant guidance for the alliances, the steering committee collected monthly feedback from each alliance facilitator (see eResources).

Strategic Planning

To help faculty define their professional objectives, each participant drafted an individual development plan (IDP) for promotion, professional development, and leadership (see eResources). In their planning, participants identified focus areas, taking into consideration their aim of obtaining promotion to full professor and their desired career and leadership trajectories. They set three goals using a SMART outline (Specific, Measurable, Achievable, Realistic, Time-bound). For each goal, they conducted a personal assessment; listed existing and needed resources; identified sources of feedback, support, and accountability; defined action steps and timelines; and assessed obstacles and possible solutions. For many faculty, advancing their scholarship (e.g., by pursuing external research funding, completing research projects, and/or publishing their work in peer-reviewed journals) was a main focus, as a lack of achievement in that area is often the greatest barrier to promotion for mid-career women faculty at PUIs.

Each IDP was also assessed using Dr. Vicki Baker's PSEI (Purpose, Scope, and Evidence of Impact) career advancement framework (Baker, 2022). This helped faculty strategically revise their IDPs to ensure that their engagement activities would advance their aspirational goals and, importantly, that they were framed in a manner that would resonate with stakeholders. Over the course of the project, faculty continued to revise their IDPs. The act of developing a three- to five-year strategic plan, coupled with focused discussions during monthly and annual meetings, helped participants identify areas in which they needed the most support to overcome barriers and served as a self-accountability check and action-driver.

Regional and All-Participant Meetings

The steering committee connected alliances through virtual and in-person regional and cross-regional meetings and virtual professional development opportunities, thereby forming an extended peer-mentoring network. Multi-alliance meetings emphasized relationship building, network expansion, and professional development.

Knowing that women's voices have been historically and institutionally suppressed, and because many of our participants acknowledged not feeling empowered in using their own voices, we chose voice positioning as our year one theme. Dr. Katrina Hutchins, author of *The Voice Positioning System: 7 Ways to Harness Your Power and Master Your Influence*, helped participants reflect on and share their voice experiences. Doing so required faculty to speak from a place of vulnerability, which would not have been possible without the relationships forged through community-building activities implemented at the outset of the project. Dr. Hutchins highlighted the importance of strategically using one's authentic voice. By providing video briefs and interactive voice coaching and train-the-trainer sessions, she helped participants build skills to make them more effective communicators and increase their success in addressing and removing advancement barriers.

Having successfully created a culture of support, encouragement, and empowerment, our year two theme focused on faculty's professional advancement planning and pursuits. We engaged Dr. Vicki Baker, author of *Managing Your Academic Career: A Guide to Re-Envision Mid-Career*, to guide participants through an assessment of their former and current professional paths and their next-stage goals. By focusing on job crafting, self-advocacy, and strategic selection of commitments through the lens of the PSEI framework, Dr. Baker outlined strategies, tools, and tips needed to bring to fruition the goals noted in participants' IDPs. As a means to inform and guide our participants on their leadership journeys, Dr. Florastina Payton-Stewart led a working session on intersectionality in academia. She emphasized advancing justice by removing systemic barriers and employing an intersectional lens in decision-making processes.

The theme of year three was strengthening relationships among alliance members and enhancing networking and collaboration opportunities while continuing to make progress on individual goals. Therefore, in place of a regional meeting, each alliance was given the opportunity to design their own meeting, choosing the date, location, length, and focus. The steering committee provided suggested activities and discussion topics, and, most importantly, participants were encouraged to enjoy themselves and their fellow alliance members!

Our final year's theme focused on supporting faculty as they assume leadership roles and work to advance workplace equity and support minoritized groups. At an all-participant meeting, Dr. Marjorie Hass, author of *A Leadership Guide for Women in Higher Education*, led sessions on sustaining leadership, managing workplace feelings, and finding joy in one's work, and Dr. Susan Elrod, an expert on leading institutional systemic change, shared resources on change leadership and management.

Regular Virtual Professional Development Workshops

In addition to the monthly alliance, regional, and cross-regional meetings, we offer virtual professional development workshops to provide frequent interactions for the ASCEND community and as venues for both steering committee members and ASCEND participants to share their expertise (see eResources). These workshops, which have included When and How to Say No with Confidence, Leading Difficult Conversations, Getting Started in Scholarship of Teaching and Learning, Leading Change From the Middle, Research Development and Proposal Submissions, Developing Your Voice in the Academy, From Girl Scout Cookies to Major Gift Fundraising, The Sustainable Professor, Taking the Leap into Mid-Level Leadership, Throw Your Hat in the Ring, and Write Away!, were especially beneficial in sustaining connections among ASCEND community members during year three, when we did not meet in person.

D. Expanding the Network

Essential to our project design was the intersection of multiple networks. While the primary relationships were developed among four to five alliance members, each of these groups interacted with other alliances within their region and, ultimately, with the entire ASCEND community. This expanding network afforded women opportunities to learn from and be supported by a larger cohort. Over the project's evolution, we were pleased to see that our individual participants became resources in and of themselves (Bruce et al., 2022b). They provided constructive feedback and guidance, lending their voices and expertise as they discovered additional support mechanisms and employed strategies to overcome barriers. As one participant said, "My voice matters, because I have not been alone in the challenges and obstacles I have faced, but sometimes I have felt like I was. Sharing my experiences and perspectives can let someone else know they are not alone" (Bruce et al., 2022b).

Lessons Learned

The peer alliance network model can establish and support a diverse array of professional networks, whether initiated by organizations, institutions, or individuals. We acknowledge that this work is challenging and that no one structure or solution works for everyone. Managing such an expansive project can be time-consuming and emotionally taxing. In creating your own peer-to-peer, cross-institutional alliances, we recommend:

- building a leadership team that can share the planning and act as a support network for the leaders
- ensuring that alliance participants share a common thread: e.g., a goal, career stage, or position
- providing but not requiring a structure with flexibility for members of each alliance to adapt meetings to their own needs
- creating a safe, confidential space
- hosting an in-person meeting soon after the network is established
- offering a variety of topics, speakers, and resources
- building in time for socializing and respite
- beginning with five participants in each alliance so that a reduction in group size would not negatively affect the alliance's ability to provide a diverse range of perspectives and experiences
- being as flexible and responsive as possible to participants' needs
- communicating with participants frequently, using a variety of modes
- employing project support personnel, including a project manager, funded organizing committee positions, and internal or external evaluators

Conclusion

Peer networks provide a sense of inclusion and empowerment that fosters resilience in the face of expected and unexpected challenges. When alliance participants feel connected, share resources, and freely express themselves, they build capacity to become better leaders and effective change agents through knowledge, confidence, and community. The potential for institutional transformation is limitless when mid-career faculty are empowered.

References

(Additional references available in the eResource.)

Angelique, H., Kyle, K., & Taylor, E. (2002). Mentors and muses: New strategies for academic success. *Innovative Higher Education, 26*, 195–209. https://doi.org/10.1023/A:1017968906264

Baker, V. L. (2022). *Managing your academic career: A guide to re-envision mid-career*. Routledge University Press.

Bruce, C., Flatt, P. M., Kirk, S. R., Roberts-Kirchhoff, E., & Schepmann, H. G. (2022a). The value of peer mentoring networks for developing leaders and inspiring change. *Journal of Chemical Information and Modeling, 62*(24), 6292–6296. https://doi.org/10.1021/acs.jcim.2c00155

Bruce, C., Kirk, S., Bertagnolli, M., Flatt, P., Roberts-Kirchhoff, E., Schepmann, H., Stone, E., Swanier, C., Turgeon, V., & Watson, M. K. (2022b, May 31–June 3). *Reducing the barriers to the advancement of mid-career female-identifying STEM faculty and driving institutional transformation to create environments where diversity is encouraged and supported* [Conference presentation]. Equity in STEM Community Convening, Washington, DC.

Cree-Green, M., Carreau, A.-M., Davis, S. M., Frohnert, B. I., Kaar, J. L., Ma, N. S., Nokoff, N. J., Reusch, J. E., Simon, S. L., & Nadeau, K. J. (2020). Peer mentoring for professional and personal growth in academic medicine. *Journal of Investigative Medicine, 68*(6), 1128–1134. https://doi.org/10.1136/jim-2020-001391

Elrod, S., Kezar, A., & de Jesus Gonzalez, A. (2023). *Change leadership toolkit: A guide for advancing systemic change in higher education*. University of Southern California, Pullias Center for Higher Education. https://pullias.usc.edu/change-leadership-toolkit/

McBride, A. B., Campbell, J., Woods, N. F., & Manson, S. M. (2017). Building a mentoring network. *Nursing Outlook, 65*(3), 305–314. https://doi.org/10.1016/j.outlook.2016.12.001

McGrath, C., Francovich, C., Smieja, J. A., Cronin, C., Lacueva, G., Sabin, R. E., Song, J. Y., Voltzow, J., & Zhong, X. (2019). Building a framework to advance the careers of women in STEM at predominantly undergraduate institutions. *Advance Journal, 1*(2). https://doi.org/10.5399/osu/ADVJRNL.1.2.1

National Science Foundation. (2019). *Women, minorities, and persons with disabilities in science and engineering: 2019* (Special Report NSF 19–304). https://ncses.nsf.gov/pubs/nsf19304/

O'Connell, C., & McKinnon, M. (2021). Perceptions of barriers to career progression for academic women in STEM. *Societies, 11*(2), 27. https://doi.org/10.3390/soc11020027

Pedersen, D. E., & Minnotte, K. L. (2017). Workplace climate and STEM faculty women's job burnout. *Journal of Feminist Family Therapy, 29*(1–2), 45–65. https://doi.org/10.1080/08952833.2016.1230987

Thomas, N., Bystydzienski, J., & Desai, A. (2014). Changing institutional culture through peer mentoring of women STEM faculty. *Innovative Higher Education*, *40*(2), 143–157. https://doi.org/10.1007/s10755-014-9300-9

Xu, Y. J. (2008). Gender disparity in STEM disciplines: A study of faculty attrition and turnover intentions. *Research in Higher Education*, *49*, 607–624. https://doi.org/10.1007/s11162-008-9097-4

Chapter 16

Building an Infrastructure for Mid-Career Faculty Advancement

Lessons Learned from Faculty Peer Networks in the UMD ADVANCE Program

Dawn Culpepper, Brooke Fisher Liu, and KerryAnn O'Meara

Overview

The UMD ADVANCE Program

Networks are an essential part of faculty professional success. When faculty members are plugged into networks, they are more productive and more agentic and, therefore, are more likely to advance (Niehaus & O'Meara, 2015). As such, many mid-career faculty development programs, including ones explored elsewhere in this volume, rightly focus on creating peer networks as a way to mitigate the mid-career malaise that many associate professors encounter (Baker & Manning, 2020).

This chapter focuses on a less-researched impact of such networks: considering how faculty peer networks, deployed over a number of years, can build a durable, sustainable infrastructure for faculty development and support that promotes a culture that is invested in faculty development across career stages. We draw from our experiences with the University of Maryland ADVANCE Program, a National Science Foundation–initiated program that supports the recruitment, retention, advancement, and professional growth of a diverse professoriate. Using the lens of social networks for organizational change (Kezar, 2014), we argue that faculty peer networks are beneficial for the faculty members, including associate professors, who participate in them, as well as the organizations in which they exist.

Program Focus

The University of Maryland ADVANCE Program for Inclusive Excellence was initially established with the support of a National Science Foundation ADVANCE Institutional Transformation (IT) grant (Award #1008117). Although the National Science Foundation's ADVANCE grant program

DOI: 10.4324/9781003428626-21

focuses on women in STEM, the UMD ADVANCE approach was to invest in the professional growth of a diverse group of women faculty in ways that also changed institutional culture, systems, and policies to become more inclusive. The grant began with a focus on tenure-track faculty but quickly expanded to include faculty members with a variety of appointment types. At the end of the grant period (2015), ADVANCE Program personnel (led by third author KerryAnn O'Meara) leveraged the program's track record of success to make the case for continued institutional support. The ADVANCE Program has been continually supported by each of the university's 12 academic colleges as well as by other academic units and by the provost's office since 2016 and is now housed in the Office of Faculty Affairs.

Recognizing the literature on the challenges of advancing from associate to full, as well as having examined institutional data that showed gender differences in time to promotion, the ADVANCE program initiated a peer network (Advancing Together, or AT) for associate professors who identified as women in 2012. A total of eight cohorts of women associate professors have participated in the peer network. The AT format has varied over the years. The most common format has been monthly seminars wherein a full professor (such as second author Brooke Fisher Liu) serves as a facilitator for a group of 5 to 12 women who meet to discuss a specific topic related to mid-career advancement. Throughout the year, other guests are invited to serve on panels and participate in question-and-answer sessions, such as women faculty who have recently been promoted to full professors, faculty who serve on campus promotion committees, and campus leaders like the provost and associate provost. Other modes have included a winter "boot camp" or twice-a-semester seminars. Each meeting includes discussion of topics relevant to associate professors (e.g., saying yes and strategically to service; strategic self-promotion) with relevant readings, learning activities, and invited speakers (see Table 16.1 for an example syllabus).

Needed Skills

Social capital is defined as "valued, actionable resources, like information, advice, or support, that people access, mobilize, and benefit from through social ties" (Benbow & Lee, 2019, p. 69). Unlike economic capital, social capital is not accrued individually but rather "flows through social ties" (Benbow & Lee, 2019, p. 72). However, the resources (e.g., information, advice, and prestige) that one receives from their social capital (Benbow & Lee, 2019) can create individual career benefits, such as status, recognition, and professional legitimacy (Niehaus & O'Meara, 2015; Williams & Williams, 2006). As we discuss in what follows, organizational and social factors can often mean that differently situated faculty members have different opportunities to access social capital and accrue its benefits (Casad et al.,

Table 16.1 Example Syllabus for Advancing Together (AT) Peer Network

Date	Topic
September	Building Connections and Discussion of Career "Joy"
October	Getting Organized
November	Charting Your Path to Full: Discussion with the Provost
January	Boot Camp (1-Day Intensive Workshop)
	• Revamping and Pivoting Research
	• Working with and Leveraging the Media
	• Feedback on Personal Narratives with Women Full Professors
February	Slam-Dunk Cases versus Cases with Questions: Advice from Promotion Committee Members and Associate Vice Provost of Faculty Affairs
March	Planning the Next Steps of Your Career
May	Creating Your Academic Legacy and End-of-Year Celebration

2021; Niehaus & O'Meara, 2015; Williams & Williams, 2006). As such, mid-career faculty members and those concerned with faculty development ought to be aware of the role of social capital and the importance of creating and leveraging organizational structures that can enhance access to it.

Rationale

There are three main organizational barriers that can undermine the extent to which mid-career faculty access social capital. First, much of the research on mid-career faculty suggests that a lack of connection and community can hinder development and advancement (Baker & Manning, 2020). One of the reasons mid-career faculty lack connections is because most colleges and universities (a) continue to rely upon dyadic (one-on-one) mentoring models and/or (b) only require/invest in mentoring for assistant professors (Buch et al., 2011; Lunsford et al., 2018). Both practices can limit the social capital mid-career faculty need to advance. A second barrier is that many colleges and universities remain highly decentralized (Campbell & O'Meara, 2014; Fleming et al., 2016; Rosinger et al., 2016). This means that most faculty members develop homophilous campus networks wherein they mostly interact with faculty members in their departments or colleges who have similar organizational experiences (i.e., same dean, same department chair). Faculty members therefore develop limited views of how things work in the context of the larger institution (Campbell & O'Meara, 2014; Fleming et al., 2016; Rosinger et al., 2016; O'Meara et al., 2019a), thereby limiting their access to social capital. Finally, academia is deeply hierarchical (Young et al., 2015), with formal and informal structures and processes that confer value and shape interactions on and among faculty members and administrators. As such, when individual faculty members experience challenges, organizational hierarchies and power dynamics may prevent them from accessing deans or provosts who could support them (Rosinger et al., 2016), and this represents another organizational barrier to the attainment of capital.

Equity and Inclusion Considerations

Each of the issues identified – a lack of connection and community, decentralization, and organizational hierarchies – has been identified as an issue that disproportionately affects the careers of mid-career faculty members from historically marginalized groups, including faculty of color and women (Baker & Manning, 2020; Covarrubias et al., 2022; Domingo et al., 2022; Williams & Williams, 2006). For instance, research shows that a lack of connection and community is exacerbated when a faculty member is the only member, or one of just a few members, of a gender and/or racial group within a department or university (Kelly & McCann, 2014; Liu et al., 2019). Similarly, hierarchical organizations tend to reproduce and perpetuate systems of social oppression that limit the full participation and advancement of individuals from historically marginalized groups (Acker, 1990; Ray, 2019). As such, peer networks are intended to disrupt the organizational forces that produce inequities in the academy by helping faculty members accrue the social capital needed to advance.

Conceptual Grounding

In the prior sections, we identified social capital as critical for faculty and identified numerous barriers that hinder mid-career faculty from accessing capital. The major way that one accumulates social capital is through one's placement in social networks. Social networks are "people loosely connected through some form of interdependencies such as values, goals, ideas, or people" (Kezar, 2014, p. 92). Researchers have shown that networks positively influence identity development for doctoral students (Baker & Lattuca, 2010) as well as retention and research productivity of women faculty (Ginther et al., 2020). Other studies show networks help faculty members become better and more inclusive teachers (Bond & Lockee, 2018) or increase the skills and connections required to attain professional promotion (Niehaus & O'Meara, 2015; O'Meara et al., 2019b). At their core, faculty peer networks (sometimes referred to as learning communities) help faculty members develop different forms of social capital, which they then leverage to advance their professional goals.

Networks are also an important but often unrecognized mechanism for facilitating organizational change in higher education (Daly, 2010; Kezar,

2014). Studies show being a part of a network can be critical for faculty members who are advocating for change in areas like hiring (Liera, 2020); promotion and recognition for non–tenure-track faculty (Kezar, 2012); and undergraduate curriculum reform (Hill, 2020), among other important change efforts. The ways that networks foster organizational change vary. Networks facilitate learning (Baker & Lattuca, 2010) and help spread and share information about organizational policies (e.g., the criteria for promotion to full professor) and how to navigate such information, thereby increasing usage and uptake (e.g., enhancing the number of associate professors who are promoted) (Kezar, 2014). When networks are composed of diverse members, they can help introduce new ideas into an organization, which can foster innovation (Kezar, 2014). Diverse networks can help build coalitions and connect change agents with central actors/decision-makers (Kezar, 2014). Networks can also enhance the trust and connectedness among organizational members that is necessary for change to occur (Kezar, 2014).

Social networks for change in this case provided a lens through which we could conceptualize multiple layers of impact for ADVANCE peer networks at the University of Maryland. At an individual level, network theories help illuminate how making connections with faculty peer networks might facilitate the attainment of social capital and contribute to advancement for associate professors. At an organizational level, network theories show how the development of networks might create connections aimed at enhancing a culture of professional development for faculty members, which can lead to long-term commitment to an organization (Lawrence et al., 2012).

Tools

Strategies for Building an Infrastructure of Faculty Support

Based on our work with peer networks at UMD, we share a list of strategies for creating mid-career peer networks over time. This list includes considerations for recruiting and structuring peer networks in ways that are supportive and sustainable.

1. Develop Diverse Ties and Share Information

    a. Encourage participation from faculty members from across organizational units and from diverse identity groups.
    b. Review department/college and campus promotion policies and expectations.
    c. Discuss differences and similarities between departmental/college norms and expectations.

   d. Provide alternative pathways to promotion; highlight individuals whose paths have been non-linear or atypical compared to what is perceived as the norm.

   e. Encourage peer network participants to share information they receive in the program with others in their department/college.

   f. Develop information repositories (e.g., research articles, worksheets, and promotion dossier examples) that are available to peer network participants after they have completed the program.

2. Foster Connection and Community

   a. Recognize peer network participants as important purveyors of knowledge and expertise.

   b. Create a peer network culture of trust and confidentiality in which members can candidly share their experiences, questions, and concerns about promotion.

   c. Share program models and outcomes with campus leaders.

   d. Create opportunities for peer network participants to continue to be involved in programs (e.g., as speakers or mentors).

3. Change the Nature of Interactions

   a. Go beyond the panel discussion by creating opportunities for mid-career faculty members to learn from administrators and share their experiences with administrators and campus leaders.

   b. Leverage insights from peer networks to inform change-related priorities and areas of policy development.

We have observed positive impacts of the peer network on individual faculty. Of the 89 women who have participated in AT, more than half have been promoted to full, with many still preparing to submit their promotion dossiers. Internal evaluation results have also been positive. In the last AT cohort (2021–2022), for instance, participants reported that the program elements, like panel discussions with promotion committee members and members of the provost's office, had increased their knowledge about the requirements, standards, and review processes for promotion to tenure and dispelled myths about promotion requirements. They also reported that program activities like working with the media, getting feedback on their personal narratives, and gaining access to information repositories had provided them with new tools for career advancement. Furthermore, participants reported that opportunities to interact with one another in an environment built on mutual trust and confidentiality had reduced isolation and added to their professional networks.

Moreover, several of the women who participated in the mid-career faculty program have gone on to be involved in other ADVANCE peer networks (e.g., a leadership development program or a program for women full professors advocating for change in their own colleges) or have become leaders within their own college or at the campus level (e.g., associate dean in the Graduate School, as was the case for co-author Brooke Fisher Liu). In these roles, they remain plugged into the network by, for instance, serving as panel speakers or dossier reviewers or helping ADVANCE program staff make connections between individual faculty members and senior faculty in their college.

Lessons Learned

Previously, we identified a lack of connection and community, decentralization, and organizational hierarchies as major barriers to creating faculty development programs and for mid-career faculty members as individuals. In our lessons learned, we focus on what we see as the main impacts of sustaining faculty peer networks over a number of years with regard to addressing these three key challenges.

Fostering Connection and Community

Through our work, we have observed that peer networks offer a new model for faculty mentoring and community building. Specifically, the Advancing Together model is grounded in group mentoring that occurs among faculty members and also at scale (i.e., one senior faculty member providing mentoring to multiple associate professors). Since the ADVANCE program started running peer networks in 2011, we have observed a growing recognition across campus that such mentorship models can be effective and beneficial, as exemplified through the adoption of peer networks in other contexts (e.g., campus-wide graduate student mentoring circles and campus-wide writing productivity groups).

Another way that peer networks have facilitated change is by providing developmental opportunities for associate professors beyond cohort meetings. Many of the Advancing Together participants are regularly invited to serve as speakers for the peer network for assistant professors, where they share advice and make connections with early-career faculty members. Because peer networks have been sustained over a number of years, there is now a robust and growing group of faculty members who remain engaged in the network (e.g., by serving as speakers or peer network facilitators). The peer networks provide a sort of anchor of connection for faculty members long after they have participated in the program.

Developing Diverse Ties and Sharing Information

Through our work, we observed that ongoing peer networks help overcome some challenges that decentralization presents by diversifying networks and creating new information-sharing channels. This clearly helps mid-career faculty who participate, for instance, by giving them concrete information about what is required to be promoted as opposed to them relying upon departmental myths. However, this also shifts organizational outcomes, for example, by changing the representation of women and faculty of color who are promoted to full professor or by reducing time to promotion. Moreover, faculty members who realize that promotion policies involve narrow definitions of productivity or lack clarity may also decide to become advocates for change in their units or at the campus level. For instance, we have observed peer network participants go on to serve as associate deans in their colleges and to advocate for changes to both workload and promotion policies that recognize the diversity of faculty contributions.

Changing the Nature of Interactions

Finally, we learned that peer networks can disrupt organizational hierarchies by helping faculty members identify and connect with central decision-makers. Many of the Advancing Together meetings involve bringing together administrators and senior faculty members who have served on college- or campus-level promotion committees. Again, the individual impact of such meetings is clear: participants gain information and, to some extent, make themselves more visible to administrators. In the long run, we have also observed that these engagements can shape policy and practice. For instance, during the height of the COVID-19 pandemic, co-authors Dawn Culpepper and Brooke Fisher Liu, as Advancing Together facilitators, learned a great deal about the challenges participants faced and the impact of those challenges on their professional pursuits. We invited administrators to the group to, on the one hand, share information with participants, but also, on the other hand, to learn about the experiences of associate professors during this time. We cannot speculate on the extent to which campus administrators implicitly or explicitly incorporated these experiences into decision-making. However, we can say that our interactions with participants deeply shaped the kinds of policies and practices that we advocated for as our institution responded to the pandemic (e.g., the necessity of recognizing personal circumstances in COVID-19 impact statements). By breaking down hierarchical barriers, peer networks help foster more communication and understanding between faculty and administrators, which can be helpful in creating more responsive policies that support faculty development.

Conclusion

Some may argue that we have painted an overly optimistic picture of the impact of peer networks in engendering a culture of faculty development, so let us be clear: Peer networks alone cannot solve every faculty development problem that mid-career faculty face. Our efforts were also greatly enhanced by the infusion of support from the National Science Foundation, which catalyzed the creation of the networks and provided resources (e.g., stipends for facilitators, salaries for program personnel, and funds for meals and curricular materials) that propelled successful program delivery. Faculty developers and institutional leaders with different or fewer resources may experience different challenges and different results.

Despite these caveats, our goal was to show that the impact of peer networks goes beyond the benefits that an individual faculty member experiences. In our view, implementing individual peer networks over a number of years created a larger network – a critical infrastructure – of women faculty members across the campus. The impact of this larger network is somewhat harder to isolate and capture, but we have witnessed and experienced ourselves the ways that it breaks down organizational silos, fosters greater connection and community, and reduces the extent to which organizational hierarchies mitigate relationships among and between faculty members and administrators.

References

Acker, J. (1990). Hierarchies, jobs, bodies: A theory of gendered organizations. *Gender & Society*, 4(2), 139–158.

Baker, V. L., & Lattuca, L. R. (2010). Developmental networks and learning: Toward an interdisciplinary perspective on identity development during doctoral study. *Studies in Higher Education*, 35(7), 807–827.

Baker, V. L., & Manning, C. E. (2020). A mid-career faculty agenda: A review of four decades of research and practice. In L. Perna (Ed.), *Higher education: Handbook of theory and research* (Vol. 36, pp. 1–66). Springer.

Benbow, R. J., & Lee, C. (2019). Teaching-focused social networks among college faculty: Exploring conditions for the development of social capital. *Higher Education*, 78, 67–89.

Bond, M. A., & Lockee, B. B. (2018). Evaluating the effectiveness of faculty inquiry groups as communities of practice for faculty professional development. *Journal of Formative Design in Learning*, 2, 1–7.

Buch, K., Huet, Y., Rorrer, A., & Roberson, L. (2011). Removing the barriers to full professor: A mentoring program for associate professors. *Change: The Magazine of Higher Learning*, 43(6), 38–45.

Campbell, C. M., & O'Meara, K. (2014). Faculty agency: Departmental contexts that matter in faculty careers. *Research in Higher Education*, 55, 49–74.

Casad, B. J., Franks, J. E., Garasky, C. E., Kittleman, M. M., Roesler, A. C., Hall, D. Y., & Petzel, Z. W. (2021). Gender inequality in academia: Problems and solutions for women faculty in STEM. *Journal of Neuroscience Research*, 99(1), 13–23.

Covarrubias, R., Newton, X., & Glass, T. S. (2022). "You can be creative once you are tenured": Counterstories of academic writing from mid-career women faculty of color. *Multicultural Perspectives, 24*(3), 120–128.

Daly, A. (2010). Surveying the terrain ahead: Social network theory and educational change. In A. Daly (Ed.), *Social network theory* (pp. 259–274). Harvard Education Press.

Domingo, C. R., Gerber, N. C., Harris, D., Mamo, L., Pasion, S. G., Rebanal, R. D., & Rosser, S. V. (2022). More service or more advancement: Institutional barriers to academic success for women and women of color faculty at a large public comprehensive minority-serving state university. *Journal of Diversity in Higher Education, 15*(3), 365.

Fleming, S. S., Goldman, A. W., Correli, S. J., & Taylor, C. J. (2016). Settling in: The role of individual and departmental tactics in the development of new faculty networks. *The Journal of Higher Education, 87*(4), 544–572.

Ginther, D. K., Currie, J. M., Blau, F. D., & Croson, R. T. (2020, May). Can mentoring help female assistant professors in economics? An evaluation by randomized trial. In *AEA papers and proceedings* (Vol. 110, pp. 205–209).

Hill, L. B. (2020). Understanding the impact of a multi-institutional STEM reform network through key boundary-spanning individuals. *The Journal of Higher Education, 91*(3), 455–482.

Kelly, B. T., & McCann, K. I. (2014). Women faculty of color: Stories behind the statistics. *The Urban Review, 46,* 681–702.

Kezar, A. (2012). *Embracing non-tenure track faculty: Changing campuses for the new faculty majority.* Routledge.

Kezar, A. (2014). Higher education change and social networks: A review of research. *The Journal of Higher Education, 85*(1), 91–125.

Lawrence, J., Ott, M., & Bell, A. (2012). Faculty organizational commitment and citizenship. *Research in Higher Education, 53,* 325–352.

Liera, R. (2020). Equity advocates using equity-mindedness to interrupt faculty hiring's racial structure. *Teachers College Record, 122*(9), 1–42.

Liu, S. N. C., Brown, S. E., & Sabat, I. E. (2019). Patching the "leaky pipeline": Interventions for women of color faculty in STEM academia. *Archives of Scientific Psychology, 7*(1), 32.

Lunsford, L., Baker, V., & Pifer, M. (2018). Faculty mentoring faculty: Career stages, relationship quality, and job satisfaction. *International Journal of Mentoring and Coaching in Education, 7*(2), 139–154.

Niehaus, E., & O'Meara, K. (2015). Invisible but essential: The role of professional networks in promoting faculty agency in career advancement. *Innovative Higher Education, 40,* 159–171.

O'Meara, K., Lennartz, C. J., Kuvaeva, A., Jaeger, A., & Misra, J. (2019a). Department conditions and practices associated with faculty workload satisfaction and perceptions of equity. *The Journal of Higher Education, 90*(5), 744–772.

O'Meara, K., Nyunt, G., Templeton, L., & Kuvaeva, A. (2019b). Meeting to transgress: The role of faculty learning communities in shaping more inclusive organizational cultures. *Equality, Diversity and Inclusion: An International Journal, 38*(3), 286–304.

Ray, V. (2019). A theory of racialized organizations. *American Sociological Review*, *84*(1), 26–53.

Rosinger, K. O., Taylor, B. J., Coco, L., & Slaughter, S. (2016). Organizational segmentation and the prestige economy: Deprofessionalization in high-and low-resource departments. *The Journal of Higher Education*, *87*(1), 27–54.

Williams, B. N., & Williams, S. M. (2006). Perceptions of African American male junior faculty on promotion and tenure: Implications for community building and social capital. *Teachers College Record*, *108*(2), 287–315.

Young, K., Anderson, M., & Stewart, S. (2015). Hierarchical microaggressions in higher education. *Journal of Diversity in Higher Education*, *8*(1), 61–71.

Chapter 17

Mid-Career but New to the Academy

A Federal Investment in ROTC Educators and Cadets

Jeffrey C. Sun and Taylor L. Pratt

Overview

In 2014, the U.S. Army's Cadet Command sought to develop and deliver a training program, in partnership with an institution of higher education, that would support mid-career Army soldiers transitioning into college-level instructional roles at Reserve Officers' Training Corps (ROTC) programs across the nation. These programs, housed within university military science departments, are designed to educate and develop college students into Army officers. In some respects, this approach is very similar to that of other professional pathways targeting workforce development through postsecondary education. However, unlike other college faculty encountering mid-career shifts (e.g., Becher, 1999), this population of college faculty (i.e., the military science faculty) are entering a new professional role with significantly different skills from those of many of their peers, skills that will be employed in a wholly different setting than that of previous work assignments. And to top it off, in most instances, the military science faculty only serve in that college teaching role for three years. Given the change in roles, timing, and organizational context, the Army's investment in these mid-career professionals has to be relatively comprehensive, quick, affordable, and relevant, while the program has to be not only effective but also skill development, equity-centered, achievable, and sustainable.

Program Focus

The University of Louisville/Army Master Educator Course (MEC), formerly known as the Cadre and Faculty Development Course (CFDC), was designed to educate Army faculty (also referred to as "cadre") teaching in Army ROTC programs, which are housed on more than 1,100 campuses across the United States. Army ROTC programs aim to "recruit, educate, develop, and inspire" cadets and serve as the largest commissioning source of officers for the Army (Gainee, n.d.; Mele, 2020; United States Army

DOI: 10.4324/9781003428626-22

Cadet Command, n.d.). The placement of ROTC programs within the organizational structure varies across institutions, but most operate as a distinct academic department (i.e., Department of Military Science) (Mele, 2020). Given the nature of ROTC programs, a mid-career professional program aimed at developing and supporting ROTC instructors needed to blend Army leader development and learning approaches with higher education concepts and principles.

MEC's educational programming addresses organization and administration of higher education, program development and assessment, diversity and equity in higher education, college teaching and learning, and instructional strategies. MEC consists of two phases delivered across two semesters. For the first phase, the "residential" experience, the program participants travel to participate in person; this portion of the program is akin to a cohort-based executive education course or training program, with intensive day-long instruction across four weeks. Following the residential experience, participants travel back to their assigned ROTC programs and begin the application phase. During this phase, participants apply lessons learned to initiatives aimed at improving their ROTC programs. After just one semester, program participants are already back in their programs, implementing their learning with the guidance of an expert higher education faculty member; this makes for a rather quick, achievable, and sustainable program that is still growth oriented and learner centered.

Teaching and learning boot camps have grown in popularity, especially in the fields of health care education and career and technical education. For instance, Rush University has a three-day boot camp for interprofessional health care education to train faculty in effective course design and learning impacts. The University of North Carolina Eshelman School of Pharmacy developed a boot camp for improving health science educators' teaching and learning practices and extended that effort to also include a boot camp for the scholarship of teaching and learning. Similarly, a team at the University of Louisville, including one of the authors of this chapter, launched a statewide initiative for career and technical education instructors, who participate in a series of day-long workshops on developmental learning and mentoring that extends over a two-year period. The required structured activities are complemented by the presence of a professional learning community that encourages the sharing of ideas and resources and offers a forum for support and positive motivation. These types of projects suggest that discipline-focused faculty development programs with a high degree of interactivity and supports via an intensive program environment are effective. Such a design attracts participation, sustains interest, and leads to teaching improvement. While this design could be implemented for early-career professionals, the boot camp approach is particularly fruitful for mid-career professionals, who are able to draw on prior knowledge more readily to improve their craft as educators. In other words, the formula of a condensed, intensive experience, which is discipline focused and models extensive interactivity, is fitting and likely desirable for the mid-career faculty audience.

Needed Skills

MEC was designed to address the Army's need to educate ROTC faculty – mid-career soldiers taking on a new instructional leadership role – on navigating and operating within higher education and on teaching cadets in ways that employ evidence-based practices. Instructional leadership and investing in its mid-career leaders are fundamental to Army training efforts. To these ends, a key Army doctrine outlines the importance of an organizational climate that encourages learning and superiors that invest in the development of their subordinates or mentees; so, as in other learning organizations, one generation inculcates values and lessons in the next (Headquarters, Department of the Army, 2012a, 2012b). Further, the Army seeks to provide soldiers with increasingly challenging educational opportunities, training, and experiences throughout their Army careers; this leadership development approach is designed to help soldiers, especially mid-career professionals, progress as leaders in the force (Headquarters, Department of the Army, 2015). Ultimately, the Army's learning goal is "develop[ing] agile, adaptive, and innovative soldiers and Army civilians with the competencies to build cohesive teams to win in a complex world" (Headquarters, Department of the Army, 2017, p. 8). Thus, the Army sought to design a comprehensive, learner-centered, sustainable program to advance the education, training, and experiences of new or incoming ROTC instructors and to address this identified need for post-secondary faculty training.

Rationale

Bearing in mind the Army's goal of investing in the leadership development of these mid-career soldiers, the design of MEC required an infusion of higher education knowledge and concepts so that the soldiers assigned to ROTC programs would be sufficiently prepared to teach and lead on a college campus. Initially, the Army sought to institute an adult learning program in line with adult education principles underpinning the Army's overarching training and education approaches (Army University, 2015; Headquarters, Department of the Army, 2012a, 2012b). However, like many outside of the field of higher education, the Army did not take into account the fact that higher education itself is a field of study. Grounding the program within the study of higher education was more appropriate because ROTC instructors needed to develop knowledge and skillsets pertaining to (1) developmental stages of young adults, (2) campus settings and experiences, and (3) structural and cultural elements of college policies and practices. Research suggests that a steep learning curve exists for professionals who transition into a faculty role as outsiders or undertake it as a "second career"; challenges can include adapting to institutional cultures and engaging in identity work (Brown et al., 2012; Crane et al., 2009; Herman et al., 2021; Trowler & Knight, 2000). As Crane et al. (2009) explain, when entering higher education as outsiders, new faculty "may experience an orientation and initiation that does not meet their particular needs" because these induction experiences are often designed for recent doctoral graduates (p. 24). Accordingly, the Master Educator Course curriculum is designed to address the higher education orientation gap that many ROTC faculty face as outsiders new to the academy, but the approach also had to connect concepts and lessons to Army doctrine, policies, and practices for the experience to be comprehensible and meaningful.

One challenge is that the field of higher education does not have professional frameworks or competencies for college instructors per se, with the exceptions of Quality Matters for online teaching, NASPA/ACPA for student affairs, high-impact practices for student retention, and general "best" practices for teaching. When the initial MEC pilot program was being developed, competency-based education (CBE) was growing; corporate training and development were continuing to expand; the field of instructional design was still evolving; and concepts such as equity, inclusion, and belonging were increasingly being researched within postsecondary contexts, especially with regard to student success practices (their infusion into instructional design and practice still being nascent). Additionally, educational technology was expanding beyond clickers and social media (e.g., virtual whiteboards, online games, and real-time presentation feedback). Wraparound services, alongside various retention supports, were becoming more common on campuses. Finally, the Army was re-envisioning holistic supports for soldiers and what the future Army might look like, including a potential shift from a focus on training objectives to one on learning outcomes that guide relevant assessment measures and activities (Asymmetric Warfare Group, n.d.). The Army needed something that integrated all these aspects, so the Master Educator Course was developed. As research and other evidence-based practices become better known, this mid-career program continues to evolve.

Equity and Inclusion Considerations

Since its inception, the Master Educator Course, which is a joint project of the University of Louisville and the Army, has incorporated a clear, equity-minded approach into several of its design elements and programmatic initiatives relating to admission of participants, academic and professional supports, and curricular design. For instance, 46 percent of program participants in the most recent MEC offering identified as a member of a racial minoritized group and 21 percent identified as women. For comparison, 2021 demographic data on the active-duty Army reported only 32 percent identifying as members of a racial minoritized group and 15.5 percent identifying as women (Military OneSource, 2021). The leadership is attentive to ensuring that a diverse range of individuals have the opportunity to participate in the program across ranks, race, ethnicity, gender, geographic location, and assigned institution, among other factors, with the goal of creating a meaningful experience for all participants.

Given the diverse needs and experiences of MEC participants, the program includes in-house writing consultants and assigned faculty advisors to address participants' individual academic needs and professional goals. MEC participants can work one-on-one with a writing consultant on any of their assignments and as many times as they would like, and a rewrite policy is in place for major assignments as an additional equity-minded practice (Artze-Vega et al., 2023). Additionally, the MEC curriculum implements and models inclusive approaches and instructional strategies for cultivating a learning environment that is welcoming and safe, such as creating ground rules for difficult discussions, mitigating stereotype threat, and designing learning with access in mind (Ambrose et al., 2010; CAST, 2018; Hammond, 2015; National Research Council, 2018; Steele, 2010). Participants practice examining and framing cadet experiences through such equity lenses. To apply their learning and improve cadet experiences, participants revise four lessons during the residential phase with an equity focus on dimensions of belonging, a universal design for learning, and the effects of learning on emotions using such artifacts as worksheets, discussion questions, slide decks, group and gamified activities, videos, assessments, and feedback on student assignments. As the needs of mid-career participants evolve and new scholarship informs equity-minded approaches, the MEC program adapts to infuse new evidence-based approaches that support equity and inclusion.

Conceptual Grounding

In its current form, the Master Educator Course is a two-semester program that aligns with the University of Louisville Master of Arts (MA) in higher education administration degree; however, it has some distinctive features. For instance, it recognizes Scholar-Army Connections by connecting Army doctrine, higher education practice, and scholarly research. The Army Learning Concept (ALC) and Leadership Requirements Model (LRM) are at the core of the MEC curriculum, which aims to blend learner-centric education, training, and experiences to develop mission-ready soldiers (Headquarters, Department of the Army, 2017). MEC incorporates a Theory-to-Practice Focus (Dewey, 1938, 1997), creating an environment in which course instructors model lessons learned through their teaching and offering opportunities for ROTC instructors to implement lessons developed throughout their coursework.

The structured learning is a massive *scaffold* experience (Bain, 2004; Vygotsky, 1978). The courses and outside classroom experiences are intentionally designed to build on and draw from one another so that students can develop their own teaching resources, lesson plans, and instructional strategies as they learn. The MEC curriculum integrates and models evidence-based research on teaching college students, including research on memory and learning. MEC participants experience instructional strategies designed to enhance their learning, such as activities that require the retrieval of prior learning, metacognitive reflection, and spaced practice opportunities (Lang, 2021; National Research Council, 2018). MEC participants are then asked to apply and implement these strategies in their own teaching. The learning is linked with demonstrated evidence to academic and professional competencies (e.g., IBSTPI, NASPA/ACPA Competencies). In short, this mid-career professional program offers a relatively comprehensive, quick, affordable, and relevant approach to making experienced soldiers into competent educators in a post-secondary setting.

Tool

The Master Educator Course (MEC)

The University of Louisville faculty had a limited background in working with the Army. A decade earlier, one of the authors had helped structure a relationship between Teachers College, Columbia University, and the U.S. Military Academy at West Point for tactical officers, but that program, while informative about the roles of mentorship and the supervision of cadets, had a different organizational structure and context; also, the Army officers in that program did not serve as college instructors, but rather filled a role more akin to that of a learning coach or mentor. To design the MEC program, in 2014, the principal investigator facilitated an integrated inquiry into ethnography and design thinking processes.

Program Design

The approach taken to designing this mid-career experience applies to other successful discipline-based, intensive delivery programs. That is, the first step is for the program designers to understand the discipline or field of study. To do so, the principal investigator of this project constructed a traditional ethnographic inquiry, in which the research sought to elucidate the military science context, the learning process (including embedded traditions and norms), the roles and functions of key actors, and the relationships between the campus and the academic program. This step relied, in part, on archival data. In addition, the principal investigator observed 16 military science class sessions and a series of labs (including a field-based training exercise and physical training sessions) on several ROTC programs. Consistent with other ethnographic studies seeking to uncover cultural experiences and implement innovative solutions to enhance those experiences (Beckman & Barry, 2007), the principal investigator took field notes about the space (e.g., learning spaces), the actors involved (e.g., people present in the classrooms and field training exercises), the activities observed (e.g., types of instruction or commands provided and reactions), the objects present (e.g., materials used in the learning environment), the actions that individuals take (e.g., struggling to comprehend and pose questions), the events observed (e.g., differences among class types), time (e.g., time of day and pacing), goals (e.g., instructional objectives), and feelings (e.g., reactions of various actors). Further, the principal investigator interviewed ROTC instructors and college students serving as cadets to expand the knowledge base, seek clarification on various observations, and gain insights about what the instructors and cadets valued, questioned, and identified as gaps in their knowledge or experience.

Continuing the ethnography principles, the second part of the study employed the Stanford design thinking framework (Plattner et al., 2011) to draw out curricular design elements from key actors behind the instructor and learner experiences. Drawing on the five-step process, a team of instructors, staff, and students engaged in an empathy exercise, which was centered on cadets' development as college students entering a new profession. Then, the participants engaged in rounds to ultimately define the needs of ROTC faculty as mid-career professionals in the Army. In other words, what is the specific problem that the Army wanted to solve when its interest is in improving ROTC faculty development? It became clear from this phase of the design thinking that the Army lacked the ability to educate ROTC faculty on how to operate within higher education and how to educate cadets in ways that employ evidence-based practices in college teaching, learning, and student development.

Moving forward with a preliminary plan, most of the participants continued the design thinking process and engaged in ideation about potential design solutions. Guided by the principal investigator, the participants brainstormed various lessons. Then the principal investigator took the hundreds of line-item recommendations and constructed learning modules and integrated them, when aligned and practical, with the NASPA/ACPA Competencies, International Board of Standards for Training, Performance and Instruction (IBSTPI) Competencies, lessons from *What the Best College Teachers Do* (Bain, 2004) and *Academic Leadership and Governance of Higher Education* (Harris et al., 2022; Hendrickson et al., 2012), and evidence-based practices from *How People Learn* (National Research Council, 2000).

Program Outline and Activities

In the first semester, Army soldiers who are selected for this program prepare for the experience by doing multiple written and reading assignments, including diagnostic writing and analysis, content pretests, and an evaluated teaching demonstration. Then the soldiers engage in an intense, four-week residential experience with 30 hours per week of direct learning time and 40 to 50 hours per week of reading and assignments. During this period, the soldiers learn about foundational concepts and cutting-edge research from respected higher education faculty concerning the organization and administration of higher education, program development and assessment, diversity and equity in higher education, college teaching and learning, and instructional strategies. Throughout this semester, the soldiers produce multiple demonstrations of learning, including a needs assessment, theory analysis, program data sheet with benchmarked data across other ROTC programs and other student populations, program improvement plan, student learning assessment, program evaluation, teaching and learning theories analysis, teaching philosophy statement, inclusive learning plan, syllabus, four lesson plans, three teaching demonstrations, an instructional toolkit (particularly technology tools/applications), and a metacognitive reflection paper that incorporates an equity-centered perspective.

In the second semester, the soldiers engage in learning through online asynchronous modules and 540 hours of applied experiences. Throughout these experiences, the soldiers also participate in a series of group and one-on-one coaching calls with a faculty mentor. At the end of these experiences, soldiers implement and test their program improvement plan, assess student learning, evaluate the program change or intervention success, and make needed improvements. In addition, the soldiers continuously practice, reflect, assess, improve, and seek guidance during their instruction. They also network across the campus and community to asset map their relationships and promote more linkages, propose new programs/interventions, design approaches that improve their performance and advance cadet success, and evaluate their progress through an equity-minded lens. Finally, they revisit the products produced in the first semester and make changes to all the plans, assessments, tools, and instructional materials in their portfolio, as well as document the changes in a metacognitive reflection paper that centers reflection via an equity-centered lens. In short, the mid-career program implements a cycle in which the participants examine their environment and approaches to excel in leadership and learning within higher education; frame their roles and impacts in meaningful ways; execute program supports and improvement plans to enhance the cadet experience; and improve operations, policies, and other practices with the mission of preparing cadets to be future Army officers.

This mid-career profession program is constantly evaluated and improved. Throughout the program delivery, the faculty and staff team, who lead the program, engage in informal and formal data collection (e.g., daily feedback and formal after-action reviews) about ways to improve the learning design and experience. The team is constantly asking: What have we learned about the Army, ROTC instructors, cadets, or universities that suggests changes to our delivery and content – whether in a macro or micro manner?

To expand the faculty and staff preparation and expertise building, every instructor and key staff member has participated in site visits to a select group of ROTC programs across the nation. One to two individuals will visit two to three campuses in a one-week trip. During these visits, the faculty or staff member learns about each visited program, much like what would happen on an accreditation site visit. The individual observes and examines the facilities, admissions/recruiting efforts, sample course instruction, techniques employed for helping skills and advising, degree and type of resources and relationships on-campus and within the community, efforts to support or expand ROTC instructor development, program key performance indicators (KPIs), and unique program and campus features. Throughout these observations, the faculty and staff search for signals of equity-minded approaches.

In sum, each lesson, assignment, activity, and improvement focuses on the mid-career professional's impact on cadets through skill development, equity-centered, achievable, and sustainable design.

Lessons Learned

Since its first "proof of principle" offering in 2015, the Master Educator Course will have served more than 1,000 graduate participants by the summer of 2023. Program successes highlight the talent and skills of these mid-career Army professionals: participants have implemented academic success initiatives (e.g., dedicated group study hours); have developed cross-campus partnerships (e.g., athletics, admissions, campus housing); have developed curriculum and continuity plans for their program; have been nominated for teaching excellence; have secured new funding (e.g., alumni donors, university budget allocations); and have improved cadet field training performance, among other initiatives and successes. In terms of program improvements, a key lesson that has emerged from program data and evaluation is the need for increased guidance on how to narrow a project or focus on a smaller, more accomplishable aspect of it within the one-semester application phase. MEC participants often plan larger initiatives that span the entirety of their remaining ROTC assignment, meaning they may not have fully completed an initiative by the end of the program. By further streamlining course assignments and advising students to design projects that are achievable within the allotted time frame, participants will be better able to take advantage of the mentorship provided by the mid-career-profession program.

Conclusion

This chapter highlighted a federal investment in ROTC educators and cadets through a program designed to educate mid-career Army professionals who are new to teaching and training students in the postsecondary environment. Though this program is federally funded, the program design and activities outlined can be applied to other parts of higher education. As discussed, faculty members leaving other professions and entering higher education as mid-career professionals often struggle to orient themselves to the new environment and can find existing programs for new faculty inadequate to address their unique needs and experiences. MEC offers an approach to designing a program that addresses the needs of mid-career-yet-new-to-higher-education faculty. The program steps and activities outlined in this chapter might be applied to designing mid-career professional programs in career and technical education (CTE), STEM, healthcare, etc., for faculty members transitioning from professional careers outside of the academy. Like MEC, such programs would need to infuse post-secondary training with the discipline, content, and field-based expertise of these mid-career professionals. Given the changing landscape of higher education, such programs – which might perhaps be led by specific colleges or campus teaching and learning centers – would work to ensure that non-traditional groups of mid-career professionals are developed and supported in their faculty roles. At the same time, this boot camp approach might be fitting for many other faculty who seek ways to improve their craft as teachers when they encounter a discipline or field of study–focused program that models a variety of instructional interactivity techniques and values faculty members' prior knowledge.

References

Ambrose, S.A., Bridges, M.W., DiPietro, M., Lovett, M.C., & Norman, M.K. (2010). *How learning works: Seven research-based principles for smart teaching.* Jossey-Bass.

Army University. (2015). *The Army University white paper.* Author. https://army-university.edu/images/AboutPageImages/Army%20University%20White%20Paper%20(Combined%20Arms%20Center%2025%20Feb%2015).pdf

Artze-Vega, I., Darby, F. Dewsbury, B., & Imad, M. (2023). *The Norton guide to equity-minded teaching.* Norton.

Asymmetric Warfare Group. (n.d.). *Adaptive soldier/leader training and education (ASTLE): An approach to implementing the army learning method.* Author.

Bain, K. (2004). *What the best college teachers do.* Harvard University Press.

Becher, T. (1999). Universities and mid-career professionals: The policy potential. *Higher Education Quarterly, 53*(2), 156–172. https://doi.org/10.1111/1468-2273.00121

Beckman, S. L., & Barry, M. (2007). Innovation as a learning process: Embedding design thinking. *California Management Review, 50*(1), 25–56. https://doi.org/10.2307/41166415

Brown, A., Bimrose, J., Barnes, S.-A., & Hughes, D. (2012). The role of career adaptabilities for mid-career changers. *Journal of Vocational Behavior, 80*(3), 754–761. https://doi.org/10.1016/j.jvb.2012.01.003

CAST. (2018). *Universal design for learning guidelines version 2.2.* http://udlguidelines.cast.org

Crane, B., O'Hern, B., & Lawler, P. (2009). Second career professionals: Transitioning to the faculty role. *Journal of Faculty Development, 23*(1), 24–29. https://eric.ed.gov/?id=EJ847797

Dewey, J. (1938). *Experience and education.* Touchstone.

Dewey, J. (1997). *Experience and education.* Touchstone.

Gainee, S. A. (n.d.). History. *United States Army Cadet Command.* www.cadet-command.army.mil/history.aspx

Hammond, Z. (2015). *Culturally responsive teaching and the brain.* SAGE.

Harris, J. T., Lane, J. E., Sun, J. C., & Baker, G. F. (2022). *Academic leadership and governance of higher education: A guide for trustees, leaders, and aspiring leaders of two- and four-year institutions* (2nd ed.). Stylus Publishing.

Headquarters, Department of the Army. (2012a). *ADP 6–22: Army leadership.* Author.

Headquarters, Department of the Army. (2012b). *ADRP 6–22: Army leadership.* Author.

Headquarters, Department of the Army. (2015). *FM 6–22: Leader development.* Author.

Headquarters, Department of the Army. (2017). *The U.S. army learning concept for training and education.* Author.

Hendrickson, R. M., Lane, J. E., Harris, J. T., & Dorman, R. H. (2012). *Academic leadership and governance of higher education: A guide for trustees, leaders, and aspiring leaders of two- and four-year institutions.* Stylus Publishing.

Herman, N., Jose, M., Katiya, M., Kemp, M., le Roux, N., van Vuuren., C., & van der Merwe, C. (2021). "Entering the world of academia is like starting a new life": A trio of reflections from Health Professionals joining academia as second career academics. *International Journal for Academic Development, 26*(1), 69–81. https://doi.org/10.1080/1360144X.2020.1784742

Lang, J. M. (2021). *Small teaching: Everyday lessons from the science of learning* (2nd ed.). Jossey-Bass.

Mele, P. A. (2020). Army ROTC and military science: Development trusted Army professionals. *New Directions for Student Leadership*, *165*, 137–148. https://doi.org/10.1002/yd.20375

Military OneSource. (2021). *2021 Demographics: Interactive profile of the military community*. https://demographics.militaryonesource.mil/

National Research Council. (2000). *How people learn: Brain, mind, experience, and school*. The National Academies Press. https://doi.org/10.17226/9853

National Research Council. (2018). *How people learn II: Learners, contexts, cultures*. The National Academies Press. https://doi.org/10.17226/24783

Plattner, H., Meinel, C., & Leifer, L. (2011). *Design thinking: Understand – improve – apply*. Springer.

Steele, C. M. (2010). *Whistling Vivaldi: How stereotypes affect us and what we can do*. Norton.

Trowler, P., & Knight, P. T. (2000). Coming to know in higher education: Theorising faculty entry to new work contexts. *Higher Education Research & Development*, *19*(1), 27–42. https://doi.org/10.1080/07294360050020453

United States Army Cadet Command. (n.d.) *Home*. Author. www.cadetcommand.army.mil/index.html

Vygotsky, L. S. (1978). *Mind in society: The development of higher psychological processes*. Harvard University Press.

Chapter 18

Using Humanities-Based Grants to Leverage Resources, Acquire New Skills, and Expand Networks

Deborah Vriend Van Duinen

Overview

"At this workshop, I've felt seen, valued, and supported. At my college, I haven't felt this way in a long time."
    – Associate Professor, English Department, Liberal Arts College

This quote, from a participant in a humanities-based faculty development workshop I led last year, speaks to what many mid-career faculty feel and yearn for as they navigate research, teaching, and service commitments at their respective institutions. The mid-career stage, for many faculty, often includes conflicting roles and responsibilities that can lead to burnout, disengagement, and stalled career progression (Baker, 2020, 2022). When it comes to pursuing grant-funding opportunities, this can be deeply problematic. Finding and securing grants is part and parcel of a faculty member's job. Grants can provide financial support for research, scholarship, and professional development. They are also often collaborative in nature and can lead to valuable networking opportunities both within and outside of higher education. Grants increase the visibility of individual faculty members and their work and benefit institutions by bringing in additional resources and expertise that advance organizational aims.

And yet, for many humanities faculty, finding grants to support their research and scholarship can be difficult. There are fewer and smaller humanities-related funding opportunities, and many of these are highly competitive. Additionally, many humanities faculty do not have the support or training they need to develop project ideas or find, apply for, and secure grants. If faculty do receive grant funding for projects, the amount of work and kind of work involved can feel overwhelming, particularly because many grants include requirements and depend on skills that exist outside of specific disciplinary training. This is especially true when grant funding requires or involves community partnerships or other collaborations.

DOI: 10.4324/9781003428626-23

This chapter aims to help mid-career faculty be more strategic, creative, and prepared in using grant funding to support their scholarship. Based on my experiences receiving local, state-level, and national grants to support my humanities-based scholarship and my work with mid-career humanities faculty, I offer two tools for faculty to use in their grant-funding efforts and implementations. These tools, rooted in social cognitive career theory (SCCT) and self-determination theory (SDT), are designed to help faculty clarify, align, and diversify their scholarly agendas. Faculty need training and support to develop the necessary skills and expertise to find, secure, and successfully implement grant-funded projects. Exploring and capitalizing on various grant-funding opportunities can help faculty experience mid-career as a "rebirth, an opportunity to evolve, and to re-envision the next phase of their career" (Baker, 2022, p. 17). When faculty are strategic about grant-funding opportunities, they can expand their scholarship's scope and dissemination and bolster their existing networks.

Program Focus

Grant funding has helped me grow my personal and professional networks and leverage existing resources. Who I am as a scholar, teacher, researcher, and leader on campus has been supported and shaped by grant-funding opportunities. To date, I have received almost 30 grants, of varying amounts, from national, state-level, and local agencies. My learning curve has been significant. I've had to learn, often through trial and error, to navigate the grant-funding world and to use grant-funding opportunities to support my larger scholarship goals. Equally hard has been learning how to run a successful grant-funded humanities-based program involving many stakeholders and partnerships. I've had to learn skills and information that I would never have otherwise learned, related to budgeting, public affairs and marketing, event planning, procurement, crisis management, evaluation methods, staff leadership, and community advocacy, to name just a few areas. I've often felt lonely, unsupported, and ill-equipped, just as the workshop participant described feeling at the beginning of this chapter.

Institutional support and training for faculty grant-funding success might seem obvious and necessary. Yet this area of faculty development remains deficient, particularly for humanities faculty and even more so for mid-career faculty. While I am now fortunate to have a supportive and well-resourced Office of Sponsored Research in the liberal arts institution where I work, this wasn't always the case and is not often the case at many smaller colleges.

Finding relevant grant-funding opportunities administered by national or international governmental agencies, private institutions, or non-profit organizations is no small task. Furthermore, preparing extensive grant proposal materials is time-consuming and labor-intensive (and feels more so with no guarantee of success). For faculty struggling to find time for their teaching, research, and service commitments, this aspect of their job can feel overwhelming and intimidating.

In March 2021, I led a three-day faculty development workshop focused on humanities-based programming and grant-funding opportunities. The workshop was fully funded by the Lilly Fellows Program in Humanities and the Arts (LFP), an organization funded by Valparaiso University, the LFP National Network, and a grant from the Lilly Endowment Inc., an Indianapolis-based private philanthropic foundation. LFP annually funds several projects for Lilly Network Institutions that are chosen because they advance the overall mission of the program and increase participation of Network Institutions in the activities and formative experiences of the LFP. The LFP identified the importance and lack of "faculty development throughout the disciplines, across a wide range of topics, and through all career ranks" (Lilly Fellows Program, n.d.). Their vision of successful faculty development projects is to have participants closely observe a campus community and, in this, to have "open invitations, interdisciplinary groups, and generous hospitality" (Lilly Fellows Program, n.d.).

My workshop focused on the intersections of literature and campus/community partnerships using an annual month-long community-wide reading program, Big Read Lakeshore, as an example of and springboard for discussing participants' experiences with humanities-based programs. Engaging 12 mid-career faculty from Lilly Network colleges and universities across the United States, the workshop addressed campus and community partnerships, book selection considerations, institutional mission alignment, program marketing and implementation, event facilitation, and research/scholarship possibilities. Various Big Read Lakeshore stakeholders, including faculty, students, local K–12 teachers, librarians, community members, and non-profit organization directors, participated in panel discussions that prompted workshop participants to share, brainstorm, and provide feedback on each other's humanities-based scholarship and programming efforts. Participants left the workshop better equipped and empowered to organize, lead, and facilitate their own grant-funded projects and programs.

In organizing and facilitating this faculty development workshop, it's important to note that I also benefited. While I learned with and from the workshop participants, I was also strategic about the opportunity to expand my existing networks and grow new skills (i.e., faculty leadership). I was explicit about this with workshop participants because I wanted to model how to use grant-funded projects to support skill development and larger scholarship and career goals.

Needed Skills

Faculty need specific skills to find and secure grant-funding opportunities and successfully implement humanities-based programming (Carlson & O'Neal-McElrath, 2008). On one level, these skills are logistical. They include knowing where to look for grants and how to make sense of their scope, topics, and eligibility requirements. There are also the skills involved in putting together a grant proposal: crafting a narrative, determining goals and objectives, identifying the audience, preparing a budget, and articulating an evaluation plan. Upon receiving a grant, there are skills required in knowing how to manage and track funds, monitor progress, evaluate success, and prepare the final report.

Many grant workshops focus on these kinds of logistical skills. What I've come to realize over the years is that these logistical skills need to be paired with strategic skills. Faculty must also clearly articulate their larger career narrative and scholarship goals, determine alignment with institutional priorities, and identify various dissemination sources (Baker, 2020). This allows faculty to be more creative, flexible, and adaptable with their research or scholarly plans. This leads to alignment with more grant-funding opportunities and the ability to craft a more compelling narrative for grant proposals. Grant funding can support new research directions and different avenues of research dissemination, such as faculty work in a local community or with a unique campus partnership. Grants can also support a diversified portfolio, including faculty professional development. Empowering faculty with the logistic and strategic skills to pursue grant-funding opportunities makes them better equipped to leverage existing campus, community, and/or professional resources, increase professional networks, and disseminate scholarship more widely.

Rationale

As Baker (2020) points out, mid-career faculty often lack, and need, mentorship and guidance. This is true within the research realm: while faculty might be experts in their areas of specialization, many, if not most, lack the skills needed to disseminate this expertise or even to partner with people outside their fields of study. This lack of faculty development can lead to high faculty burnout rates, disengagement (Baker, 2022), and an under-actualized program potential on campus and/or in a college or university's larger geographic community.

In addition, there remains little to no collaboration and few conversations across institutions about humanities-based programs and faculty involvement, even though such programs often establish important and relevant connections and collaborations for institutions and their surrounding communities. Humanities-based programming can initiate and encourage campus and community conversations about timely and relevant issues. Faculty involved in such programming initiatives are well positioned to be thought leaders and change agents on their campuses, in geographic communities, and worldwide. Yet a gap remains in faculty development around these experiences both within and across higher education institutions.

Equity and Inclusion Considerations

Research on mid-career faculty suggests that women and faculty of color traditionally spend more time on their teaching, service, and leadership (Perry, 2014; Strunk, 2020) and that these commitments often do not contribute to their professional advancement (Baker et al., 2019) or to the furthering of their research and scholarly work. It is hard to find the time and energy to proactively find and apply for grant-funding opportunities, let alone initiate and successfully implement a grant-funded project. In addition, faculty of color can face the challenge of epistemic exclusion, the devaluing of their scholarship (Dotson, 2014; Settles et al., 2021).

Many women and faculty of color have little guidance or motivation in advancing their careers (Misra & Lundquist, 2015). Too often, faculty lack the specific knowledge to find and apply for grant-funding opportunities and the support to learn how to do grant-related tasks and responsibilities that fall outside the realm of their academic training or expertise. Mid-career faculty need specific tools and strategies to successfully navigate grant-funding opportunities for their projects and their work within these projects. Supporting all mid-career faculty with grant-funding opportunities and skills is important, but providing this support for women and faculty of color is especially important.

Theoretical Grounding

Supporting mid-career humanities faculty in finding, securing, and successfully implementing grant funding requires skill development. I draw on two theories to conceptualize how faculty must approach their scholarship goals and grant-funding opportunities.

Social Cognitive Career Theory (SCCT)

SCCT emphasizes the role of social and cognitive factors in career development and decision making (Bandura, 1986; Lent et al., 1994). Focusing on the importance of personal goals, self-efficacy beliefs, and outcome expectations, this theory provides a framework for how faculty can approach career decisions in the academy. Gonzalez et al. (2019) used SCCT to explore the supports for and barriers to researcher development for new faculty members. They found that barrier categories included lack of mentoring, workload, and lack of resources. Support categories included a supportive university environment, funding, and effective research collaborations. Seo et al. (2017) identified core competencies needed to advance the careers of female associate professors by drawing on an SCCT framework. Their findings include making important connections, fulfilling responsibilities in academia, being politically savvy, managing personal and professional obligations, developing a sense of self-agency about one's career, and believing in oneself in the context of academic work. Their study provides helpful suggestions for supporting faculty research and practice.

Related to grant funding, SCCT suggests that it is important to have a clear understanding of the expected outcomes, a strong motivation to apply for and seek grants, and the necessary knowledge and skills with which to do so. SCCT research suggests that faculty development around grant-funding needs to support faculty beyond giving them practical tips and tricks for submitting grant materials. Rather, conversations about and support for grant funding, on an individual and institutional level, need to occur within a larger context of relationships, self-reflection, and career goals.

Diffusion of Innovations Theory (DOI)

DOI considers how new ideas and innovations spread and are adopted within a social system. Originally developed by sociologist Everett Rogers in the 1960s, this theory identifies five main categories of adopters of new innovations: innovators, early adopters, early majority, late majority, and laggards (Rogers, 2003). Innovators are the first individuals to adopt new innovations, and they tend to be risk-takers and highly knowledgeable about the innovation. Early adopters are the second group to adopt new innovations, and they tend to be opinion leaders and respected within their social networks. DOI considers factors that contribute to innovation, including the compatibility of the innovation with existing values and practices, its complexity, its perceived value, and its observability.

The DOI model has been used within faculty development contexts, exploring how academic institutions adopt and implement new practices or technologies. For example, Smith et al. (2020) used the DOI model to develop a faculty development fellows program at a regional comprehensive university. Bennett and Bennett (2003) used DOI to guide the development of a faculty technology training program. They attributed the program's success to how it explicitly addressed factors that impact an individual's choice to innovate. DOI provides insight into faculty experiences with grant-funding opportunities, such as what might encourage or hinder them in pursuing and successfully carrying out grant-funded initiatives. Identifying these factors can help faculty mentors, leaders, and institutions develop more effective strategies for supporting faculty members' grant-funded projects.

Tools

I present two tools, grounded in SCCT and DOI and designed to promote conversations with faculty about their scholarship goals. The tools can be used individually but are better suited to being used in a dialogue between a faculty member and a mentor or colleague who knows the faculty member and their scholarship well. Both tools are adapted from support I received from Hope College's Office of Sponsored Research (Kehoe & Fleischmann, 2021). These assessments should be completed before searching for grant-funding opportunities because they are designed to expand possibilities and potentials for what, how, when, with whom, and why projects could occur. Too often, faculty start with a specific grant-funding opportunity in mind and then try to fit their agenda into the grant's parameters. This is the wrong approach! Only after brainstorming and articulating larger scholarship goals and possibilities and identifying new resources, stakeholders, and collaborators should grant-funding opportunities be explored.

The Scholarship/Project Assessment worksheet guides faculty in reflecting on different categories relevant to their scholarship with questions that prompt new ideas and connections. These categories are particularly relevant for humanities faculty, who often need to position their scholarship in various ways to find and use funding opportunities.

Table 18.1 Scholarship/Project Assessment Tool

Scholarship and Project Scope	• What does your scholarship focus on? • What projects (past, present, future) fit within this scholarship? • How might your project ideas be broken into different stages/phases? • Who are possible stakeholders for your scholarship or specific projects? • Who might be interested in or benefit from your work?
Alignment with the Institutional Mission/Goals	• How does your project further your institution's mission and goals? • What does your institution value (i.e., student research), and how might this be incorporated into your project?

(Continued)

Table 18.1 (Continued)

Existing Resources, Skills, and Networks	• What existing resources can you draw on to support your project in your department, division, or college? • What skills or strengths do you bring to your project? (i.e., detail-oriented, visionary, interpersonal) • How might you draw on your existing network to support your scholarship?
Campus Partnerships	• Which faculty members on your campus might have similar interests, goals, and expertise? • Which campus programs or departments might be interested in your project? • Whose expertise on campus might you draw on in your project?
Community Partnerships	• What are possible partners in the geographic community surrounding your campus? (i.e., educational institutions, non-profit organizations, businesses) • Whose expertise in the community might you draw on in your project? • Who might be interested in hearing about your results and findings?
Peer/Institutional Networks	• Who does similar scholarship/research in other institutions or related fields? • What opportunities for connection, support, and collaboration might there be?

Table 18.2 Grant-Funding Considerations Tool

Clarifying Your Project/Scope of Research	• Articulate the problem that your project is responding to and how your project aligns • Identify all possible stakeholders and research/ scholarship dissemination sources • Identify different "entry" points to your project or different stages of your project (be creative in thinking about how different kinds of funding could support your overall project)
Deciding What You Want to Do With Grant Funding	• Support an aspect of a larger project • Support your writing project • Travel to do research somewhere (i.e., Newberry Library) • Participate in an activity or professional development opportunity (i.e., NEH Summer Institute) • Connect with an individual or institution (for mentorship, networking) • Develop an aspect of your CV (i.e., support for publication, awards, prizes)

Finding Grant-Funding Opportunities	• National and international governmental sources • National and international private institutions, foundations • Your institution's office of sponsored research • SPIN (Sponsored Programs Information Network); SMART (SPIN Matching and Research Transmittal Service) (requires an institutional membership) • Professional societies and organizations (i.e., National Council of Teachers of English) • Word of mouth among people in your field, at your institution • Institutional/funding agency's websites (i.e., Smithsonian Institute, Lilly Fellows Program) • Acknowledgments in published articles/books related to your research/scholarship (grants or funding are often mentioned)
Understanding Specific Funding Opportunities	• Topic of the grant (i.e., annual theme vs. general topic) vs. your subject matter • Eligibility requirements for the grant (i.e., level of degree, citizenship, career stage, geography, discipline-specific, institution-specific, etc.) • Timing of the grant vs. your timeline (often an annual cycle; plan around future dates) • Allowances vs. what you need covered (i.e., course buyout, supplies, equipment) • Awarded directly to individual vs. awarded to an individual's institution
Applying for Funding	• Ask your institution's office of sponsored research for support • See if/what support is required from your institution and initiate these conversations/asks • Email the funding agency/institution to ask questions; attend Q&A sessions/webinars to learn more about the granting agency and the specific call for proposals • Talk with previously successful grantees; ask to look at their proposals • Ask to see the proposal rubric
Receiving and Using Funding	• Determine who needs to be involved; some grants go straight to faculty members, while others need to go through your institution • Share the news with your department chair, dean, and institution's public affairs and marketing office • Review what you included in your proposal to make sure you carry out your proposed plan • Find out what you need to include in your final report (i.e., what data to collect, what questions are posed) • Follow deadlines (i.e., for submission materials, final report, etc.) • Evaluate your work (often a required part of a grant) • Submit final report • Disseminate your findings/publications to your stakeholders (i.e., granting agency)

The Grant-Funding Considerations worksheet is a more practical tool designed to support humanities faculty in looking for and determining which grant funding might be the best fit for their career and scholarship goals.

Lessons Learned

It can be difficult to navigate the complex and complicated world of grant-funding opportunities. Writing grant proposals can be very time- and labor-intensive, and success rates in receiving grants can be quite low. Grant work and final reporting can also feel overwhelming, particularly if faculty don't have the personal and professional support needed to carry out a successful project or program. However, when grant-funded projects can be used to contribute to larger career and scholarship goals, there is much to be gained.

I wanted to share this approach to grant-funding opportunities with the humanities faculty participants in my workshop. At the end of the workshop, participants reported that they appreciated the specific advice related to finding and applying for grants and the chance to learn in-depth about a grant-funded program. However, what resonated the most was finding a space to feel seen, heard, and supported in their grant-funding goals, attempts, and experiences and to be encouraged to approach grant-funding opportunities strategically.

Conclusion

Finding and securing grant-funding opportunities is essential to the work that humanities faculty do. Finding and securing grant-funding opportunities that support larger humanities-based scholarship agendas and faculty career development is also essential. Grant funding in the humanities can be creatively approached in ways that support faculty research agendas, service, and teaching commitments. It can also provide the impetus for faculty to think about new ways of collaborating with campus or community partners and disseminating their work in broader ways.

References

Baker, V. L. (2022). *Managing your academic career: A guide to re-envision mid-career*. Routledge.

Baker, V. L. (2020). *Charting your path to full: A guide for women associate professors*. Rutgers University Press.

Baker, V. L., Lunsford, L. G., & Pifer, M. J. (2019). Patching up the "leaking leadership pipeline": Fostering mid-career faculty succession management. *Research in Higher Education, 60*, 823–843.

Bandura, A. (1986). *Social foundations of thought and action: A social cognitive theory*. Prentice-Hall.

Bennett, J., & Bennett, I. (2003). A review of factors that influence the diffusion of innovation when structuring a faculty training program. *The Internet and Higher Education, 6*(1), 53–63.

Carlson, M., & O'Neal-McElrath, T. (2008). *Winning grants step by step* (3rd ed.). John Wiley & Sons.

Dotson, K. (2014). Conceptualizing epistemic oppression. *Social Epistemology, 28*(2), 115–138. http://dx.doi.org/10.1080/02691728.2013.782585

Gonzalez, L. M., Wester, K. L., & Borders, L. D. (2019), Supports and barriers to new faculty researcher development. *Studies in Graduate and Postdoctoral Education, 10*(1), 2134. https://doi.org/10.1108/SGPE-D-18-00020

Kehoe, M., & Fleischmann, R. (2021). Finding short-term research funds [Internal Webinar]. *Hope College*. https://hope.edu/offices/sponsored-research-programs/

Lent, R. W., Brown, S. D., & Hackett, G. (1994). Toward a unifying social cognitive theory of career and academic interest, choice, and performance. *Journal of Vocational Behavior, 45*(1), 79–122.

Lilly Fellows Program. (n.d.). *Lilly Fellows Program*. www.lillyfellows.org/about/about-us/

Misra, J., & Lundquist, J. (2015, June 26). Diversity and the ivory ceiling. *Inside Higher Ed*. www.insidehighered.com/advice/2015/06/26/essay-diversity-issues-and-midcareer-faculty-members

Perry, D. M. (2014, June 23). But does it count? *The Chronicle of Higher Education*. www.chronicle.com/article/but-does-it-count/?cid=gen_sign_in

Rogers, E. M. (2003). *Diffusion of innovations* (5th ed.). Free Press.

Seo, G., Mehdiabadi, A. H., & Huang, W. (2017). Identifying core competencies to advance female professors' careers: An exploratory study in United States academia. *Journal of Further and Higher Education, 41*(6), 741–759. https://doi.org/10.1080/0309877X.2016.1177167

Settles, I. H., Jones, M. K., Buchanan, N. T., & Dotson, K. (2021). Epistemic exclusion: Scholar(ly) devaluation that marginalizes faculty of color. *Journal of Diversity in Higher Education, 14*(4), 493–507. https://doi.org/10.1037/dhe0000174

Smith, T. W., Greenwald, S. J., Nave, L. Y., Mansure, V. N., & Howell, M. L. (2020). The diffusion of faculty development: A faculty fellows program. *To Improve the Academy: A Journal of Educational Development, 39*(1). http://dx.doi.org/10.3998/tia.17063888.0039.107

Strunk, K. K. (2020, March 13). Demystifying and democratizing tenure and promotion. *Inside Higher Ed*. www.insidehighered.com/advice/2020/03/13/tenure-and-promotion-process-must-be-revised-especially-historically-marginalized

Section 5

Conclusion

Chapter 19

From Reactive to Sustainable

Advancing the Practice of Mid-Career Faculty Development

Vicki L. Baker, Aimee LaPointe Terosky, and Laura Gail Lunsford

Introduction

One doesn't have to look very hard to find stories of dissatisfied workers. The Gallup Poll "State of the Global Workplace 2023" found that worker stress has reached "historic highs," which is negatively impacting worker productivity and performance (Gallup Poll, 2023, p. 2). Higher education reflects these global trends, as faculty survey after faculty survey highlights increasing levels of career dissatisfaction and rising concerns about the changing nature of the academic career (Azubuike et al., 2019), especially among the ranks of mid-career faculty (Baker & Terosky, 2022; Welch et al., 2019). Because of concerns about worker disengagement and attrition, institutions and organizations are being asked to rethink how best to support their employees' professional and personal growth and well-being (Gallup Poll, 2023). The old way of doing things is not effective, as numerous authors in this book have noted.

All ranks of academia face challenges and barriers; however, the mid-career stage is distinctive due to the oftentimes abrupt and significant increase in service, administrative, and leadership responsibilities following the awarding of tenure and promotion (Neumann & Terosky, 2007). These new responsibilities at mid-career are, unfortunately, rarely accompanied by robust and supportive professional development or support staff/services, thereby exacerbating an already challenging transitional time (Welch et al., 2019). This long-standing pattern in higher education – loading up mid-career academics' plates with new tasks while simultaneously overlooking this career stage's need for professional growth supports – is deeply concerning. Much of what mid-career faculty members are asked to do lies at the core of a college or university's mission or purpose: namely, leadership in academic affairs and shared governance, mentoring of junior and departmental colleagues, and development of academic programing and advising of students (Harris et al., 2022). This context facing mid-career faculty is alarming and requires high-level structural changes,

DOI: 10.4324/9781003428626-25

changes that will take time and concerted effort on the part of key stake-holders in higher education. Fortunately, many scholars, practitioners, and organizations are already striving to address these concerns at the individual, institutional, and consortial levels. Sharing the strategies and tools of these change agents is the purpose of this book.

As we conclude this volume, we first recap each chapter to highlight the cross-cutting lessons for developing faculty at mid-career. Second, we aim to propel the field of mid-career practice forward by presenting four critical considerations to aid mid-career professionals' efforts to build a robust portfolio of programming, tools, and strategies. At mid-career, faculty members are expected to have mastered their disciplinary teaching and scholarship. Yet for tenured associate professors, the service and leadership demands are increasing for a group of faculty members whose numbers are fewer than those in the assistant and full ranks (NCES, 2019). Because there is limited research on how the needs of mid-career faculty members in other appointment types are supported, we seek to pave the way forward for career advancement at mid-career, regardless of appointment type.

Volume Recap

The challenges and opportunities associated with the mid-career stage are multifaceted, requiring varied tools, strategies, and sources of support. In an effort to both acknowledge and highlight that reality, we organized a volume that addresses core needs of faculty members and institutional leaders at the mid-career stage. We join the growing chorus of those who are refuting the notion that career advancement is an individual endeavor in which one must simply "work harder" to advance (Social Sciences Feminist Research Group, 2017; Trahar, 2023). Such a mindset contributes to the greater disparities confronting underrepresented groups in the academy, particularly women faculty, women faculty of color, and faculty of color (Matthew, 2016; Truong, 2021). The contributions in this volume illustrate that mid-career advancement requires collaboration and partnerships. We are inspired by the work featured throughout this volume, which may enable institutional leaders to enhance and sustain their career development portfolios. Likewise, we hope the tools might inspire mid-career faculty members to envision a path forward. As an editorial team, our aim was to provide insight into what is possible as mid-career faculty members seek to address the question "What's next?" We also sought to offer tangible tools and strategies for mid-career professionals that can serve as a road map for addressing the "How to navigate?" question that plagues mid-career professionals. Our inclusion of the four section themes was purposeful, to inform sustainable mid-career faculty development programming and practice.

Section 1 targets mid-career faculty members and mid-career leaders by offering guidance on critical skill development. Starck's chapter helps mid-career faculty demystify the grant-making process, particularly for those seeking to serve as primary investigators. The behind-the-scenes insights provide a much-needed toolkit for navigating this often-challenging aspect of the faculty career. Boland and Baker offer a three-phase framework for re-envisioning the sabbatical, which they argue is the most important professional development opportunity available to mid-career faculty members. Their model accounts for pre-planning, engagement, and academic re-entry phases; along with the worksheet tool, it serves as a useful guide for mid-career faculty and those who provide guidance to them during this transition. Reddick and Hughes make a case for the importance of mentoring at mid-career. They acknowledge that the needs of mid-career faculty differ from the needs of those at other stages, thus necessitating new strategies and approaches to giving and receiving mentoring support. Lunsford and Baker also offer guidance on mentorship by describing tools department chairs and deans can use to mentor their mid-career faculty colleagues. They make a case for critical mentoring skill development in institutional leaders to ensure a strong, robust pipeline of well-equipped mid-career leaders. Finally, Terosky and Footman offer guidance to mid-career faculty members to help them safeguard time, space, and place to pursue passions and priorities. Through the use of a job-crafting framework, they guide mid-career faculty members in crafting more personally and professionally meaningful lives.

Section 2 features institutional efforts that we hope will inspire and motivate our peers to invest in mid-career programming for all appointment types at their respective institutions. Hastings shares details about the mid-career faculty program she helped develop and implement at Texas State University. Via a cohort model, mid-career faculty members propose a career development project and receive peer and one-on-one support as they refine their ideas and seek funding to advance their efforts. Drinkwater highlights the importance of mid-career faculty support at a selective liberal arts college (SLAC). Her chapter makes a case for the need for dependable, consistent programming that focuses on the varied yet targeted needs associated with mid-career. Mumpower and Wojton focus on identity-informed mentoring by describing their offering of an annual Faculty Mentoring Institute. Dahlheimer and colleagues provide a blueprint for mid-career programming focused on non–tenure-track teaching faculty in a cohort model that also connects faculty members across different appointment types. As the academy continues to rely on contingent and part-time faculty, chapter authors make a case for why adapting tenured faculty–focused mid-career supports misses the mark. They share insights into career advancement resources and programming that better meets the needs of this faculty population. Finally, Strickland-Davis describes a faculty development effort at a community college driven by an institutional-level strategic planning effort. At its core, the mid-career programming seeks to equip mid-career faculty with the knowledge and skills to support a diversifying student body.

In Section 3, we learn about how members of consortiums and professional associations envision career advancement strategies and related support at mid-career. Whether in a tenure system or not, the mid-career stage can be a daunting and isolating phase in one's professional (and personal) journey. Consortiums and professional associations can provide resources alongside those found in the institutional context. Boyd and colleagues share their experiences as creators and facilitators of multi-campus faculty learning communities in the Associated Colleges of the South (ACS). Cross-campus learning and engagement facilitate psychological safety and visibility and foster a much-needed career advancement community for mid-career faculty. The challenges and opportunities of mid-career are not only germane in the US; they transcend global boundaries. Elçi and colleagues describe their experiences building a voluntary faculty development network in Türkiye, YÖMEGA: the Higher Education Professional Development Network. By supporting the professional development of teaching staff in the areas of technology and teaching and learning, YÖMEGA serves as a model for the role of inclusive, grassroots networks in facilitating career growth and development. Programming that supports full-time and part-time faculty and staff is demonstrated in the chapter by Colclough and Deal, which features the North Carolina Teaching and Learning Hubs. The Hubs complement and supplement work at the community college level to ensure that faculty and staff are knowledgeable about evidence-based strategies to increase equitable student success outcomes. In the last chapter of this section, Heasley and Baker feature a session that is part of the Mid-Career Faculty Workshop, hosted by the Association for the Study of Higher Education (ASHE) and the Council for the Advancement of Higher Education Programs (CAHEP). By undertaking a dynamic SWOT Analysis, mid-career faculty can get guidance on how to navigate their career trajectories, while other professional associations can learn from this chapter how to invest in community-level professional development.

In Section 4, the final section of our volume, contributors highlight the role of grant-funded initiatives to spur on much-needed programming and mid-career support; they also shed light on how to sustain those efforts after initial funding ends. Schepmann and colleagues illustrate the power of regional inter-institutional peer alliances through their Advancing STEM Careers by Empowering Network Development (ASCEND) initiative, funded by the NSF. The possibilities are great when mid-career faculty and administrators can work collaboratively on career advancement strategies and practices. Culpepper and her co-authors share their experiences directing an ADVANCE program at the University of Maryland's campus. While NSF funding helped launch the program, their chapter features the efforts pursued to sustain and broaden the reach of the program on campus. Sun and Pratt illustrate the importance of investing in mid-career professionals whose roles are evolving. Via the Master Educator Course, soldiers are enrolled in a graduate-level program on college teaching and learning, student success, higher education administration, and organizational change as they prepare for their college-level faculty roles. In our final content chapter of the volume, Van Duinen reflects on her experience leading a Lilly Network Exchange to support mid-career faculty advancing humanities-focused projects. She shares strategies and lessons learned while navigating the maze of external funding in the humanities.

Sustaining Mid-Career Programming: Critical Considerations

As we reflect on the knowledge gleaned from the collective wisdom shared throughout this volume, we highlight four critical considerations to ground mid-career practice:

1. The importance of providing opportunities for all mid-career stakeholders,
2. The need to be intentional about equity and inclusion throughout all phases of mid-career development and career advancement,
3. Harnessing collaboration and capacity building to sustain mid-career programming, and
4. Managing the tension between sustainability and agency.

Our hope is this knowledge propels the practice of and sustainability efforts aimed at mid-career advancement.

Supporting All Mid-Career Stakeholders

Faculty development programming for tenured or tenure-track faculty is neglecting more than half of the academic workforce. The myriad of faculty appointment types in higher education is increasing, with tenure-track, full-time faculty working alongside non–tenure-track, teaching, clinical, part-time, or contingent faculty. This shift is demonstrated in recent COACHE data that surveys not only tenure-track but also non–tenure-track faculty members' perspectives on contemporary academic work (Azubuike et al., 2019). As higher education grapples with the changing landscape of faculty appointment types, it is clear that traditional professional development approaches modeled on short-term, one-size-fits-all paradigms are no longer sufficient (Baker et al., 2017, 2018). As noted repeatedly by this book's chapter authors, innovative approaches that consider the full breadth of faculty audiences are paramount. How might an institution better support a non–tenure-track program director? How might a part-time faculty member craft their work in ways that are professionally and personally meaningful? How might a new department chairperson be guided in inclusive practices? How might a professional organization develop programs to re-engage a mid-career faculty member who is "quietly quitting," a new term associated with employee disengagement following the COVID-19 pandemic (Gallup Poll, 2023, p. 4)? Fortunately, this book provides chapter after chapter of navigational strategies to immediately support mid-career faculty and institutional leaders. Through the tools provided by our authors, we hope to better equip mid-career faculty, and the institutions charged with supporting their professional growth and advancement, with tangible resources that speak to all appointment types.

Intentional Equity and Inclusion

We can and should do more to support policies that enable historically marginalized faculty (HMF) members to flourish at our institutions. Sotto-Santiago and colleagues (2019) argue that targeted faculty development programming can make a difference for such faculty members in terms of retention, productivity, and leader development. Recent reports suggest there is a greater awareness of the work to be done. For example, a 2023 American Association of University Professors report finds that the percentage of contingent faculty in the United States has increased from 47 to 68 percent over the last 30 years. Further, a greater proportion of these appointments are held by women and underrepresented minority faculty members than in the past (Colby, 2023). A 2019 European University Association report emphasized a greater need for a "holistic system-level approach" (p. 8) across universities to improve awareness and implementation of policies supporting diversity, equity, and inclusion (Claeys-Kulik et al., 2019) for students, faculty, and staff. Developing the talents of all faculty members is a workforce imperative for all nations.

The chapter authors point to their efforts to overcome problems of hidden labor, biases, and inequitable service burdens for women and historically underrepresented faculty members. Tokenism, recruitment bias, and unequal expectations are additional challenges scholars have identified for HMF (Sotto-Santiago et al., 2019). The chapters in this volume highlight concrete steps to create inclusive learning communities and a sense of belonging through mentorship, job crafting, sabbatical policies, and more.

HMF are defined differently depending on institution type and discipline. Personal attributes such as gender and ethnicity are considered in relationship to the discipline. For example, women faculty members are underrepresented in STEM but not in nursing. Diversity also encompasses the varied appointment types mentioned earlier. Thus, three main points emerge from the tools in this book. First, as non–tenure-track faculty members take on more of the academic work, it is important that faculty development programs address their needs. Second, tailored faculty development programming, for example through mentorship, hubs, and job-crafting exercises, can increase a sense of inclusion and belonging among underrepresented or non–tenure-track mid-career faculty members. Third, a strategic institutional approach is needed that leverages existing campus resources, which can improve and sustain faculty work at the departmental and institutional levels.

Harnessing Collaboration and Capacity Building to Sustain Mid-Career Programming

Resources for faculty development are often limited, and faculty development programming might not be enough to overcome the natural disciplinary silos at universities. Faculty developers need to view themselves as institutional change agents who live in the sometimes-uncomfortable space of the *intersection* of individual needs and organizational goals (Baker et al., 2017). There are also intersections between administrators and faculty members and between departments and disciplines. Sustaining change efforts is hard. Programming often disappears when the champion (e.g., the director of faculty development) leaves or changes jobs. Thus, it is critical to engage in collaboration and intentional capacity building when designing and delivering faculty programming. The tools in this book (e.g., those related to refreshing sabbatical policies and creating identity-informed mentoring opportunities) provide examples of how to build capacity through policy changes that involve a critical mass of faculty members.

The Alignment Framework for Faculty Development (Figure 19.1) provides a useful model to think through the key stakeholders for a project and their needs (Baker et al., 2017). This framework highlights two important roles for faculty developers. First, it is important to regularly assess faculty members' needs at mid-career, using either local or national surveys (such as the COACHE survey used by Wojton and Mumpower in Chapter 8). Second, faculty development programming must be aligned with institutional strategic plans. This alignment is one way to justify resources allocated to faculty development. Strickland-Davis, in Chapter 10, for example, aligns a new faculty development center with institutional goals.

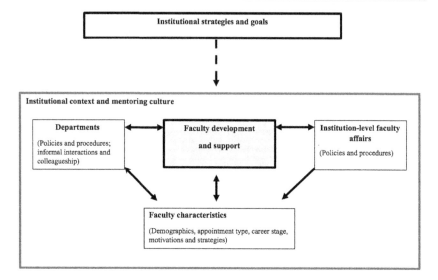

Figure 19.1 Faculty Development Alignment Framework

We can also borrow the idea of *small wins* from community psychology (Weick, 1984). Small wins focus on sustained, small interventions that garner support and interest while not attracting the attention of detractors. Quality, targeted faculty development programming that is consistent and strategic and that slowly builds offerings can create momentum in developing a sustainable portfolio to better serve faculty needs.

Managing the Tension between Sustainability and Agency

We view the navigational tools and expert commentary in each chapter as beneficial to mid-career faculty and higher education institutions. However, we would be remiss, as the editors and authors, to ignore the tension between career sustainability and assertion of individual agency. Trends such as cuts to higher education budgets, reductions in tenure-track faculty and support staff lines, diminished positive perceptions about the value of higher education in society, and increasing workload demands on mid-career faculty illustrate the point that the sustainability of the traditional faculty career is in question (Harris et al., 2022). Scholars have noted that scholarly passion and meaningful engagement with knowledge consumption and production alongside students are key draws of the academic career. And yet faculty studies often highlight that the time and space for this type of "passion" work are in limited supply (Neumann, 2009, p. 10), thereby raising red flags around the current and future status of faculty engagement and retention. Through scholarship and practice, the editors and authors of this book attempt to balance the ideal with the real. Ideally, we strive to serve as catalysts for a much-needed, larger structural reform in faculty development in the hope of furthering the creation of academic careers that are inclusive, sustainable, and purpose filled. Realistically, we provide on-the-ground wisdom of practice and navigational tools for mid-career faculty members' immediate use in hopes of supporting individuals' sense of agency (O'Meara et al., 2008) in their professional careers and personal lives.

Concluding Remarks

As we conclude, we highlight the collaboration and capacity building on full display throughout this edited volume. The editorial team, along with the volume contributors, are deeply passionate about and committed to advancing the study and practice of mid-career faculty members and the institutional leaders tasked with supporting them. Our hope is that the collective wisdom featured here inspires others to advocate on behalf of this critically important population of faculty members and that it will provide a road map for action across the academy. As the academy continues to evolve, so too must the career advancement strategies employed to ensure a robust pipeline of diverse, *engaged* individuals at mid-career; we need their knowledge, their wisdom, and their talents to propel us forward.

References

Azubuike, N.O., Benson, R.T., Kumar, A., & Mathews, K. (2019). *COACHE summary tables 2019: Selected dimensions of the faculty workplace experience.* https://coache.gse.harvard.edu/files/gse-coache/files/aacu19_coache_butwhataboutfaculty_datahandout_v20190125.pdf

Baker, V.L., Lunsford, L.G., Neisler, G., Pifer, M.J., & Terosky, A.L. (2018). *Success after tenure: Supporting mid-career faculty.* Stylus.

Baker, V.L., Lunsford, L.G., & Pifer, M.J. (2017). *Developing faculty in liberal arts colleges: Aligning individual needs and organizational goals.* Rutgers University Press.

Baker, V.L., & Terosky, A.L. (2022). Bridging the research-practice nexus: Resources, tools, and strategies to navigate mid-career in the academy. *New Directions for Higher Education*, 1–7. https://doi.org/10.1002/he.20401

Baker, V.L., Terosky, A.L., & Martinez, E. (2017). *Faculty members' scholarly learning across institutional types* (Association for the Study of Higher Education's Monograph Series). Jossey-Bass.

Claeys-Kulik, A., Jørgensen, T.E., Stöber, H. (2019). *Diversity, equity, and inclusion in European higher education institutions.* European University Association. https://eua.eu/downloads/publications/web_diversity%20equity%20and%20inclusion%20in%20european%20higher%20education%20institutions.pdf

Colby, G. (2023, March). *Data snapshot: Tenure and contingency in US higher education.* American Association of University Professors. www.aaup.org/sites/default/files/AAUP%20Data%20Snapshot.pdf

Gallup Poll. (2023). *State of the global workplace 2023.* www.gallup.com/workplace/349484/state-of-the-global-workplace.aspx?thank-you-report-form=1

Harris, J. T., Lane, J. E., Sun, J. C., & Baker, G. F. (2022). *Academic leadership and governance of higher education: A guide for trustees, leaders, and aspiring leaders of two- and four-year institutions.* Stylus.

Matthew, P. A. (2016). What is faculty diversity worth to a university? *Atlantic.* www.theatlantic.com/education/archive/2016/11/what-is-faculty-diversity-worth-to-a-university/508334/

National Center for Education Statistics. (2019). https://nces.ed.gov/programs/digest/d19/tables/dt19_315.20.asp

Neumann, A. (2009). Protecting the passion of scholars in times of change. *Change: The Magazine of Higher Learning, 41*(2), 10–15.

Neumann, A., & Terosky, A. L. (2007, May/June). To give and to receive: Recently tenured professors' experiences of service in major research universities. *Journal of Higher Education, 78*(3), 282–310.

O'Meara, K., Terosky, A. L., & Neumann, A. (2008). *Faculty careers and work lives: A professional growth perspective* (ASHE Higher Education Report no. 34(3)). Jossey-Bass.

Social Sciences Feminist Network Research Interest Group. (2017). The burden of invisible work in academia: Social inequalities and time use in five university departments. *Humboldt Journal of Social Relations, 39*, 228–245.

Sotto-Santiago, S., Tuitt, F., & Saelua, N. (2019). All faculty matter: The continued search for culturally relevant practices in faculty development. *The Journal of Faculty Development, 33*(3), 83–94.

Trahar, J. (2023). Why working harder doesn't work. *Greatest Common Factor.* https://gcfactory.com/the-pov/2023/2/3/why-working-harder-doesnt-work

Truong, K. A. (2021, May 27). Making the invisible visible. *Inside Higher Ed.* www.insidehighered.com/advice/2021/05/28/why-and-how-colleges-should-acknowledge-invisible-labor-faculty-color-opinion

Weick, K. E. (1984). Small wins: Redefining the scale of social problems. *American Psychologist, 39*(1), 40.

Welch, A. G., Bolin, J., & Reardon, D. (2019). *Mid-career faculty: Trends, barriers, and possibilities.* Brill.

Index

Note: Page numbers in *italics* indicate a figure and page numbers in **bold** indicate a table on the corresponding page.

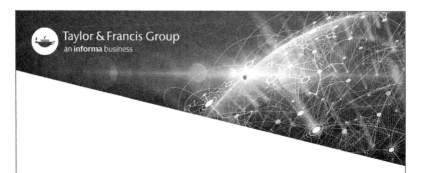

Printed in the United States
by Baker & Taylor Publisher Services